The International Library of Sociology

THE FIRST YEARS OF
YANGYI COMMUNE

Founded by KARL MANNHEIM

The International Library of Sociology

RACE, CLASS AND SOCIAL STRUCTURE
In 21 Volumes

THE FIRST YEARS OF YANGYI COMMUNE

by

ISABEL and DAVID CROOK

Routledge
Taylor & Francis Group

LONDON AND NEW YORK

First published in 1966 by
Routledge
2 Park Square, Milton Park, Abingdon, Oxfordshire OX14 4RN
711 Third Avenue, New York, NY 10017

First issued in paperback 2014

Routledge is an imprint of the Taylor and Francis Group, an informa business

British Library Cataloguing in Publication Data
A CIP catalogue record for this book
is available from the British Library

The First Years of Yangyi Commune
ISBN 0-415-17626-3
Class, Race and Social Structure: 21 Volumes
ISBN 0-415-17826-6
The International Library of Sociology: 274 Volumes
ISBN 0-415-17838-X

ISBN 978-1-138-87376-6 (pbk)
ISBN 978-0-415-17626-2 (hbk)

Publisher's Note
The publisher has gone to great lengths to ensure the quality of this
reprint but points out that some imperfections in the original
may be apparent

CONTENTS

v

Contents

Contents

TABLES

APPROXIMATE EQUIVALENTS

1 *mu*   = $\frac{1}{6}$ of an acre or $\frac{1}{15}$ of a hectare

1 *jin*   = 1·1 lbs or $\frac{1}{2}$ a kilogram

1 *yuan* = 3/- or 43¢.

ILLUSTRATIONS

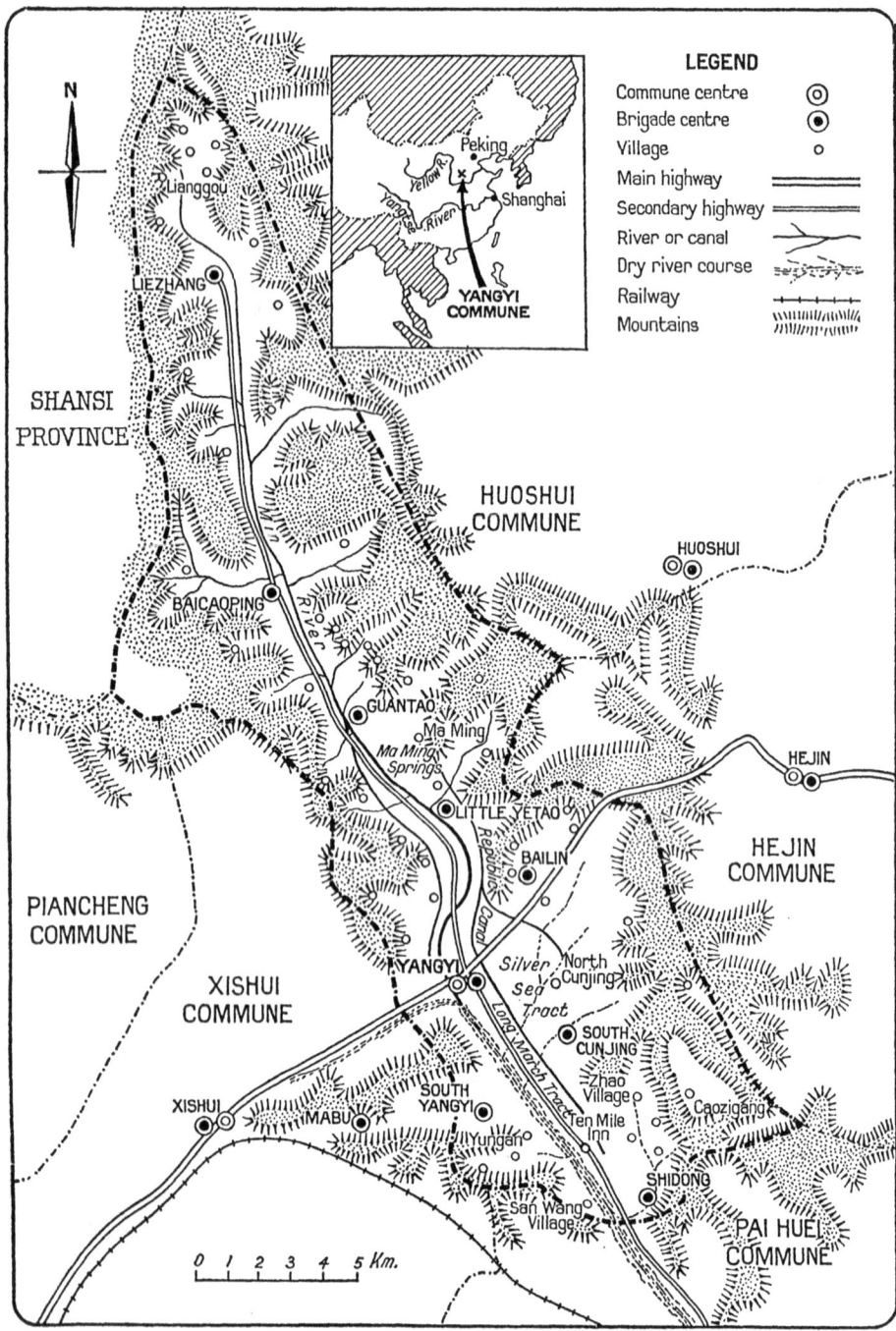

LEGEND
Commune centre ◎
Brigade centre ⊙
Village ○
Main highway
Secondary highway
River or canal
Dry river course
Railway
Mountains

N

SHANSI
PROVINCE

Lianggou
LIEZHANG

BAICAOPING

HUOSHUI
COMMUNE

HUOSHUI

GUANTAO
Ma Ming
Ma Ming
Springs
LITTLE YETAO
BAILIN

HEJIN

HEJIN
COMMUNE

PIANCHENG
COMMUNE

XISHUI
COMMUNE

Republic's Canal

River

YANGYI

Silver Sea
Tract

North
Cunjing

SOUTH
CUNJING

Zhao
Village

Caoziqang

XISHUI

MABU

SOUTH
YANGYI

Yungan

Ten Mile
Inn

SHIDONG

San Wang
Village

PAI HUEI
COMMUNE

Long World Track

0 1 2 3 4 5 Km.

Peking
Yellow River
Yangtze River
Shanghai
YANGYI
COMMUNE

PROLOGUE

OVER a fifth of mankind live in people's communes. To turn a blind eye to such a social organism is to deny a primary fact of twentieth-century life. For the commune, whether one likes it or not, has taken root and flourishes. Despite the doubts of some friends and the fears and obstructions of enemies its influence is spreading and will spread further in the course of the present decade.

It would be pretentious for two individuals like ourselves to attempt an overall appraisal of so vast and significant a subject. That is one reason why our study is strictly limited as to time and place. It deals with the first two years of one commune. But despite the variety, flexibility and adaptation to local conditions which characterize China's tens of thousands of communes, we cannot claim that it is unique any more than that it is typical.

Our first acquaintance with what is now Yangyi Commune was made before communes existed. That was in 1947–48, during the civil war against Chiang Kai-shek's Kuomintang, when we lived for eight months in Ten Mile Inn, a village in the communist-led Liberated Areas.[1] There we made a study of the recent history of the village[2] and observed a campaign which completed the land reform.

The Chinese revolution was then at a turning point. Within a year its leaders had left their mountain strongholds for Peking, and the centre of gravity of the revolution had shifted from the country-side to the cities. We too followed in its wake. For the next ten years or so we studied events in the countryside both from Peking (where we were teaching) and during visits to various parts of China. In the summers of 1959 and 1960 we returned to Ten Mile Inn. It is mainly on material gathered during these two visits that this book is based.

Even by the first of these visits, Ten Mile Inn was already a brigade of Yangyi Commune.

Yangyi is in Shexian, the southernmost county of Hopei Province, in the dry and rugged Taihang Range. It is about 275 miles south-west of Peking and 600 north-west of Shanghai. Yet it is neither

---

[1] Scattered areas mostly in North China, with a total population of 140 million. In 1947 they consisted of sixteen separate Border Regions, so called because they were situated on the borders of different provinces, remote from the centres of Kuomintang provincial authority. Ten Mile Inn was in the Shansi-Hopei-Shantung-Honan Border Region, which had a population of 30 million.

[2] *Revolution in a Chinese Village—Ten Mile Inn*, Routledge & Kegan Paul, London, 1959.

xi

geographically nor historically remote, for such areas as this were at
the very hub of China's revolution from almost the end of the
thirties until the People's Republic was set up in 1949. Even today
mention of the Taihang Mountains recalls the epic era of the old
revolutionary bases, from which the Communist-led forces emerged
to drive out first the Japanese and later the Kuomintang armies
from the whole of mainland China.

In the area which now forms the Yangyi People's Commune the
first Communist Party Branch was set up in 1938. Soon over a
thousand local peasants had joined the 8th Route Army[3] and over
twelve thousand were in the militia. In 1943 combined army and
militia forces fought a battle at Yangyi, inflicting 1,300 casualties on
the Japanese and their Chinese puppet troops. Later these same
forces fought Chiang Kai-shek's American-armed troops in the
civil war which ended with the setting-up of the Chinese People's
Republic in 1949.

Veteran guerilla fighters of the thirties and forties play a leading
role in Yangyi Commune today; and boys who then smuggled
messages through the enemy lines or guarded the gates of their
villages armed with red-tasselled spears have become secretaries of
Communist Party branches or leaders of brigades.[4]

The commune area, shaped like a willow leaf, is thirty-three
miles by ten[5] and runs north-west to south-east across Shexian
county, along the generally dry Min River. As it approaches Yangyi
townlet the valley broadens out and from then on, to its south-east
end, the commune land is broad, flat valley bottom. But towards the
north-west the valley grows narrower and narrower, the mountains
steeper and higher, till at the very tip they rise to the ridges of the
Taihang range which separates Hopei from Shansi Province.

Here, cleft from the crags lies the most inaccessible village of the
commune, Lianggou. From the late thirties and throughout the war
against Japan this inaccessibility was a vital asset, for Lianggou
housed an 8th Route Army arsenal. Here, in rock-hewn caves and
thatched farm buildings of sun-baked mud, gunpowder was made,
and hand-grenades, land-mines and even primitive rifles and mortars
were turned out. Three times the imperial Japanese forces fought
their way up the Min River valley, harried by guerrillas thrusting at
them from the ravines which branch from the bed of the river like the
veins of a leaf from its stem. Once, the invaders got within a mile of the
village. Then they were driven back. 'One good man and a machine-
gun could hold that pass against an army,' declared a guerrilla

[3] The Communist-led army operating in North China throughout the war
against Japan—successor to the Red Army founded in 1927 and predecessor of
today's People's Liberation Army (P.L.A.).
[4] For definition, see p. 35.
[5] Yangyi has since been split up into four communes. See p. 34 f.n.

veteran. Yet in the end the Japanese did penetrate Lianggou. A landlord guided them on a wide detour to the western side of the mountain range and showed them where ropes could be lowered over the face of the cliff. Taking the defenders unexpectedly in the rear they gained control of the arsenal. The Japanese held Lianggou for twenty days before they withdrew. They demolished all they could, but their retreat was hardly completed before the arsenal was working once more.

Lianggou was never captured again, but its natural features, which were such an asset in wartime later became a liability.

More accessible but little better favoured by nature is Little Yetao, ten miles down the valley. 'One tenth farmland, two tenths water, seven tenths hills—all as bald as a monk's pate,' ran the old description of the place. One of these 'bald-headed' hills was the scene of a skirmish during the war against Japan, in which a group of encircled cadres[6] shot their way out to freedom with a machine-gun seized from the enemy. In those days, when the landlords, rich peasants and Japanese formed a triple scourge, the life of Little Yetao's 600-odd people swung from poverty to beggary and back.

Today there are murals on the walls along the narrow, flag-stoned village streets, and the hillsides have been planted with apple, peach and mulberry trees. The straggling, boulder-strewn old river-bed is for the most part dry, though green with newly-planted willows—and the water runs in a newly-dug channel. The brooks which once poured down the hillsides are channelled, too, and drive a generator beside the mill. Half-way up the hill beyond the village, an old temple, with its curved, tiled roof and 'devil-scaring' gargoyles, its ancient incense burners and fat, impassive Buddhas now houses the brigade poultry. Below are terraces of rabbit-hutches and pig-pens.

Quite different is Yangyi townlet further down the valley. For centuries a local market, its narrow, twisting cobbled street is still lined with wooden-shuttered shops selling anything from harrows to thermos flasks—though today all are commune-run stores. Between the shop fronts grey stone gateways, with red or black lacquered doors, lead to unexpected strings of courtyards surrounded by pomegranate trees and latticed windows. These former homes of Yangyi traders of old, now house community dining-rooms, commune nurseries and a 'home of respect for the aged'. At one end of the main street is the commune tractor station and farm-tool workshop; at the other is a sizable stonelined pond, built with landlord capital years ago. The water which the villagers now freely use was once sold at three coppers a bucket.

[6] 'Cadre' is the current translation of *ganbu*, a term covering various types of government and Communist Party administrative and political workers—officials, civil servants, leading personnel and staff at all levels.
For a technical definition of this and other classes, see table following p. 4.

Prologue

Water is still a vital matter. Two miles northeast of Yangyi the 1,400 family townlet of Bailin sprawls on rolling uplands. The lie of the land and the quality of the soil are favourable for farming—if only the rain falls. In dry years people once used to carry water all the way from Yangyi—if Yangyi had it to spare. Once, during a drought, an old man carried two buckets of water from Ma Ming springs in the hills above Little Yetao, over seven miles away. When he got home he stumbled on a stone and spilt it all. The next day he left the village with a curse, swearing he would never go back. That was in the days when the people of Bailin paraded the temple gods through the village streets in order to bring on rain.

It was much the same in Ten Mile Inn five miles to the southeast The village stands beside the Min River, but beyond where the stream peters out and flows underground. Its boulder-strewn bed is dry, except during years of flood. 'Don't marry your daughter into Ten Mile Inn,' went the saying—for she would have to carry buckets of water on a shoulder pole, at times for a mile or more.

Nevertheless legend has it that 'The Seventh Fairy Maid' forsook her home in the Milky Way to marry a boy of the village. She was captivated, it seems, not only by his looks but also by his skill—for he span yarn and wove brocade so fine that it was used for the Emperor's clothes. The story has survived in one of the operas still loved by the local people. So, too, has his skill, for women of Ten Mile Inn won the county prize for spinning and weaving during the war against Japan.

Entrenched on the terraced hill beside the village is the Fort. With its cobbled causeway climbing to a massive stone gate and the backs of its stone houses rising sheer from the hillside, cut away below to form a cliff, the Fort still looks what it once was—a citadel from which the landlords dominated the peasants in the village below.

This lower village is commonly called The Street. Only a dozen years ago a highway linking two county towns ran right through The Street. But it was so narrow and so blocked at each end by old gatehouses, that a few heavily-loaded pack-mules and donkeys could cause a traffic jam. In recent years a broad dirt highway has been cut through the threshing floors between the Fort and The Street. But the old thoroughfare is still the heart of village life. Here are the community dining-rooms, with groups of old women round their doorways, gossiping as they clean the vegetables, the village general store in a fortress-like building once owned by a rich peasant usurer, and the new kindergarten and sewing-centre.

Lianggou, Little Yetao, Yangyi, Ten Mile Inn—each has its individuality. Together they make up a cross-section of the fifty-eight villages and hamlets which formed the commune. A glance at the recent history of one of them will throw some light on the rest.

PART ONE

Two Years' History
of Yangyi Commune
1958 – 1960

Chapter I

THE YEARS BEFORE THE COMMUNE
(1938 to 1958)

THE 'NEW DEMOCRATIC REVOLUTION' IN TEN MILE INN[1]

BEFORE the land reform 70 per cent of the people of Ten Mile Inn lived for most of the year on husks, wild herbs and watery gruel 'so thin you could see the reflection of the moon in it.' It was no rare thing for a family of five to share one ragged quilt, sleeping in a circle on the *kang* (heated brick bed), feet in the middle and heads out all round. In the very poorest families husband and wife might share one pair of trousers, to be worn by whoever went out. In a nearby village there was a farmhand who scraped together enough for a suit of clothes when he married. He wore it for thirty-two years. This, however, was unusual, for by prevailing standards, a suit was expected to last only nine years: for the first three it was called new and worn on holidays; for the next three it was an ordinary suit; and only during the last three years was it looked on as getting old and shabby.

In 1937 there were just over 1,400 people in Ten Mile Inn, and just under 700 acres of land. This would have worked out at half an acre a head—if it had been evenly shared. But it was not. Eight households of landlords and rich peasants owned 120 acres; and landlords living in other villages owned another 90 or so. There were 40 families of upper-middle peasants who had enough to get along on and even to put aside a little each year. The remaining 373 families had only 218 acres between them. This again was not evenly distributed. In the household of the present secretary of the village Communist Party Branch there were then four people; they had one-sixth of an acre between them.

This was how it was in 'normal' times. But in 1940 the Japanese imperial troops swept up the valley bringing with them death and destruction.

[1] Mao Tse-tung divides the Chinese revolution into two steps: the democratic and the socialist. The democratic step in turn is divided into 'old' and 'new'; the former occurring in the period following the Opium War of 1840, and being led by the bourgeoisie; the latter following the Russian 'October Revolution' of 1917, and being led by the working class. See 'New Democracy', Mao Tse-tung, *Selected Works*, Vol. III, Lawrence & Wishart, London, 1955.

Two Years' History of Yangyi Commune

TABLE 1: *Definitions of Rural Classes*[2]

Landlords are those 'who own land, but do not engage in labour or engage in only supplementary labour, and who depend on exploitation for their means of livelihood'. Their major form of exploitation of the peasants is exacting rent, but they also lend money and hire labour.

Rich peasants, 'generally speaking, own the better means of production and have some floating capital. They take part in labour themselves, but as a rule depend on exploitation for most or a part of their means of livelihood. Exploitation by rich peasants is chiefly in the form of hiring wage labour (long-term labourers)'.

Middle peasants 'depend wholly or mainly upon their own labour for their living. In general they do not exploit others. Many of them themselves suffer exploitation on a small scale in the form of land rent and loan interest. But generally they do not sell their labour power'.

Upper-middle peasants 'practise a small degree fo exploitation, but this is not of a constant character and the income from it does not constitute their main means of livelihood'.

Lower-middle peasants 'on the whole are self-sufficient but suffer some exploitation through paying rent or interest'.

Poor peasants 'in general have to rent land for cultivation and suffer exploitation in the form of land rent, loan interest or hiring out their labour in a limited degree. The selling of labour power for limited periods is the basic feature distinguishing them from lower-middle peasants'.

Workers (including farm labourers) 'generally have neither land nor farm implements . . . They depend wholly or mainly on the sale of their labour power for their living'.

And then, as the peasants said, 'The sun arose in the West.' For units of the Communist-led 8th Route Army, driving eastwards from their bases in the heart of the Taihang Mountains, organized the peasants to defend themselves.

In 1942–43 in the midst of bitter struggle against the enemy, famine struck.

---

[2] These definitions were based on two documents issued in 1933 by the Democratic Central Government in Ruijin, Kiangsi Province, then capital of the Soviet Area in south-east China. These documents were re-issued, with slight modifications, by the Central Committee of the Communist Party in 1948, for use in the land reform in the Liberated Areas. They were brought up-to-date and published in 1950 for use throughout the country. (See *The Agrarian Reform Law of the People's Republic of China and Other Relevant Documents*, Foreign Languages Press, Peking, 1959.) Other definitions, used briefly after 1948, were: old and new middle peasants and old and new rich peasants, 'old' referring to those who had belonged to the class in question before land reform and 'new' to those who did so only after it. The new rich peasants practised capitalist exploitation (rather than the primarily feudal exploitation practised by old rich peasants). The swift success of the co-operative movement prevented their ever becoming a significant force in the countryside.

For untold generations famine had been a regular feature of Chinese rural life. It had brought death and disease to millions and forced millions more into beggary.

It had broken up families, forcing parents to sell, give away, abandon—even kill—their own children, rather than see them starve.

The famine of 1942–43 was exceptionally severe and in adjoining areas under Kuomintang administration the misery of the people was on a scale and of a nature which hardly bear description. The Communists, however, though they had only just established themselves in the Ten Mile Inn area, called on the people not to yield to famine as they had done in the past. On their initiative a militant peasant union came into being, which seized the hoarded grain of the landlords and rich peasants, cooked it in great cauldrons and served it to the hungry.

But these efforts, especially in the face of the Japanese onslaught, had their limits. They lessened suffering. They could not prevent it. People still went begging, sold their children, hanged themselves. In 49 of Ten Mile Inn's 400-odd families, 59 people starved to death.

Thoroughgoing social, political and economic reforms were clearly a matter of life and death to the majority of the people—for 70 per cent of them were poor peasants or hired hands. It was these who rallied most closely around the Communist Party and it was mainly from among them that new Communists were recruited during campaigns for the successive reforms the Party introduced. These included reduction of rent and interest, progressive taxation, mutual aid and at last the land reform, which was completed in 1948. Starvation no longer hovered at the peasant's elbow. The number of draught animals increased. Houses were built. The standard of living of the peasants improved.

All this was done on the basis of equitable individual ownership of the land. But though half an acre of land per head may make for justice, it does not permit prosperity. The individual farmer no longer starved to death. He lived. But his life was still one of poor food and harsh toil—so long as he hoed his own row, with next to no capital and with tools which had changed but little in two thousand years.

The first step towards overcoming the limitations of small-scale individual ownership was the large-scale development of mutual aid. This had begun back in 1942 during the war against Japan. With the land reform, which took place between 1946 and 1948, it surged forward. By 1948 there were 485 mutual aid groups in the area which was later to become Yangyi Commune, embracing half of the households. In 1951 there was a fresh upsurge of mutual aid which raised the number of groups to some 700 and included 85 per cent of the households in the area. Most of these groups consisted of ten

5

to twenty families and a system of accounting grew up to record man and animal labour days given and received.

Again production went up. Living standards rose—for the majority. But not for all.

The delicate balance of the family unit might be destroyed by illness or death. And tradition held that when a parent died, his or her share of the land should be sold to ensure a proper burial. Some had bad luck. Li Bao-hui, formerly a poor peasant, at first gained a growing share of the new prosperity by buying and selling draught animals. He made quick profits—until he bungled his biggest deal and had to sell five *mu*[3] of his new-won land to meet his obligations. A few farmers were lazy or inefficient. Fu Chou-tze, widely known as a loafer, had received four *mu* at the time of the land reform. But he neglected his fields and his yields were low, so to pay taxes and buy clothes he sold small plots of land each year; at the end of three years he had parted with half his holdings. Others neglected their land for different reasons. They spent so much time and energy on public service that they had little left for their fields.

On the other hand some were far better off than the average—through having exceptionally good land, plenty of hands and few dependents in the family and through seizing any chance to buy land put on sale by those stricken by misfortune. These stayed out of the mutual aid groups and hired labour to work their extra land. Those at the other end of the scale—who had little land left—also withdrew from the mutual aid groups, to work for those better off. The political and economic reforms ensured that they were paid what were regarded as reasonable wages, but they were still exploited.

In short, within a few years of the land reform some were getting richer, others poorer. Land, houses, draught animals and tools were being put on sale and were finding buyers. In 1951 alone, in the area now covered by Yangyi Commune, 200 families sold land and 100 sold housing. Class differentiation was reappearing.

Individual farming, even with mutual aid, was no general or lasting solution.

The land reform had destroyed the old semi-feudal land system and brought victory for the 'new democratic' revolution in the countryside. But ahead of it lay two roads. One, that of 'every man for himself', led to capitalist farming. The other, that of 'each for all and all for each' would lead to socialist co-operative farming.

On the side of the 'capitalist road' lay the whole weight of tradition and age-old habit—not to mention the drive and ambition of those families who were buying land and animals.

On the side of the 'socialist road' lay first and foremost the Communist Party with its great prestige won through successful

---

[3] A *mu* is roughly one-sixth of an acre, or one-fifteenth of a hectare.

leadership in driving out the Japanese, defeating the Kuomintang armies and carrying out the land reform. 'The Party' was no distant or alien outside force. Each village had its branch and in some cases had done so for ten years or more; and into each branch had been recruited those villagers who proved themselves most able, daring and self-sacrificing in different phases of the struggle. On the socialist side, too, were those peasants whom circumstances had forced to sell their land and labour and who feared above all a return to the bad old days.

At the time of the land reform the majority of peasants were not yet aware of the fork in the road ahead. Yet, in a sense, it lay within themselves. For they had a dual nature: on the one hand they were tillers of the soil and producers of its fruits, on the other they were owners of the land and sellers of its produce. The former characteristic predisposed them towards socialism, the latter towards capitalism.

The struggle to win the majority for socialism was the main task in the next stage of the socialist revolution in the countryside. Mutual aid had been the first step in this direction; the second was the organizing of farming co-operatives.

SETTING OUT ON THE SOCIALIST ROAD

Mutual aid made possible some rationalizing of labour. In busy seasons such as sowing and harvesting, a team of farmers with draught animals could be concentrated in the fields of one team member after another, instead of each family doing the job without enough hands for efficient division of labour, often without any draught animals. In slack seasons mutual aid made it possible for some farmers to be released from all work on the land. These could earn money doing trade-and-transport,[4] brick-making or other side-occupations. But mutual aid had its limitations. It rationalized the use of labour, not the use of land. Each farmer planted what his family needed, not what his land was most suited for. Once the advantages of rationalizing labour had been grasped, some naturally began to think of extending the principle to land. This put elementary or semi-socialist co-operatives on the agenda.

In the winter of 1951–52 three experimental farming co-operatives were set up in the county. One of them, organized by the National Labour Hero Ren Qing-mei, was in Little Yetao, not ten miles from Ten Mile Inn. Here the proceeds were evenly split, one half being shared out according to the amount of land each family had invested, the other half according to the amount of work it had done.

---

[4] The buying of raw or processed materials (such as coal or cotton seed cakes) or handicraft products (such as pottery) at the point of production, transporting them by cart or carrying-pole to a market some way off and re-selling at a small profit plus carrying charges. See also Chapter XIII, p. 146.

In the first year of the co-operative's existence output on its land was 38 per cent above the village per *mu* average.

In the winter of 1952–53, the Spinning Heroine Guo Heng-de of Bailin, following in Ren Qing-mei's footsteps, persuaded 16 families in her village to pool their land and labour. The 16 families dwindled to 6 when disease struck the co-operative's herd of sheep and goats. But these 6 weathered the storm and reaped a bumper harvest. Their average yield per *mu* was 30 *jin*[5] higher than that on land worked by mutual aid and 50 *jin* above that on land farmed individually.

Time and again during 1953 some of the cadres of Ten Mile Inn raised the question of organizing a farming co-operative in their village. But in China as a whole experience in setting up and running such co-operatives was considered too scanty to warrant a general switch-over. Meanwhile the policy, summed-up in the words 'only successes—no failures allowed', was for just a chosen few to take the step. Ten Mile Inn had to wait. The only places in the county permitted to organize trial co-operatives were those where the local Party Branch had exceptionally high prestige and where the local cadres had shown themselves to be especially able. If at this early stage co-operatives had sprung up everywhere, it was felt, the general run of cadres might have found themselves unable to cope with the problems which were bound to arise. In this event they might have made serious mistakes, or the co-operative might have failed altogether. In either case the bulk of the villagers would have been prejudiced against the new type of organization.

For these reasons the number of co-operatives in the area was kept down to twelve. These first twelve were watched with hope by some, with doubts or even hostility by others.

Even within the Communist Party there had been controversy over whether to start on co-operation immediately or to wait. Some said that since China was not industrially advanced and so not yet in a position to mechanize agriculture, it was impossible to achieve co-operation quickly. Others prophesied that a rapid realization of co-operation was bound to lower agricultural output. Still others feared that it would impair the unity of the peasants by making not only the rich, but the upper-middle peasants dissatisfied with Government and Party policy, or even hostile to it, and leaving only the worse off in favour. But the majority position was to 'strike while the iron was hot', to move towards socialist farming before capitalist farming had a chance to consolidate itself in the countryside.[6]

The question was: could co-operatives achieve higher yields

[5] One *jin* equals roughly 1·1 pounds or half a kilogram.

[6] See Liu Shao-chi, 'The Victory of Marxism-Leninism in China', *Ten Glorious Years*, Foreign Languages Press (F.L.P.), Peking, 1959, p. 11.

than individual farmers? Each area had to provide its own answer. In Yangyi the autumn harvest accounting for 1953 showed that per *mu* output on the land of the twelve co-operatives in the area was well above the average. The figures were:

On farms individually worked:	190 *jin*
On farms worked with mutual aid:	210 *jin*
On farming co-operatives:	230 *jin*

Co-operatives achieved higher yields—in Yangyi and elsewhere in China—not simply through collective work on collectively-managed land. They had applied four basic principles. These were: that all members benefit, not just some at the expense of others; that management of land, labour and capital be steadily improved; that farming technique—seed selection, use of fertilizer and insecticide, etc.—be constantly advanced; and finally that the means of production be expanded, with more land being brought under cultivation, more water conservancy being undertaken and the number of draught animals and farm implements increased.

In the winter of 1953–54 there was a nation-wide movement to study the Communist Party's General Line for the Transition to Socialism[7] and the socialist transformation of the countryside through the organizing of co-operatives, was singled out for special attention.[8] Following this study movement peasants throughout the county began converting their mutual aid groups into farming co-operatives. In the county as a whole the number of co-operatives rose to 105, taking in 18 per cent of the households and 13 per cent of the land.[9] The biggest of these was led by Ren Qing-mei of Little Yetao and comprised 125 households. It was at this time that Ten Mile Inn set up its first co-operative consisting of 19 families. The organizing of co-operatives continued rapidly throughout the year. By the end of 1954, in Bailin, with its 1,400 families, 24 had been formed, comprising 1,020 families—72 per cent of the people in the village.

Not all who joined were whole-hearted. Some had mixed feelings. In Yangyi townlet there was an upper-middle peasant named Meng. There were four in his family and they had six acres and a

[7] That is, the period from the setting up of the People's Republic until the establishment of socialist relations of ownership and production. The General Line was: to bring about step by step, socialist industrialization and the socialist transformation of agriculture, handicrafts and capitalist industry and trade.

[8] 'Decisions on the Development of Agricultural Producers' Co-operatives' promulgated by the Central Committee of the Chinese Communist Party, December 1953. These decisions were based on a summing-up of experience in carrying out the Draft Decisions circulated in December 1951.

[9] By May 1954, as an outcome of this nationwide movement, there were over 95,000 farming co-operatives with a total membership of more than 1,700,000 households.

mule. When the local co-operative had won initial success, Meng, enticed by the higher yields and urged by his Young Communist daughter-in-law, became a member. But he found the work uncomfortably strenuous for he had become accustomed to hiring labour at rush periods. But what irked him beyond endurance was to see his mule used by fellow co-operative members as if it were their own. Besides, quite a number of the better-off peasants had not joined the co-operative. So Meng decided to pull out. His daughter-in-law (his son was away at college) felt that this would be wrong and did her utmost to make him change his mind but without success. As a last resort, feeling she could never be happy in such a family she threatened to apply for a divorce. Meng had to choose between his daughter-in-law and his mule. He chose the mule. He reasoned: 'My son will always be able to find himself another wife, once he's graduated. But it won't be so easy for me to get another mule. Inside the co-op I can hardly call my mule my own. Out of it, I've got my mule and my son. And in time I'll have another daughter-in-law as well.'

The daughter-in-law, however, changed her mind. Old Meng, after all, was her father-in-law, not her husband. And this was 'the new society'. She gave up the idea of a divorce and said she would insist on her husband and herself setting up their own separate household. This meant dividing the property—the land and other means of production, including the mule. Old Meng was in a dilemma.

The girl, as a Youth League member, took the matter up with the village Communist Party Branch. They said to her that 'dividing the family' would be very hard on the old man. It would mean putting undue pressure on him. The peasants must have freedom to join, stay out of or withdraw from the co-operatives of their own free will. They must be convinced by facts.

So the girl agreed to give the old man a year's grace and father-in-law and daughter-in-law went on farming in the old way. It was a hard grind. The family's yield for the year turned out to be 210 *jin* per *mu* (remarkable for an individual effort). The co-operative's was 245 *jin*. Old Meng applied for readmittance to the co-operative and after being made to cool his heels for a while was accepted.

About this time a little verse became popular in the locality. It ran:

> You can't build a wall with only one stone,
> You can't build a house with one beam.
> The co-op's far better than working alone;
> Together our strength is supreme.

The year 1955 started off with a debate on the relative merits of the two courses open to farmers: to hoe their own row or to co-operate. This made the advantages of co-operation clearer than ever and immediately following it the number of co-operatives rose to 214, with a membership of 78 per cent of the households. Eighteen of these comprised 100 or more households each.

Organizing continued throughout the year. By the end of it virtually every peasant was in a co-operative. Ten Mile Inn had twelve comprising 97 per cent of the village population. The picture was the same in the surrounding villages. 1955 was a year of great advance in co-operation.

This advance was not only of number but of kind. The debate led to general agreement that 'the co-op's far better than working alone', but raised the question what sort of co-op it was to be. How was the increased output to be distributed? Up to this time, 50 per cent of the proceeds had gone to dividends on the land invested by the members, the other 50 per cent to labour performed. Those peasant families with relatively little land and plenty of able-bodied workers were all for increasing the payment for labour and reducing that for land, even for dropping it altogether. Those with more land than labour and those who preferred to give up labour on the land in favour of trading or other more profitable activities tended to think the opposite. Some of the cadres feared that if payment on land was reduced or done away with, the better-off peasants might withdraw from the co-operatives. Nevertheless a change was made. Payment on land was reduced to 30 per cent and that on labour raised to 70 per cent. Despite the cadres' fears, very few well-off peasants withdrew, for though they might have liked to, they feared that they would be unable to hire labour.

At the same time other problems emerged, such as how to improve farm implements and make the best use of land, labour and draught animals.

The land at this time was still privately owned and invested by its owner in the co-operative he joined. Holdings were scattered and some of the Ten Mile Inn villagers, for instance, owned plots in other villages, while some peasants of other villages owned plots in Ten Mile Inn. This not only involved a waste of time walking to and fro but also interfered with ploughing. And things had not yet developed to the point at which one co-operative would plough another co-operative's land for it—except in isolated cases where obstructive boundary markers were surreptitiously moved out of the plough's way! This hardly fostered the spirit of co-operation. Nor did disputes over the different crops to be planted by different co-operatives working adjoining fields. If sorghum, for example, which grows to a height of eight feet or more and has spreading roots, were to be planted on both sides of low-lying crops like sweet potatoes, the latter would be deprived of sunlight, air and nutriment. Sometimes agreements were negotiated on such matters. But these agreements were not always kept. One Ten Mile Inn co-operative agreed with its neighbour not to plant sorghum on a certain plot though this crop had long been grown there. Later it had second thoughts about the change, feeling that sorghum would grow best there after all. So it went back to its original plan. Members of the other co-operative, considering they had been cheated, pulled the grain up by the roots.

Private ownership and collective use of implements and draught animals also involved contradictions. Sometimes, just when an animal was to carry manure to the fields, up would come its owner saying that he needed it for grinding grain at the mill, or that his wife wanted to ride it on a visit to a relative in another village.

There was also the question of management. Collective labour on collectively-managed private holdings presented entirely new problems. Inexperienced cadres were taxed to the limit; sometimes beyond it. This was a nation-wide phenomenon.

This period of rapid change in which co-operatives increased in number and size and changed in nature, in which they were still finding their feet, gave rise to divergent estimates on how co-operation was progressing. Was its growth healthy? Or had things got out of hand? Was a drastic curtailment called for? Some urged a slowing down, or even a retreat because they felt that the movement had 'gone beyond the cadres' experience' and that it would prove impossible to consolidate even those co-operatives already set up.

Then, on 31 July, 1955, Mao Tse-tung made a speech on 'The Question of Agricultural Co-operation' which started:

> Throughout the Chinese countryside a new upsurge in the socialist mass movement is in sight. But some of our comrades are tottering along like a woman with bound feet, always complaining that others are going too fast. They imagine that by picking on trifles, grumbling unnecessarily, worrying continuously and putting up countless taboos and commandments they are guiding the socialist mass movement in the rural areas on sound lines.[10]

Granting that the socialist revolution was new and that the Party had no experience of socialist revolution, Mao Tse-tung asked, 'How are we to get such experience: by sitting back and waiting for it, or by throwing ourselves into the struggle for socialist revolution and learning in the process?'

When the rush work in farming was over for the year, there was a movement to study this speech. Cadres who earlier in the year had been daunted by the newness of the task facing them and lacked confidence in their own ability to cope with it, now began to feel they were on firmer ground. They criticized themselves for their 'boundfoot' approach and took a fresh look at the co-operative

---

[10] Mao Tse-tung, 'The Question of Agricultural Co-operation', F.L.P., Peking, 1956.

movement and the tasks before them. The conclusion of this discussion in Ten Mile Inn, as in the whole of the Chinese countryside, was that an advance must be made to fully socialist co-operatives in which distribution would be based entirely upon the amount of work done and the land would be owned collectively.

Some such co-operatives already existed in the county. The leading villagers of Ten Mile Inn went to see how they were run and to talk things over with their members. They became convinced that such co-operatives meant still bigger yields; and that they had the ability and resources to set them up. So in 1956 Ten Mile Inn removed all its boundary stones, merged all its small, semi-socialist farming co-operatives, and established a fully socialist co-operative in which the land was collectively owned. It embraced the entire village. The farmers called it a 'high level co-op' as distinct from the 'low level co-ops' in which land was collectively worked but individually-owned and whose system of distribution was based partly on investment.

The establishment of the socialist co-operative in Ten Mile Inn brought to an end both private farming and the buying and selling of the main means of production and the tendency for an exploiting and an exploited class to emerge among the farmers. It made for more rational use of land, labour and draught animals, and for more efficient irrigation. The concentration of resources permitted investment in more efficient implements. Seventeen two-wheeled, double-shared ploughs were bought. More important still, with the removal of boundary stones, tractors could be and were used for the first time.

Another historic development was the starting of the first public system of security for the aged, the orphaned, the widowed and the disabled who had no means of support. The co-operative gave them supplies of food, clothing and fuel, provided education for the young and promised proper burial for the old. These were known as the 'Five Guarantees'.

LOCAL REVOLUTIONARY LEADERS

Completion of the New Democratic Revolution and the initial success in the Socialist Revolution were not bestowed on the people of Yangyi by a corps of revolutionaries from outside. They were achieved by the process of 'taking root and sending forth branches', or 'discovering and training activists among the farm labourers and poor peasants, and through them forming ties with the masses and setting them in action'.[11] Three of such local 'activists' illustrate the

[11] Teng Tse-hui, Director of the Department of Rural Work of the Central Committee of the Communist Party of China, speech at the 8th National Congress of the C.C.P., 1956. *Documents of the 8th National Congress*, Vol. II, F.L.P., Peking, 1956.

process in the Yangyi area. Ren Qing-mei of Little Yetao and Guo Heng-de of Bailin played key roles in the land reform and in mutual aid. Jin Han-cheng, also of Bailin, was too young; but he joined them when they went on to head the movement to establish farming co-operatives.

Ren Qing-mei, born amidst the 'bald-headed' hills of Little Yetao in 1901, was the first person in the Yangyi area to join the Communist Party.

'My family were tenant farmers,' he relates. 'Most of the time we ate husks and wild herbs. Now and then the men would have a bit of millet, but never the women. For two months a year I went around bare from the waist up. If I did manage to get a new suit of home-spun cloth for the new year's holidays, I wore it for three days and then put it away till the next new year. It had to last me at least six or seven years.

'I only had three months' schooling as a child, when I was nine. It wasn't till after I'd joined the Party at the age of thirty-seven that I learned to read and write. As a young man I worked for a landlord. He had over two hundred *mu*. And he ran an inn, too. So every morning I had to get up at dawn and before breakfast I had to fill five big vats with water. It all had to be carried from half a mile away and I had a bad back. But the landlord cured that for me. There were quite a few of us hands working for him and at noon we ate and rested in the fields. But he wouldn't let us rest in the shade. There were only a few trees and he said that we'd start quarrelling over who was to be in the shade—so we all had to stay in the sun. It was hot all right—but the heat seemed to cure my back.

'He wasn't so kind in other ways, though,' went on Ren. 'When I went to the fields in the morning I had to carry a great load of manure. And when I came back in the evening I had to lug a big stone that could be used for building. He squeezed all the work he could out of us—and all for twelve silver *yuan* a year. That wouldn't buy even a *jin* of grain a day—and you needed more than that for what he made you do.

'I couldn't afford to marry till I was twenty-seven' (old by prevailing standards) 'and even then I only managed it because my parents joined a sort of club. The members paid into a pool so that each family in turn would have enough to buy wedding gifts. My wife's family didn't expect much because they were famine refugees from Shansi.

'That was in 1928. And that was the sort of life I led, the life of a hired hand or a poor peasant, for the next ten years. The country was in a state of chaos, with petty warlords fighting each other for power and plundering the people. In 1937 at the beginning of the war against Japan, in this area alone there were a couple of dozen of them—The Twenty-four Commanders they were called—but they were nothing but bandits, robbing, raping and looting wherever they went.

'Then as the Japanese army approached, they faded away—and a new sort of soldier arrived. They were the vanguard of the 8th Route Army, which was led by the Communist Party. They were different from that KMT rabble of The Twenty-four Commanders. They wore simple, patched uniforms and straw sandals and were kind and helpful to the people. I got to know one of the political instructors, Wang Tie. He said that the landlords led an easy life while the poor suffered—he didn't need to tell me that—but that the day would come when we poor people would own the land we tilled and be the masters. That was something new. And he told me about the Long March and the hardships that Chairman Mao himself put up with. So gradually I grew to understand that the Communist Party was the party of the working people, of people like me. And that same year, 1939, I joined it.'

Ren Qing-mei threw himself into the work of the Party. He was active in every reform it carried out and in every campaign it launched in Little Yetao. He helped to set up the local militia and to organize the evacuation of the village during Japanese mopping-up thrusts. He was at the forefront of the struggle against the landlords and rich peasants, first for the reduction of rent and interest, then, in 1944–45, for the elimination of old debts contracted at exorbitant rates of interest. He was a founder of one of the early (pre-land reform) mutual aid groups. And in 1946 he played a leading part in the struggle to win the land for the tiller.

This was a bitter and complex class struggle, for the landlords and rich peasants did not passively concede defeat. They even won some partial and temporary victories. One of these occurred in 1947 when they launched a slander campaign against Ren Qing-mei, and the township government and Party leaders, hearing of accusations from 'the village masses', suspended Ren from his posts as Party Branch Secretary and village cadre pending investigation. He never doubted that he would be cleared and in the spring of 1948, when the whole affair was brought into the open, he emerged with greater prestige than ever.

'I was elected a Labour Hero in 1950,' he relates, 'and was sent to a conference at Baoding. There I saw a film about the Soviet scientist Michurin. It showed that by using his methods you could make a poor mountain area prosperous. From that very moment I was determined to follow in Michurin's footsteps.'

This was not Ren Qing-me's first step towards enriching his village, for during the 1943 anti-famine production drive he had pioneered the planting of wheat there. 'But the Japanese came and set their horses to graze in the wheat-field.' After they left, wheat was planted again, but in 1946 it was struck by blight; so Ren went down to the plains to get better seed. Then, from his harvest in 1947, the first after land reform, he distributed thirty *jin* of seed among all the households in the village.

To follow in Michurin's footsteps and cover the hills with fruit trees meant first of all raising saplings. Ren had just under an acre and a half after the land reform for a family of six, and he set aside almost a quarter of it for the saplings. This meant just that much less for grain, and so his second son, a boy of eight or nine, asked his father why he did it. Ren Qing-mei replied: 'The Party's calling on us to do it, and if it weren't for the Party I'd have no land at all.' When the saplings grew he distributed them among the villagers.

When relatives and friends urged him to be more 'practical', meaning that he should keep them for himself or sell them, Ren replied: 'I'm a Communist. I'll be rich when everybody's rich.'

*   *   *

The first woman in Yangyi area to join the Communist Party came from Bailin, the large, sprawling village on the dry uplands two miles from Yangyi townlet. Her name was Guo Heng-de.

Before Guo Heng-de was born (in 1919) her father died, leaving his wife two *mu* of land. For a lone mother and daughter to survive on that, in the landlord-ridden, warlord-ravaged Chinese countryside of those days, took strength of character. Both mother and daughter had it. As a child Heng-de scoured the hillsides for fuel and carried back crushing loads. By the time she was thirteen she was a skilful spinner. When she was fifteen she married, but her husband was soon forced by poverty to leave for the far North-east to try and scrape together a living.[12] Meanwhile the young wife supported herself by needlework. When she was seventeen her mother died.

Two years later, in 1937, news of the Communists' activities further up the valley reached Bailin. By 1938 guerrilla detachments had made the village too hot for the Japanese to hold and communist cadres were already operating in it, though still precariously. Following the Communist practice of relying on the poorest peasants, a woman cadre, named Guo Jing, found shelter in Guo Heng-de's home. She ate the same food as the poor peasants—husks and wild herbs—wore coarse home-spun cloth and spoke in homely language. 'We were soon like sisters,' said Guo Heng-de. Guo Jing stayed with Guo Heng-de two years and this close contact helped set the course for Guo Heng-de's life.

[12] Nothing was heard of him for years, as he did not know how to write and could not save enough money to go home. He was able to do so only after the North-east was liberated. He returned to Bailin to find his wife (whom he hardly knew) an outstanding cadre. The couple were reunited and brought up a family, but though the husband supported Guo Heng-de in her activities as a cadre, he never aspired to become one himself. In 1960 he was a cook in one of Bailin's community dining-rooms.

When Japanese forces drove through the area on mopping-up expeditions, Guo Heng-de showed the communist cadres to secret caves, cooked for them and hid their documents. When a landlord threatened her with death for associating with the 'red bandits' she was not intimidated. 'I never wavered,' she said. 'I knew they were for the poor. I would have given my life for them.' In 1942 when she joined the Communist Party, she was only twenty-four; but her whole life made her feel that the communist-led reforms were just, and that she should fight for them.

In the same year she was elected head of a small spinning group, set up as part of the movement to fight famine by increasing production. Later she headed an 8th Route Army relief centre, which distributed grain and cotton and saved 140 people from starvation. 'That was a terrible year,' said Guo Heng-de. 'Over four hundred people left the village to go to Shansi Province as beggars. But it was a bad time for begging. A hundred and twenty-odd starved to death. And here in the village it was the same. In Guo Da-cheng's family of five, two starved to death, one daughter was given away as a child bride and one son as a child bridegroom. There were suicides, too. Guo Ru-zhi couldn't pay his rent so he hanged himself. His cousin scraped together enough to pay it, but then he had nothing left. So he hanged himself too.' In one family the husband wanted to sell the children rather than hear them whimper with hunger, but the wife threatened to leave him if he did. Guo Heng-de gave them food saved from her own scanty meals and half a bushel of grain bought with money she had earned by spinning. This saved the marriage. (Today the couple live happily together; one of their children is at university; the other in the army.) 'There were seven families like that,' said Guo Heng-de. 'Guo Jing and I helped them all—because we were Communists.'

Guo Heng-de helped young wives, too, to stand up to tyrannical mothers-in-law.[13] In 1944 she was elected Spinning Heroine, First Class, at a conference of the whole Border Region.[14] The same year she became head of the Bailin Women's Association.

In 1945 there was a movement to implement the law for Reduction of Rent and Interest. Though this law had long been on the Kuomintang statute books, it was carried out only in the Liberated Areas, and even there only after a struggle. Peasants over whom the landlords had so long had the power of life and death were often afraid that some day the Communists (there were only six in the village then) would go, and Kuomintang landlord rule return. So the more timid paid the reduced rates by day, and secretly made up the

---

[13] The old-style patriarchal family, which existed in the feudal or semi-feudal countryside, gave rise even among the poor to the notorious 'tyrannical mother-in-law'.

[14] The Shansi-Hopei-Shantung-Honan Border Region.

balance to the landlords at night. Guo Heng-de and the other village Communists worked tirelessly among the peasants, explaining that the Communist Party would always stand by the people; and that as long as the peasants followed the Party's lead in the struggle for their rights the oppressive old régime could never be restored. Gradually even the more timid peasants were won for Reduction of Rent and Interest; and for the land reform and mutual aid which followed.

Guo Heng-de headed the first mutual aid group, of eight families in Bailin. Then in 1952, when she first heard about farming co-operatives, she went to the Party Committee and volunteered to take the lead in organizing one in her village. The co-operatives were new then and the Committee were doubtful if a woman, even such a woman as this, could manage it. But Guo Heng-de went to Little Yetao and conferred with Ren Qing-mei about the one he was successfully leading. On her return, with the help of the Party Branch, she built her mutual aid group up to sixteen families and persuaded the members to change it into a semi-socialist co-operative, sharing 40 per cent of the proceeds according to land invested and 60 per cent according to work done.

It was not all plain sailing. The co-operative bought sheep and goats in the mountains to the west but lacked experience in raising them. They died off one by one until the flock had dwindled from 126 to 20. Three families of middle peasants began grumbling and saying that the co-operative was no good. Many of the other members lost heart and in the end ten of the sixteen families withdrew. But once more Guo Heng-de 'didn't waver'! 'We six families that are left,' she said, 'can still get a bumper harvest.' And they did. Their yield was 30 *jin* per *mu* higher than that of the mutual aid groups and 50 *jin* higher than that of peasants working their land individually. Then those who had withdrawn asked to come back. Guo Heng-de and the others who had stood by the co-op welcomed them, but not without reservations. First they wanted to point out the lessons to be drawn from this experience. This was done in the winter of 1953 when classes were set up to study the 'General Line of the transitional period'. When this course of study—illustrated by what had happened in the Bailin co-op itself—had driven home the advantages of co-operation, those who had backed out were readmitted. But not all at once. The poor peasant families were accepted first, on the grounds that the 'rural semi-proletarians' stood to gain the most from the socialist transformation of agriculture and in the long run would be its staunch supporters.

Guo Heng-de's co-operative grew steadily after that. It soon consisted of 33 households, more than double the original membership. Then new co-operatives sprang up one after another until there were 6 in the village, with a total membership of 99 families.

The Years Before the Commune

In the spring of 1954 a further study movement was launched, this time of the Draft Constitution of the People's Republic (adopted in September 1954). This movement, which clearly showed the significance of co-operatives in the transformation of agriculture, swept through the whole village. By the end of 1955 eighteen more co-operatives had been set up. This brought the total to 24, embracing over 1,000 households, more than 70 per cent of the village population. In 1956 Guo Heng-de took the lead in transforming Bailin's semi-socialist co-operatives into fully socialist ones. At the same time, to help solve the vital problem of irrigation, she led a movement for the digging of rain storage tanks.

In the course of each new task—fighting the Japanese, overcoming famine, organizing mutual aid, setting up co-operatives—Guo Heng-de never tired. Her years of revolutionary work won her the name 'The Unfading Red Flower'.

*　　　*　　　*

Jin Han-cheng, like Guo Heng-de, was a native of Bailin. But when the Communists first reached the village in 1938 he was only seven.

'My father was a skilled carpenter,' he relates, 'but his skill did him little good. He inherited debts from his father and so he soon fell into the clutches of a landlord. We ate coarse grain' (sorghum and millet) 'all through the year and were lucky to get a little wheat at New Year. Even then it would only be three *jin* or so—just enough for a bit of a treat for the holiday. Often we had nothing to eat in the house. Mother would bring the pot of water to a boil and then go out to try and borrow something to put in it. If she had no luck I'd go.

'My father was full of illusions. He believed the old tale that people like himself were dependent on the landlords and thought it was kind of the landlord to provide him with a job. He couldn't see that it was the landlord who depended on him.'

Jin's father and grandfather had both been illiterate and they thought that their own ignorance rather than landlord rule was the root of their misfortune. So the family pinched and saved to send Han-cheng to an old-style school. 'But all the teacher ever did,' Jin continues, 'was to make you learn the classics and beat you. So I left. Not long after that the 8th Route Army set up a 'Resist Japan' school and my father was delighted to have me go there. He thought any sort of schooling was bound to bring good fortune.

'But that was before land reform and life was still bitter. I hardly had clothes to go to school in, though some of my classmates were sons of well-to-do peasants, and their parents even let them run up a bill at the dumpling shop. But it was a "half-work, half-study" school and they were so soft and pampered that the work was too

C　　　　　　　　　　19

much for them and they dropped out. After I'd been at school only a month or so the Japanese began to advance and the headmaster urged me to go home. Things were getting dangerous, he said. I didn't want to leave that school, but I had to in the end. The headmaster himself was killed, gun in hand, fighting the Japanese.'

From the age of thirteen to sixteen his schooling was constantly interrupted by the war, but somehow he kept it up, to say nothing of teaching at a spare-time school and doing propaganda work for the New Democratic Youth League.[15] He finally finished the senior primary course and went on to a teachers' training school at the age of sixteen. This was not a 'half-work, half-study' school but Jin was forced to make it so. His family had received a little land in the first wave of land reform in 1946, but it was hardly enough to make ends meet and the boy did part-time work as a builder and as a porter, carrying eighty-pound loads on a pole. With a great effort his mother managed now and then to send him something good to eat —but that was not what he wanted. All he cared about was buying books.

He was an outstanding student, but when his father fell ill and was unable to work, Jin prepared to leave the training school. The authorities would not hear of him going and secured financial aid for the family from the Liberated Area Government. Then after further training in Handan (then capital of the Border Region, now of the region) he went to teach in a senior primary school in the prosperous townlet of Beiyen. There he was outstanding for excellent relations with his pupils and was elected a model teacher. He liked his work as a teacher, but in 1951 he felt he should respond to an urgent call for young cadres, made by the administration.

So at the age of twenty Jin Han-cheng became a cadre. Two years later, after taking part in the movement against waste, corruption and bureaucracy, he joined the Communist Party. This fulfilled an ambition first fired by the headmaster who nine years before had died fighting the Japanese.

Jin Han-cheng, Guo Heng-de and Ren Qing-mei were of the same social origin, having been born into families of poor peasants. It was these once exploited and all but landless 'rural semi-proletarians' whom the Communist Party relied on to fight for its policy in the countryside. And it was tested cadres like these three who guided the people of Yangyi along 'the road to socialism'. Jin Han-cheng himself said, when looking back on this period of the co-operatives: 'Many cadres were steeled in the struggles of the co-operative movement. 380 Party members and old cadres became leaders of co-ops; 873 young people also became cadres, either of co-ops or of production teams. Some old cadres and Party members

---

[15] Predecessor of the Communist Youth League.

dropped behind, but people like Guo Heng-de and Ren Qing-mei were always in the van.'

'THE GREAT DEBATE'

Around Yangyi the transition from individual to collective farming fell into three main stages. First had come mutual aid, starting in 1942 with seasonal groups formed for collective labour and developing into year-round groups involving some division of labour or specialization and the running of group-owned enterprises such as oil-presses, brick or lime kilns and herds of sheep or goats. This first stage took ten years or so. Then came the stage of semi-socialist farming co-operatives, starting with returns based equally on land and labour and going on to higher returns for labour and lower ones for land. After four years the third stage of fully socialist co-operatives was reached, in which the land became collective property and dividends were paid on labour alone.

The purpose of these changes had been to increase output and bring the mass of peasants bigger incomes. But to achieve this it was necessary to exploit the possibilities for technical improvements in farming created by improved organization. So throughout the period of transition there had been a series of production movements—for collecting fertilizer, improving tools and seed and introducing new crops.

With the setting up of socialist co-operatives a draft National Program for Agricultural Development[16] was drawn up. This was a blue-print for the modernizing of Chinese agriculture within twelve years (1956–67). Its forty points covered every aspect of rural development from mechanization and electrification to beautifying the countryside with flowering trees and shrubs, wiping out illiteracy and taking care of the aged.

With the popularizing of this program among the members of the new socialist co-operative, to which everyone in the Yangyi area now belonged, there was a marked upswing in rural construction and the stage was set for a leap forward in production. This was prevented by exceptionally bad weather, spring drought being followed by such heavy summer rains that the Min River, usually dry, became a torrent. Hail storms, too, did much damage, especially to the wheat crop. But though some co-operatives suffered losses, others actually maintained the increased yields of 1955. Thus disaster was staved off. This raised the prestige of the co-operatives, for most farmers felt that without them the year would have been calamitous.

It still was a year of battle, and not only against the weather.

16 Published as a pamphlet, F.L.P., Peking, 1960.
21

Managing a farm four or five hundred times as large as the traditional family holding called for whole new sets of procedures. Some
co-operatives in the county could not cope with this and suffered
losses; some just managed to get by. But others achieved remarkable
results despite the difficulties.

This lack of uniformity of achievement was to be found throughout the country and it fostered a fresh divergence of views within the
Communist Party. Did the cases of poor management show that the
co-operative movement had been pressing on too fast? Or did the
striking successes of the best units show that the way to consolidate
the weaker ones was to push ahead? (Actually in the winter of
1956–57 there was a general slowing down in the nation as a whole.
Soil and water conservation projects were far fewer than in the
previous winter and campaigns to accumulate fertilizer were also
less keen. The total area sown to food crops was ten million acres
less than in 1956.)

The difference between these two approaches was part of a
bigger struggle which came to a head in the 'anti-rightist' campaign
in the summer of 1957. At top Party and Government levels the
outcome of this battle in the political and ideological field was a
defeat for those who called for slowing down and victory for those
who pressed for speeding ahead.

In the autumn following this movement at the top, the Party
organizations at basic levels throughout the countryside launched
rectification movements.[17] These too developed into hard-fought
battles against 'right deviationist conservative ideas'.

In Yangyi, the local Party branches, once convinced that the
solution to the difficulties in their co-operatives lay in pressing ahead
rather than in drawing back, prepared to improve management.
Accordingly, in the winter of 1957, each co-operative in the Yangyi
area carried out a check-up on five points. First it looked into the
way it had handled distribution, to ensure that reasonable ratios
had been set between payment to members and public funds for
running expenses. Some co-operatives were found to have erred on
the side of accumulating funds at the expense of the immediate
well-being of the members; others had depleted their funds by paying
out too much to members. Each co-operative also considered its
division of authority between the chairman and his committee at the
top and the team leaders below. This brought to light in many cases
a tendency to refer too much to the chairman, with a consequent
bogging-down of activity all along the line. Following this, systems
for fixing responsibility for farm tasks were looked into. A check

[17] In 1942 in a speech on the need to 'drive out' subjectivism, sectarianism
and jargon from Party work, Mao Tse-tung used the term, *zhengfeng*—a pun
meaning 'rectification' and 'a gust of wind'. The Chinese Communist Party has
used it ever since to denote movements for improving ideology and style of work.

was also made on whether co-operatives were being run 'industriously, thriftily and democratically', any expenditures which did not contribute to production being condemned. Methods used by co-operative cadres to get members to play a part in administration were also investigated. The fifth and final target of the check-up was the overall planning and publicity done among members on the future of co-operation in general and their own co-operative in particular.

After this check-up had been going on some time it broadened into a movement for education in socialism among all the people in the countryside. This took the form of a 'Great Debate' to thrash out the question of 'which road China's farmers should take—the road to socialism or the road to capitalism'. It was conducted by 'stating facts, making comparisons and reasoning things out'.

In and around Yangyi support for the socialist co-operatives was widespread. But it was not universal. A minority were lukewarm, sceptical or even opposed. According to an investigation in the village of South Yangyi, for example, five-sixths of the families were strongly for socialism, but nearly a sixth had their doubts and a handful were definitely hostile.[18]

In the old days before the land reform there had been a poor peasant in South Yangyi, called Su Wen-he. His family's land yielded less than half a pound of grain per person per day, so they had to live largely on husks and wild herbs. They never ate meat even during the New Year festival. Su had four sons but he was too poor to arrange a marriage for more than one of them. In the famine of 1942 Su and his youngest son both died of hunger. With the land reform the family's holding was increased to nearly five acres and they received two donkeys. Within a short time the two remaining bachelor sons got married and it was not long before Su's widow found herself with a family of three sons, three daughters-in-law, four grandsons and three grand-daughters, 'with twelve silk quilts, five cotton quilts and ten pairs of rubber overshoes'. When she died, shortly before the Great Debate, she was buried in a fine coffin and the leaders of the co-operative came to pay their respects to the bereaved. When Su Wen-he had died in 1942 he was buried in a reed mat. Not even this had been possible for the youngest son. He was buried in a hole by the side of the road.

All this was told by Su Wen-he's sons during the Great Debate. It reminded many listeners of their own past, moving them to anger at the thought of the old landlord rule, to resentment at those who opposed the reforms, and in some cases to remorse. One peasant had been so poor in the old days that he had no home of his own and slept in temples or under the eaves of other people's houses. After

---

[18] See Chapter XVII.

23

TABLE 2; *Table of per mu Yields for Grain in Yangyi Area*[19]
(from before the land reform to fully socialist co-operatives)

	Whole area
I. *After the Anti-Japanese War and before the Land Reform (1945–47)* Yungan Village 120 *jin*	130 *jin*
II. *After the Land Reform (1948)* Yungan Village 146 *jin*	152 *jin*
III. *During the Developing of Mutual Aid and the Emergence of Co-operative Farms (1953)* Farms worked individually Farms using mutual aid Co-operative farms (12 farms in 10 villages comprising 1·6 of households in the county) Yungan Semi-socialist Co-operative 183 *jin* (1954) Ten Mile Inn (1954) Farms using mutual aid 166 *jin* Semi-socialist co-operative (19 families) 200 *jin*	190 *jin* 210 *jin* 230 *jin*
IV. *Period of Widespread Semi-Socialist Farming Co-operatives (1955)*	245 *jin*
V. *Period of Socialist Farming Co-operatives (1956) (a year of floods and hail-storms)* Yungan Socialist Co-operative 230 *jin* Ten Mile Inn Socialist Co-operative 258 *jin*	227 *jin*
VI. *Following the General Line for Socialist Construction (the eve of the commune) (1958)* Yungan Socialist Co-operative 272 *jin* Ten Mile Inn Socialist Co-operative 316 *jin* Yangyi Socialist Co-operative 369 *jin* Little Yetao Socialist Co-operative 382 *jin*	313 *jin*

[19] Tables such as this, and most other local statistics, are based on figures compiled by brigade or work team accountants, mostly young people recently graduated from village primary schools. Generally speaking the figures may be taken as showing broad trends rather than as accurate in detail.

the land reform he became an 'upper-middle peasant', and when the co-operative was set up he gave it no support. 'I drank the water, but forgot those who dug the well,' he said during the debate. 'If it weren't for the Communist Party I'd have been dead long ago. How could I have failed to support the co-op? I was black-hearted.' And he struck himself.

In Ten Mile Inn there was a former rich peasant named Wang Jia-wen. 'Now that a man can't buy land any more,' he had complained, 'things are worse than before liberation. You can't even eat decently any more.' During the Great Debate a lean, wiry young man named Wang Ling-rong retorted to him: 'You talk as if you represented all of us. But you don't. You just represent yourself and a couple of others like you. I certainly wasn't better off before. Now we all get enough to eat—including you. What gets you is that the rest of us are as well off as you are now and you can't throw your weight around any more. So you think you're worse off than you used to be.'

This was what was meant by 'stating facts, making comparisons and reasoning things out'.

The effect of the debate was not merely to win over some of the waverers and even to convince a few of those opposed. More important was the effect on the majority, who already supported co-operation. The debate deepened their understanding of the past and the present and gave a clearer view of what lay ahead—mechanization, electrification and full-scale irrigation.

A new spirit pervaded the countryside following the debate. There was a fresh upsurge of enthusiasm for the 'socialist road'.

Chapter II

THE BIRTH OF YANGYI COMMUNE
(Summer, 1958)

THE new spirit which pervaded China's countryside after the debate between the 'two roads', took on tangible form.

In the six months from October 1957 to April 1958, over 58 million acres of land were brought under irrigation. This was 13 million acres more than in the eight years since the founding of the People's Republic; and 18 million more than in the thousands of years of China's previous history.[1]

During the same six months, fifteen and a half million tons of fertilizer was accumulated by farmers all over the country. This averaged a ton and a half an acre—three times as much as in 1956. And in the first four months of 1958, 48 million acres were afforested —one and a half times as much as in the previous eight years.

Then, when the farming season started, cadres and Party members in hundreds of thousands of co-operative farms began to run small experimental plots for various crops—wheat, maize, rice, cotton—on which they set new records and ended old ideas as to what could and could not be achieved.

As a result of all these efforts and of the unprecedented amount of work put into field management, the 1958 harvest was 35 per cent above that of 1957.[2] This was the Great Leap Forward in agriculture.

The burst of energy was not confined to farming. To provide a basis for rural industrialization, co-operative farms set up improvised blast furnaces. The whole countryside started smelting iron and steel.

In the Yangyi area water and soil conservation went on apace in co-operatives along the Min River during the winter months. A hundred members of Little Yetao co-operative took on the task of reclaiming over 300 acres of bare mountain-side. On its lower slopes they filled in ravines, built terraces and channelled in water, to make some seventeen acres of vegetable gardens. Higher up, by repairing

---

[1] Liu Shao-chi, 'Report on the Work of the Central Committee of the Communist Party of China to the Second Session of the Eighth National Party Congress, May 5, 1958', (F.L.P., Peking.)

[2] Corrected figure (after earlier over-estimates) given in 'Communique of 8th Plenary Session of the 8th Central Committee of the C.C.P.', *Documents*, F.L.P., Peking, 1959.

old terraces and building new ones, they reclaimed 45 acres for orchards, in which 5,000 fruit trees were planted. 'Fish-scale' pits —miniature terraces covering only half a square yard, so named because of their shape—were dug all over the steeper slopes. In each of these pockets of earth hardier trees were planted. By the end of the winter, when the work was finished, the once bare slope was covered with 15,000 saplings. Three channels were dug to bring water from the Ma Ming springs in the hills above the village down to the co-operative fields. And on one of these channels a power plant was built—the first in the Yangyi area. Every home in the village was fitted with electric lights—which many of the villagers had never even seen before.

Bailin co-operative had neither bare mountain slopes nor springs. Its problem was to conserve water for its dry, rolling upland fields. The solution was rain storage tanks—vat-shaped, small-necked, full-bellied holes in the ground, with a capacity of a few cubic metres. They were dug at carefully chosen folds in the ground which formed tiny natural drainage basins, fed by rivulets during every fall of rain.

Throughout the winter, soil and water conservation went on in all parts of the Yangyi area. At the same time those co-operative members who were not building up terraces or digging pits, rain storage tanks or channels were busy collecting fertilizer. By the spring of 1958 the whole area was ready to start ploughing and sowing on fields improved by four solid months of work.

A new movement now swept up almost all the Party members and co-operative cadres. This was for the running of high yield experimental plots. By the end of the 1958 farming season the following records had been set:

1958 RECORD YIELDS FOR STAPLE CROPS
IN YANGYI AREA

maize:	3,000 *jin* per *mu* on	5 *mu*	
	2,000 *jin* per *mu* on	28 *mu*	(round figures)
	1,000 *jin* per *mu* on	230 *mu*	
sweet potatoes:	10,000 *jin*[3] per *mu* on	62 *mu*	
millet:	2,612 *jin* per *mu* on	1 *mu*	(Guo Heng-de)
	1,056 *jin* per *mu* on	8 *mu*	

That year (1958) total farm output in the Yangyi area rose to 313 *jin* per *mu*. In Ten Mile Inn it went up from 258 *jin* of grain per *mu* in 1957 to 316 *jin*; and from 80 to 115 *jin* per *mu* for unginned cotton.

[3] In production statistics sweet potatoes are included under grain, 4 *jin* of sweet potatoes being counted as 1 *jin* of grain.

But before this record harvest was brought in the movement for smelting iron and steel began to gain momentum. In Yangyi it started with a discussion of whether farmers could make iron and steel at all. At the outset some thought they could not. The conclusion of the debate, however, was that they not only could but must, in order to bring about an early technical revolution in farming, iron and steel being essential for mechanization.

There is both iron and coal in the hills only a few miles from Yangyi townlet—the coal only twelve yards down—and as the movement got into its stride clusters of small furnaces appeared in co-operatives up and down the Min valley. Along the roads flowed a stream of ore from the local mines.

Each of the movements started since the winter of 1957–58 had raised its own problems. With this one the big question was transport. One pack animal could carry only a hundred-weight and a half; a cart drawn by two animals could carry ten times as much. Ten Mile Inn and other big villages on the highways had long done carting as a side-line. Villages off the highways, however, had only pack animals, which besides being inefficient for transport were needed for farm work. If only the big highway villages could cart the coal and iron, not just for themselves but for their neighbours! But each village formed a separate co-operative.

Transport was only one of the problems pointing to the need for a larger organization. Another more vital still was water.

In the winter soil and water conservation drive, though all the co-operatives could boast of successes, only Little Yetao could claim a measure of security from the vagaries of the weather. This was partly because the Ma Ming springs were in the hills just above it. Villages like Ten Mile Inn and Bailin, in spite of the recent improvements, were still very much at the mercy of the heavens. They needed channels from the springs not only for irrigation but to put an end once and for all to their shortage of drinking water.

The water flow at Ma Ming springs was normally about a cubic metre a second. But it was not efficiently used for irrigation. Besides, it was the cause of constant friction even after the socialist co-operatives were set up and 'socialist emulation' between Bailin and Yangyi was not unmixed with a memory of quarrels over water. In 1956 there had been a drought and Bailin's newly-established socialist co-operative had posted guards every third of a mile along the stream from Ma Ming to prevent interference with the flow of what little water there was. But it was no use. The people living along the stream knew the lie of the land and the flow of the water far better than those from Bailin; and they diverted 'their' water for their own use. None of it ever got to Bailin in spite of the guards.

Leaders of the different co-operatives broached the idea of a joint water conservancy and irrigation project. The response was far from whole-hearted. The people in the villages upstream were not interested, because they had their own water and those far downstream swore the water would never reach them. One man in Bailin said, 'If a drop of water ever flows here from Little Yetao I'll crawl between your legs three times.' Only the villages in the middle reaches favoured the project, but they lacked the resources to undertake it alone.

This was not the only reason for the idea being dropped. A channel from Little Yetao to Ten Mile Inn, for example, would have to run through the land of several co-operatives; so property boundaries and land utilization also entered into the picture.

The farmers pondered and discussed these matters. They knew that in the Soviet Union there were big collective farms. They had seen films about them at the mobile cinemas and some had been to conferences in the provincial capital or even in Peking, where they had heard delegates report on visits to the Soviet Union. Couldn't the Yangyi area set up some sort of collective farm as well? During the summer of 1958 cadres from several villages in the locality went more than once to the county government proposing that their co-operatives be merged into one big collective farm.

Many of those who pressed for such a merging or federating of co-operatives into a bigger unit, considered the question to be mainly one of size. As long as the unit was large enough to rationalize the use of water, they felt, the problems of land and labour could be solved.

But there were others, mainly cadres and Party members, who saw the question as one not only of size but of scope. Most villages, for instance, had four different types of co-operative. There were the agricultural producers' co-operatives for farming; supply and marketing co-operatives to supply these farming co-operatives with implements and fertilizer and to sell their produce for them; credit co-operatives (sometimes separate, sometimes, as in Ten Mile Inn, a branch of the supply and marketing co-operative), which made loans to the farming co-operatives to help them push forward production. Many villages also had handicraft co-operatives— usually groups of blacksmiths and carpenters making simple farm tools. As early as 1953 the Central Committee of the Communist Party (in its Resolution on Co-operatives) had pointed out that these different forms of rural co-operative, though different were complementary; that they interlocked and acted on each other, and that through them the economy was being integrated. What was needed now, it seemed, was some organizational form to co-ordinate all these separate units.

By 1955, in areas where co-operation was well advanced, local leaders were already stressing the need for co-ordination. The Party committee of one county in the Taihang Mountains, summing up

29

the tasks ahead of it, said: 'In the fields of administration and law, finance and economy, culture and education and public health and in mass organizations, all-round co-ordination of the various types of work is lacking.'[4]

With the socialist co-operatives embracing whole villages, the one-time village administration was swallowed up. The only duties remaining to the village heads were now registering births and deaths and mediating family quarrels.

In 1956, following a State Council directive, a merging of townships had taken place to keep them from coinciding with the growing co-operatives. Even so, the functions of the townships and the co-operative overlapped, for example in the field of tax collection.

By 1958, with the studying of the newly-adopted General Line, many cadres and Party members began to feel that more than co-ordination was called for. What they wanted was a broadening of the functions of the basic social unit.

THE GENERAL LINE

The new General Line, in fact, was already exerting an influence on all aspects of work and life in the countryside. The tasks of the previous General Line had been to carry out step by step socialist industrialization and the socialist transformation of private industry, agriculture, handicrafts and trade. With socialist transformation in the main completed by the winter of 1955–56, the new General Line was to make China a great socialist country with modern industry, agriculture, science and culture in the shortest time possible. It called on the people to 'show the communist spirit of daring to think, speak and act'; and to 'go all out and aim high, for greater, better, faster and more economical results in building socialism'.[5]

These phrases expressed the prevailing mood. Study of the General Line opened up a vista of a land free from poverty and ignorance. With this prospect before them the co-operative farmers went about their work not slowly and steadily, but like people long homeless coming into possession of all they needed to build new homes. They hurled themselves into it with enormous energy. On the walls of their mud-brick houses a new slogan appeared:

> Three years of bitter struggle!
> Ten thousand years of joy!

The new general line had been taking shape during the previous

---

[4] *The Socialist Upsurge in China's Countryside*, edited by Mao Tse-tung, F.L.P., Peking, 1957, p. 357.

[5] Liu Shao-chi, 'Report of the Work of the Central Committee of the C.C.P.', delivered at the 2nd Session of the 8th National Congress. See *Peking Review*, No. 14, 3 June, 1958.

eight years, so it brought together in a systematic form a number of major principles already put to the test.

These included a set of policies known as 'walking on two legs'. One of the 'pairs of legs' was the simultaneous development of agriculture and industry.

Explaining the necessity for this Liu Shao-chi pointed out[6] that in such a vast agricultural country as China the 500 million farmers are a most important force, in revolutionary struggle and in construction; and they must play an immense role in industrialization. They would provide both heavy and light industries with the biggest domestic market in the world and with unlimited opportunities for growth. They would produce the food needed by a rapidly growing industrial working class and the materials needed for a fast expanding light industry. They themselves would build small industrial enterprises in the villages.

Another pair of legs was the simultaneous development of national and local industries.

The efforts of the whole people were needed for the development of industry, Liu Shao-chi pointed out, for 'the fire burns high when everyone piles on the wood'. This meant exploding the myth that industry could be run only by specialists. 'It is only when all central and local authorities at every level down to the co-operatives go at it . . . that we can achieve greater, faster, better and more economical results.' If this were done, he went on, 'Industrial plants will soon dot every part of the country like stars in the sky . . . This will inevitably speed up the pace of the nation's industrialization, of the mechanization of agriculture and of reducing the differences between the city and the countryside.'

Liu Shao-chi went on to warn, however, that such developments would give rise to many new problems hard to foresee at the moment.

The rapid building of 'a great socialist country with modern industry, agriculture, science and culture,' required effective measures in education, and the general line called for the wiping out of illiteracy, the instituting of compulsory primary education and the bringing of secondary schools to the townships and higher educational institutions and scientific research bodies to the regions[7] and even to many counties.

'It is man that counts. The initiative of the masses is a mighty driving force.' This was the spirit of the new General Line. It meant drawing the masses of the people into every aspect of national development, combining centralized leadership with de-centralized management. And with four-fifths of the people in the countryside it

---

[6] Ibid.
[7] *zhuanqu*, literally 'special district', in effect a sub-province.

31

meant that industry, agriculture, science and culture must all take root and flourish in the rural townships or farming co-operatives.

It was soon clear that with the wider activities devolving upon the countryside there was going to be increased overlapping between the township and the co-operatives. Ever since the setting-up of the high level co-operatives, comprising as they often did an entire village or even several small villages, there had been some duplication of administration, even though the township had been enlarged. Now with the contemplated larger co-operative or collective farm, this duplication would again spread upwards to the township. In addition, there would be overlapping in local industry as well as competition for local raw materials, man-power and capital.

Such problems brought forth a variety of solutions in different parts of China. In some places co-operatives were merged into 'state farms', in others into collective farms and in still others into some type of federation. Throughout the summer of 1958 Party and Government leaders were in the countryside studying these new ventures.

One particular merger of co-operatives took upon itself all the functions of both co-operative and township, of production and social services. Mao Tse-tung, after visiting it, christened this new, as yet nameless social unit a 'people's commune'. His subsequent comment on this and other experimental units he had visited was splashed in large headlines in *The People's Daily*.[8] It was: 'Best of all is the people's commune.'

In August 1958, the Communist Party Central Committee met to discuss the coming stage in the development of socialist co-operatives, and on August 29 its 'Resolution on the Setting-up of People's Communes in the Rural Areas' was published. This immediately received wide publicity and study.

'Chairman Mao said the communes were best. And the district leaders said we ought to learn what they were and how they were run,' recalled a member of the Yangyi Commune Party Committee. The people in such places as Yangyi, Little Yetao, Bailin and Ten Mile Inn held meetings every night and the ferment of discussion even bubbled over into the day's work in the fields.

The commune, the farmers concluded, was 'big and public'. It combined larger size with more varied functions than those of the socialist farming co-operative. Just how wide these functions were came out in the course of study and discussion. First it became clear that the commune not only engaged in farming in all its aspects (including field work, forestry, animal husbandry, side occupations and fishery); but that it also ran industry.

But the differences lay not only in broadening the scope of

---

[8] National organ of the Chinese Communist Party.

production. The commune also undertook exchange, in other words trade and banking.

And the wider functions did not stop at economic activities, for the communes were also to take over culture and education as well as defence.

With all these functions—to say nothing of social and welfare services for all its members from the cradle to the grave—it became clear that the commune absorbed and replaced both the co-operative and the township. It was a new, all-inclusive social unit.

At the end of a week's discussion 430 Ten Mile Inn households sent in applications for the setting up of a commune in the locality. It was much the same with all the surrounding villages and in September 1958, 33 socialist farming co-operatives merged to form the Yangyi People's Commune.[9]

10,000 households with 37,000 people came under unified leadership. 16,000 acres of land came under a control plan. When land reform was completed in 1948 this land was in family farms of less than two acres each. Ten years had brought a 10,000-fold increase in the size of the basic unit.

[9] In the first half of 1958 there were 740,000 farming co-operatives in China. By the end of the year these had merged into 26,000 communes.

Chapter III

YANGYI COMMUNE TAKES SHAPE
(Autumn and Winter, 1958)

THE founding of the Yangyi Commune in September meant, to begin with, little more than the replacing of ten township and thirty-three co-operative councils with a single commune council. The actual merging of these forty-odd units came later. Meanwhile a Commune Party Committee was set up to guide developments. Ren Qing-mei and Guo Heng-de, while remaining leaders of their own villages, both became vice-heads of the commune and members of its Party Committee.

The merging was no simple matter. It involved problems not only of size and organization but of ownership and distribution, the solution of which called for theoretical guidance. This was found in the 'Resolution on the Establishment of the People's Communes in the Rural Areas' passed by the Central Committee of the Communist Party in August 1958. This Resolution, however, which summed up the experiences of farming co-operatives in various parts of China striving for a larger social organization, gave guidance only in the broadest terms. It left ample room for local initiative and experiment.

With regard to size, the Resolution advised that communes should be based on single townships and should comprise about 2,000 households. Considerable variation was allowed for, however. In some places several townships might merge and form one commune comprising 6,000 or 7,000 households, if this suited topographical conditions and the needs of production. In Yangyi even this figure was exceeded, ten whole townships and parts of two others, with a total of 10,000 households, being combined. This brought together all the poorer co-operatives of the rugged upper reaches of the Min River and some of the more prosperous ones where the valley broadened out. The Resolution had allowed for such a situation, stating that while the setting up of communes of 10,000 or even 20,000 households was not to be encouraged, it need not be opposed.[1]

---

[1] Actually this proved too large and in the winter of 1960–61 Yangyi Commune divided into four, thus bringing the size closer to that advocated by the Resolution. This was a nation-wide trend. By the end of 1962 the number of communes had risen from 26,000 to over 70,000. See Liao Lu-yen, 'Collectivisation of Agriculture in China', *Peking Review*, No. 44, November 1963.

34

1. Living-quarters hollowed out of a mound in the centre of the Silver Sea Tract, with the tower of Heroic Ambition at the end.

2. Village mural showing advancing peasant cleaving the mountains in his path. Figures in foreground are cadres from county headquarters. (County Head Wang De-hen in dark uniform.)

3. Village mural showing the advantages of raising livestock.

4. Mural on a Yangyi townlet wall. Inscription reads: "Advance triumphantly and overfulfil this year's plan ahead of time."

The initial procedure advocated was to 'change the top, let the bottom stay put'. Accordingly the newly-formed Yangyi Commune Council reorganized existing township committees into Commune Departments of Industry and Trade, Culture and Education, Security and Defence.

Meanwhile the constituent co-operatives went on farming as before—but under the new name of 'production brigades'.

The task of the newly-formed Commune Council, Party Committee and Departments was to carry the reorganization down to these brigades and their work teams; and in doing so not merely to avoid disrupting production but to stimulate it—to say nothing of leading campaigns in water conservancy and steel making.

Speaking of this period Jin Han-cheng, one of the secretaries of the Commune Party Committee, said: 'We had a hard time keeping pace with events, especially with so many new tasks facing us right on top of the autumn harvest and ploughing.'

Nevertheless, the merger went ahead, with the new commune leadership keeping one eye on the August Resolution, the other on possible problems or mistakes.

As to ownership the Resolution merely warned that it should continue to be by the collective and should not be converted into ownership by the whole people. But the exact nature of this collective ownership was not laid down. In Yangyi it was decided to make the commune itself the owner of the chief means of production. This meant, among other things, that the commune took over funds and the heavier farming equipment. Thus the three tractors owned by three of the down valley brigades now became commune property, and as such belonged to all thirty-three brigades. They went to form the nucleus of the newly-founded Commune Tractor Station on the outskirts of Yangyi townlet. The power plant at Little Yetao, too, now became commune property and its power lines were extended to the commune centre.

The commune also assumed ownership of donkey and mule carts, ploughs, harrows and other large implements (not of hoes, picks and hand tools). This did not as a rule involve their removal from the brigades, but with the transfer of ownership the commune council could and did re-allocate some animals and implements, mainly from the better-off brigades to others that were in need of them. At the same time some of the flocks from brigades in the mountains were distributed among those down the valley to give them a start in animal husbandry.

On the whole the changes appeared to be made quite smoothly. Nevertheless certain problems did come to the attention of the Commune Council and the Party Committee.

'When they heard something about handing over all funds to the commune,' said Party Secretary Jin, 'the cadres in Zhao Village—

where they have all those fine vegetable gardens—rushed out and bought three bicycles. Not for themselves, of course. For the brigade.' As a large and flourishing co-operative Zhao Village had saved up enough for the bicycles and the cadres realized that it might be some time before the commune could afford to provide all its brigades with such things.

Yangyi, another of the most prosperous brigades did something different but for similar motives. During the socialist co-operative period the members had pooled their carts and draught animals thus allowing the co-operative to engage in the profitable side-line of short-distance transport. Out of the proceeds the original owners were to be paid back within five years. When arrangements were being made to transfer funds and farming equipment to the commune, the Yangyi brigade cadres hastily re-paid the original owners of these carts and animals in full—three years ahead of time.

Such actions as these depleted the commune's capital.

Another incident, too, gave the commune leadership food for thought. In Shidong, between Zhao Village and Ten Mile Inn, a donkey-cart and two ploughs were left out in the fields to rot and rust. Now that they were commune property, the brigade no longer felt responsible for them.

Pay, as well as ownership, was broadly dealt with in the Resolution. It was to be 'socialist in character', that is, based on the principle: 'to each according to his work.' There was no need to hurry the change from the original system of payment, the Resolution advised; what was necessary was to avoid any unfavourable effect on production. The exact system of payment should be determined according to specific conditions. 'Where conditions permit, the shift to a wage system may be made,' stated the Resolution. 'But where conditions are not ripe the original system of payment according to work days may be temporarily retained.'

In Yangyi conditions were considered ripe for a shift not only to wages, but to wages and free food. The yield on land sown to grain in 1958 came to 313 *jin* per *mu*, which meant an average of about 630 *jin* per person. These figures were unprecedented, and the farmers voted themselves free food. They called this their 'iron rice-bowl' as against the old term 'broken rice-bowl', which had been used before land reform when a peasant lost his means of livelihood. This was more advanced than anything the Resolution called for.

The idea of free food was no sudden local inspiration. Before land reform, starvation hovered over 70 per cent of the peasants. Every year they eked out the time between 'the yellow and the green' (the autumn and the spring harvests) by eating bark and chaff and the roots of wild plants. And each year in the villages people died of hunger. In years of flood or drought, which occurred on an average every two years in one area or another, people fled as refugees and many never lived to go home. At frequent intervals these disasters were so serious and widespread that millions lost their lives in a single year, as happened in 1936, 1942 and 1943. Corpses lined the roads. Thus warm homes and clothes, machines to lighten their labour, leisure—such things as these the mass of China's peasants did not aspire to. What they did dream of was a plot of land on which to raise enough food to keep body and soul together.

The land reform realized this dream. Together with other Communist-led reforms it banished famine. But it did not provide plenty. The reforms made it possible for the farmers to keep themselves and their families alive—but not to eat their fill the year round. Right until the time of the co-operatives women, who did not do the heaviest manual work, eked out their grain with chaff for part of the year—as even the women of rich peasant families had done before land reform. The better part of the grain was left for the men who burnt up more fuel in their heavier work in the fields. Even they could not be said to have plenty to eat. A full stomach was no part of the Chinese peasant's everyday experience. As late as 1957, 30 per cent of China's rural population received government or village aid to tide them over.[2]

Then in 1958 came a harvest double that of the peak year before land reform—250 million metric tons of grain.[3] And with this harvest came the setting up of communes and a revision of the distribution system established by the co-operatives. These two coming together gave rise to free food in various parts of China.

Besides free food Yangyi introduced another innovation in the pay system which had not been proposed in the Central Committee resolution. This was the paying of wages directly to the individual who earned them instead of to the head of the household, for in the mutual aid groups and co-operatives the pay of all the members of a family was handed to the family head. This remnant of the patriarchal family system was now given its final blow.

Rates of pay and the issue of free food were worked out on a commune-wide basis, varying only according to the category of the worker. These categories themselves, however, did not vary as between brigades; and the only work records now kept were of absenteeism—for which deductions were made from the month's wages. The actual quantity or quality of work done by the individual worker was no longer taken into account.

[2] Li Ching-chuan, 'The People's Communes are the Inevitable Outcome of China's Social Development', *Ten Glorious Years*, F.L.P., Peking, 1960.
[3] Verified figures given by the Central Committee correcting earlier exaggerated estimates. See 'Communique of the 8th Plenary Session of the 8th Central Committee of the C.C.P.', F.L.P., August 1959, Peking.

With these sweeping changes in the system of payment, too, problems of various kinds came to light.

The commune leadership noticed quite early that right on its very doorstep, in Yangyi brigade itself, the tempo of work was slowing down. Word had started going round the brigade: 'They're taking it easy up there in the hills in Liezhang. They think they don't need to work so hard or be so thrifty now that they're in with us and the other valley brigades.' The Commune Party Committee looked into this and found it to be true. Everyone in remote Liezhang was singing the praises of the commune—but quite a number were working with less than their old doggedness to dig a living out of their stony mountain soil. As even the Liezhang Brigade Party Secretary himself said with satisfaction: 'We're all a hundred per cent in favour of this merging of the co-ops into a commune. We've only got a *mu* of stony soil per head up here. Now we can get help from the brigades down in the valley.'

CONTRADICTIONS BETWEEN POORER AND
BETTER-OFF BRIGADES

The new commune leadership, despite having 'a hard time keeping pace with events', kept themselves informed on the various problems of the merger and subjected them to careful study. What they were after, in their own words, was to sort out 'the main contradiction'.

'In the end,' said Party Secretary Jin, 'we came to the conclusion that the main contradiction in our commune was the one between the poor and the better-off brigades. The better-off brigades—the ones with the most and best land—as co-ops had had the highest income. Now they thought that as brigades of the commune they'd be brought down to the level of the poorer brigades. The poorer brigades, on the other hand, thought that by joining up with the better-off ones they'd be all right no matter what happened.'

In short, contrary to the whole spirit of the General Line, some of the better-off as well as some of the poorer brigades were not going all out, and production was slowing down. The solution of this problem was considered to be the key to the commune's consolidation.

Accordingly the Commune Party Committee launched an education campaign to convince the poorer and the better-off brigades that the commune benefited them both. And that both should go all out—in its interests and their own.

The Committee pointed out that in every advance from land reform on, the larger the operational unit, the higher had been the yield per *mu*.[4] Therefore, they reasoned, with the commune, which was thirty times as large as the socialist co-operative, this trend

[4] See table on page 24.

38

would continue at a faster rate than ever. In other words, said the Party Committee, there was every prospect that the 1959 plan would be fulfilled. And it called for an average yield per *mu* 20 per cent higher than that reached by the commune area in the unprecedented harvest of 1958. This was more than the better-off brigades themselves had ever achieved. Even this figure was regarded as a minimum quota which could be absolutely guaranteed. The actual target, which there seemed every possibility of reaching, was 400 *jin* per *mu*.

With the poorer brigades deep in the mountains, a different point was stressed. This was that the commune made possible more diversified farming and more rational use of land. This had been proved by the Little Yetao brigade, which though in the mountains was one of the most prosperous in the commune. Such facts were used to dispel the idea of dependence on the better-off brigades and strengthened the spirit of self-reliance.

To clinch matters two new systems were introduced among the poorer brigades: 'Guarantee of work and output' and 'Grading of working force.' These meant that within each work team, individual workers were given norms based on their skill, strength and previous performance.

Such were the leadership's measures—educational and organizational—to offset any trends likely to hamper the growth of the infant commune.

POLITICAL AND ADMINISTRATIVE STRUCTURE

The commune had now taken shape. The people of Yangyi had a single organization embracing industry, agriculture, trade, education, military affairs and welfare services. This new and complex socioeconomic unit combined within itself 'management' (which would continue to develop and be perfected), and 'state power' (which was ultimately to 'wither away').

The highest body of management and state power was the Commune People's Congress, which was to be elected every two years by all commune members, men and women, of sixteen and over, and to meet twice a year or oftener if need be. (This was the body that elected deputies to the County Congress, and thus indirectly to the National People's Congress in Peking.) This Commune Congress had the task of deciding on the measures necessary for carrying out Party and Government policy under the conditions actually existing in the commune. This involved overall economic planning of production and distribution, the laying down of plans for the welfare of commune members, and so on. It also had the duty to serve as a sounding board for the views of members in all branches of work and all parts of the commune. Deputies were expected to present the views of their constituents. Its third duty was supervision of the Commune Council, the body entrusted with the work of the Congress when it was not in session. At its sessions the Congress was to check and see that its decisions had been carried out, and that there was no corruption or incompetence among the cadres.

The Commune Council, consisting of thirty-one members elected by and responsible to the congress, had four departments, an office, and a technical station under its direction, with a staff of twenty full-time workers. These departments were: Security (equivalent to police); Military Affairs (in charge of the militia and the call-up); Industry and Trade; and Education and Culture.

Each of these departments had branches in the sub-divisions of the commune, named 'managerial districts',[5] which employed altogether twenty-five full-time workers. These sub-divisions were considered necessary because the commune stretched almost thirty miles, and cadres travelled mainly on foot and occasionally by bicycle.

Such was the administrative structure of the commune. Assessing the changes which had been brought about, one of the Commune Party Secretaries said, 'The commune organization makes for concentrated leadership and economy of cadres, as well as for unified planning and action. It makes things more convenient for the members and helps to promote production.'

The only significant organizations remaining in the area not merged into the new unit were the local branches of the Communist Party, the Communist Youth League and the Women's Federation.[6]

FIRST FRUITS

While carrying out the merger the commune leadership had also been spurring on mass movements for water conservancy and steel making. At the same time it was paying attention to field management in order to ensure the biggest possible autumn crops and to ploughing and sowing winter wheat.

The very month that the commune was set up an attack was launched on the age-old enemy, drought. A five-mile arm was added to the Republic Channel, which till then ran only from Little Yetao to Yangyi. The new extension took the water on as far as Ten Mile Inn, where a deep, stone-lined pond was dug to hold it. The digging took 2,800 labour days and passed through land which not long before had belonged to different co-operatives. Now these, instead of posting guards along their old channels contributed labour to build the new one.

[5] *Guanliqu*, hereafter called 'districts'.
[6] See Part Three.

Yangyi Commune Takes Shape

Celebrations marked the completion of the channel and the pond, which made it possible to irrigate 100 acres—a seventh of all Ten Mile Inn's farmland. At the same time, of course, it solved the village's ancient drinking-water problem. Now not even the most doting of mothers need fear to marry her daughter into Ten Mile Inn.

Before the commune was fifty days old it had turned out 3,000 tons of iron and 750 tons of low grade steel, suitable for the making of farm tools. Limited though this output was in quantity and quality, it was enough to lay the foundations of local industrialization. The setting up of the commune Farm Implement Manufacture and Repair Shop with its diesel motor, steam pumps and lathes, provided a nucleus for this. Meanwhile a movement was under way to get loads off shoulders and onto wheels, as well as to improve wheeled transport by providing the old-style creaking wooden-wheeled carts with ball-bearings and rubber tyres. Sixty-seven mule-carts were soon so equipped.

These achievements, coupled with the Great Leap in agriculture, brought a big increase in the commune members' income. This was to be reflected in a sharp rise in the sale of consumer goods during the following six months. Sales for this period (the first half of 1959) were three times as high as those of the first half of 1958—just before the Great Leap in farm output and the setting up of the commune.

Improvement in the standard of living took the form not only of goods but of services. Community dining-rooms, together with the nurseries, kindergartens, tailoring shops and maternity and old folks' homes which were set up in the more socially advanced villages such as Bailin, were to free women from their kitchens and courtyards for paid work in social services and economic enterprises as well as in the fields. Work was no novelty for these women. What was new was working in a collective instead of at home, and, above all, receiving payment into their own hands. This was a revolutionary advance even for those women who had worked in the fields before.

These were the achievements of Yangyi Commune during the first months of its existence.

Chapter IV

TEMPERING THE WINDS OF COMMUNISM
(Spring, 1959)

SHEXIAN, like hundreds of counties all over China, summed up the early achievements of its communes and their problems, as well as the measures taken to deal with them. And it was on the basis of a mass of such summaries and of its own work and study in the field that the Central Committee of the Chinese Communist Party, in December 1958, passed its 'Resolution on Some Questions Concerning the People's Communes'.[1]

Referring to the communes as 'a new social organization, appearing fresh as the morning sun above the broad horizon of East Asia', the Resolution went on to clarify many aspects of their structure and working systems in the light of the first few months' experience.

The Resolution was studied and discussed—first by the leaders of Hopei Province, then by those of Shexian County. After this the County Party Committee called a conference which was attended by cadres of five levels: region, county, commune, district and brigade. Its purpose was to measure up the situation in each of the county's communes against Central Committee policy and to work out how the resolution could be implemented locally.

In Shexian, as elsewhere in the country, the verdict was not only that the communes had proved their worth but that they had galvanized every aspect of life and work. As for mistakes, which were to be expected in the course of such a vast and complex undertaking, the conclusion was: in the first flush of enthusiasm the mark had been overshot, the level of production and of the farmers' political understanding had been over-estimated. As the saying had it: 'The winds of communism blew too hard.' Two specific mistakes were briefly formulated in the words: 'levelling' and 'transferring'.

A member of the Yangyi Commune Party Committee explained these as follows:

'When we first set up the commune, for instance, and introduced wages and free food, we thought we ought to even things out. So we took the whole commune as one unit and worked out average rates. The "levelling" meant automatically raising pay in the poor brigades

---

[1] 6th Plenary Session of the 8th Central Committee of the C.C.P. (pamphlet), F.L.P., Peking, 1958.

and lowering it in the better-off ones—regardless of work and conditions. That didn't call forth the best efforts of either. Rates of pay and of free supply should have been fixed separately within each brigade according to what it produced.

'Our second mistake was in "transferring" property from the brigades to the commune or from one brigade to another without compensation. That is how the commune council came to take over 71 mule carts and 118 donkey-carts from brigades along the highway; and how the sheep and goats were transferred from the mountain to the valley brigades—all without payment. This sort of mistake also dampened enthusiasm.'

The County Conference interpreted the general spirit of the Central Committee's resolution as being that ownership of the means of production by the commune (as distinct from by the brigade) was a good thing—but that the time was not yet ripe for its full implementation. To make this clear and to set right the mistakes of 'levelling and transferring', the following six principles were laid down:

1. There should be ownership at three levels, the chief being the brigade.[2]
2. There should be unified leadership, with management at different levels (commune, brigade, work team), and more power than before at the lower levels.
3. There should be accounting at each of the three levels and each should be responsible for its own profit and loss.
4. Property and labour exchanged between brigades should be paid for.
5. The Commune Congress should decide on the distribution plan—including an appropriate figure for accumulation—and should be responsible for the allocation of manpower.
6. Payment should be according to actual work done, with recognition of the differences between poorer and better-off brigades.

The whole trend of these six principles was to place more power in the brigade; but the top level leadership by the commune council was still upheld.

The next step was to straighten things out in the commune in the light of these six principles. So in April 1959, a Yangyi Commune Communist Party Conference was called, at which the Party members elected a new Commune Party Committee and new Party cadres. Then a congress of the whole commune was convened at which a new Commune Council was elected. After that, with the newly-elected leadership at the helm, the straightening out of the commune began.

[2] Experience of the next year or two showed that in many communes the time was not ripe even for making the brigade the chief level of ownership and emphasis was accordingly shifted to the work team.

Three main tasks were tackled: the adjusting of ownership; the dispersing of management; and the working out of a more suitable system of distribution.

MAKING THE BRIGADE THE CHIEF LEVEL OF OWNERSHIP AND MANAGEMENT

First the brigade was made the chief level of ownership. In doing this much revolved around accounting. The carts, mules, donkeys and so on, which had been transferred from the brigades to the commune were returned; and if any brigade property which had been taken over was damaged or used up, it was paid for. Altogether the commune paid 110,000 *yuan* to the brigades. An account was drawn up, as well, of work done by one brigade for another, and proper payment made. In addition, individual contributions made to the brigade—the pots and pans, benches and tables 'blown by the winds of communism' out of private homes into community dining-rooms—were now returned or paid for.

By the end of the check-up a clear picture of the modified system of ownership had emerged.

The commune owned the big hill pastures and afforestation projects, the three tractors and other large implements, the large enterprises, such as the Farm Implement Manufacture and Repair Shop, an iron mine, which it had put into operation that year, a a small reservoir and dam which it had built. (By the autumn of 1960 a small steel mill was to be added to its industrial holdings.)

The brigades, being the basic level of ownership, owned almost all the arable land, the smaller pastures and areas planted to trees, the draught animals and medium-sized farm implements (such as ploughs, harrows and seeders), carts, oil presses, brick and lime kilns and small capital construction projects such as the Ten Mile Inn pond.

The work teams owned what small enterprises they set up and ran, mainly handicraft industries, condiment shops serving their own canteens and so on.

In addition to these three main levels of ownership there remained some individual or household ownership of means of production such as private allotments, trees around dwellings and small hand tools.

All the above, of course, applied to ownership of means of production. Ownership of the 'means of living'—homes, furniture, clothing and other personal effects, as well as private bank deposits—was in a different category. 'Such things are and always will be private possessions,' stated the Resolution.

This briefly was what the principle 'Ownership at three levels, the chief being the brigade', meant in Yangyi Commune.

In accordance with the second principle of the April check-up—
'Unified leadership with management at different levels, and more
power than before to the lower levels'—considerable decentralizing
took place.

One feature of the 1958 merging of the thirty-three co-operatives
and ten townships into one commune had been the simplification
and rationalization of the administrative set-up. Previously each of
the ten townships had had a congress and a council with departments for security, industry, culture, trade and so on; while each of
the thirty-three co-operatives had had its own congress and council,
concerned mainly with agriculture, though some also had offices to
deal with animal husbandry, afforestation, finance, side-occupations
or other activities. All in all there had been much duplication. In
the newly set-up Yangyi Commune these forty-odd congresses and
councils were replaced by one congress and one council.

With the April check-up a new internal structure began to
crystallize. While the keynote of the first phase had been unifying and
streamlining, that of the second was decentralizing—particularly
increasing the authority vested in the brigade.

Yangyi Commune emerged from the April check-up with three
clear-cut levels—commune, brigade and work team—and with
definite decentralization of functions. But only at the commune level
had the internal structure crystallized.

In accordance with principle 5 of the check-up the Commune
People's Congress was to decide on distribution plans, including the
proportion of accumulation, and on the guiding lines for allocating
man-power. At its sessions elected representatives were to discuss
current production plans, output quotas, the amount of grain to
be sold to the state, the purchase of major implements or equipment
—such as tractors or diesel motors. The development of local
industry, electrification, mechanization, construction of major
irrigation works and so on was also its concern. So was education.
The carrying out of these decisions was put in the hands of the
commune council.

Though the April check-up made clear the functions of the
brigade and work team it left their internal structure in a formative
state.

The brigade—generally embracing the former high level co-
operative—was the unit actually managing agriculture, industry,
trade, education and defence in a given village or group of small
villages and forming a business accounting unit for its twelve to
fifteen hundred men, women and children. Most brigades had a
collective leadership which called meetings of the entire membership
whenever major questions arose. For ordinary affairs the brigade
leaders simply consulted the leaders of the dozen or so work teams.
The work team—coinciding to some extent with the mutual aid

groups of the land reform period or with the semi-socialist farming co-operatives of the 1954–55 period—was the basic unit of labour organization.

The major remaining task of the check-up was to work out the details of a system of distribution suited to both the existing level of production and the understanding of the majority of commune members.

The guiding principle set forth in the 'Resolution on Some Questions Concerning the People's Commune' was: on the basis of industrious and thrifty running of the communes, the amount set aside for accumulation (after deducting production costs, administrative expenses and taxes) should increase; and at the same time the amount used to meet the individual and collective needs of the commune members should also increase. Thus they would livᴄ better and better each year.

In Yangyi, after careful calculation of the financial position of the commune and its brigades the following decisions were taken by the Commune Congress:

First of all the gross income of the brigade should be divided into two parts. 40 per cent should be set aside for expenditure and 60 per cent for distribution to the members. However, a leeway of 5 per cent should be allowed, so that in any particular brigade expenditure might take up 45 per cent and distribution 55 per cent.

Expenditure should cover the following items:

Taxes (one unified agricultural tax)	7%
Accumulation and welfare (handled partly by the commune, partly by the brigade)	10%
Production costs (fertilizer, seed, fodder, etc)	20%
Administration costs (pay for full-time cadres, office expenses etc.)	2%

The 10 per cent set aside for accumulation and welfare should be divided between the commune and the brigade. Of the accumulation fund 40 per cent should be kept by the brigade and 60 per cent be handed over to the commune; of the welfare funds, on the other hand, 80 per cent should be left in the hands of the brigade and only 20 per cent administered by the commune. All in all the total sum contributed by the brigade to commune accumulation should range from 4 per cent to something under 10 per cent.

So much for the 40 per cent set aside for expenditure. As to the 60 per cent to be distributed to brigade members, the guiding principle on the system of payment put forward in the Resolution was: to combine individual pay, based on work done, with free

46

supply. This in essence embodies the socialist principle of 'to each according to his work', but includes the beginnings of the communist principle of 'to each according to his needs'.[3]

A few months of practical experience had shown that neither Yangyi Commune nor its neighbours had as yet an economic basis for completely free food. This proved to be the case in many communes throughout the country. But the Central Committee did not condemn it. Instead it put forward measures for preserving what was practicable of these 'shoots of communism' and for ensuring their growth. Different provinces consequently worked out what they regarded as the conditions which a commune should satisfy in order to institute free food and wages. Hopei Province laid down five stipulations. These were:

1. The leadership of the commune must be strong.
2. The political consciousness of the commune members must be high.
3. The income of commune-owned enterprises must make up at least half of the total income of the commune.
4. The net income must reach 1,000 *jin* of grain and 150 *yuan* per person.
5. The management of the commune must be efficient.

Yangyi Commune had fallen far short of stipulations 3 and 4. Income from commune-owned enterprises in 1958 amounted to only 4·2 per cent of the total; and though that year's harvest was unprecedented it still amounted to an annual average grain income of only 630 *jin* per person, while money income came to about 75 *yuan* per person. Though these figures represented a big advance they showed that the commune had gone only a little over half-way towards the set targets.

These targets had been set by the province as a guide. But Yangyi Commune, taking into account the big differences between its various brigades, made provision for individual brigades to introduce free food and wages before the commune as a whole had reached the necessary level. Thus any individual brigade, so long as it fulfilled the five requirements, would be permitted to introduce free food.

Even with this modification, free food clearly still lay some years ahead. In the meantime a certain amount of free supply was to be retained; but its scope was to be carefully controlled, a ratio between pay and free supply being laid down so as to guarantee that at least 90 per cent of a brigade's members would have a steadily increasing income. The ratio was as follows:

[3] In all official Chinese statements, socialism and communism are differentiated in accordance with Marxist principles which define socialism as the lower or earlier stage of communism.

Brigades with an average annual income per member of	Funds for Distribution	
	Free Supply	Pay in Cash or Kind
	%	%
70 *yuan* or over	30	70
50 to 70 *yuan*	20	80
Under 50 *yuan*	10 to 15	85 to 90

This meant that the brigade was to set aside 10, 20 or 30 per cent of the amount for distribution and then decide in what form to give the free supply. In all cases the young, the old and the disabled were provided for. This was the commune's social insurance.

The remaining 70, 80 or 90 per cent as the case might be, was to be paid in cash or kind to brigade members according to work points earned. This meant that the better-off a brigade was, the higher would be its rates of pay and the greater its amount of free supply.

This was how the main income was to be disposed of. But it did not cover additional income received from over-fulfilling targets. For income from this source there was a whole set of separate regulations.

Any income over and above the target was to be kept within the brigade and evenly divided between it and the particular work team producing the surplus. The brigade was to keep most of its share for accumulation funds, but to distribute 25 per cent directly to its members. Thus every brigade member would benefit both directly and indirectly from the success of any of the work teams; and everyone would have a stake in the success of every team.

Of the work team's half of the surplus, part was to be set aside for accumulation, which would help the team secure still bigger bonuses in the future. One quarter was to be divided among the rank and file team members and the rest to go in prizes or bonuses to individuals or groups who had played an outstanding part in achieving the team's success.

While for the able-bodied members of Yangyi Commune this distribution system, instituted as a result of the April check-up, was undoubtedly a socialist one based on the principle of 'to each according to his work', it also provided free education, simple medical care and social insurance (in the form of the Five Guarantees)[4] as well as a certain amount of free supply. Thus it had within it the 'shoots of communism'.

*   *   *

In August 1959, a few months after the check-up, the Central Com-

[4] See p. 13.

mittee of the Communist Party met again. Taking stock of the communes in general and the check-up in particular, it stated:

> The people's communes . . . have overcome the tendencies which, owing to lack of experience, occurred during the initial period of their existence—tendencies towards over-centralization, equalitarianism and extravagance—and have taken the road to sound, consolidated development.[5]

The Resolution went on to affirm the value of the communes, particularly their advantages over the socialist co-operatives.

> In this way the advantages of the people's communes will come into play more and more clearly. Being large and having a wide range of activities, they can plan their production and distribution in a unified way; they can mobilize and use rural labour power more fully and rationally than the agricultural producers' co-operatives; they can undertake construction which the co-operatives could hardly handle; they can facilitate: the speedy and integrated development of agriculture, forestry, animal husbandry, side-occupations and fishery and also of industry, agriculture, trade, education and defence; the mechanization of farming, the steady increase of the farmers' income, rapid progress in rural life as a whole and the development of collective undertakings such as community dining-rooms and nurseries; they can also provide that a certain portion of their distribution is in the form of free supply . . .

Yangyi Commune itself had come into being in September 1958 because, in the words of Commune Party Secretary Jin, 'the relations of production were fettering the forces of production.' That is, the farming co-operatives had been too limited in size and scope to solve the problems of soil and water conservation, rural industrialization, and the mechanization, 'chemicalization', and electrification of agriculture. Speaking of the consolidation of the commune following the April check-up Secretary Jin said: 'At last we had solved the contradiction between the forces and the relations of production.'[6]

[5] 'Resolution on Developing the Campaign for Increasing Production and Practising Economy', in the '8th Plenary Session of the 8th Central Committee of the C.C.P.', *Documents*, F.L.P., Peking, 1959.
[6] The matter was actually more complicated than appeared, and it was not until nearly three years later that the *People's Daily*, following the 10th Plenary Session of the 8th Central Committee of the C.C.P., stated editorially, 9 November, 1962: 'The socialist transformation of agriculture has now been achieved; individual, small peasant economy has been transformed into collective economy.'

Chapter V

THE EIGHT POINT CHARTER
(Spring, Summer and Autumn, 1959)

YANGYI COMMUNE'S production, now 'unfettered', struck out on a fresh advance. The same energy was put into soil and water conservancy as during the previous winter—even though a number of the best workers went off to help build the Jinan-Taiyuan railway, which skirted the southern edge of the commune.

Little Yetao again achieved the most striking results of all the brigades. Realizing the importance of increasing the output of grain, its farmers 'rearranged the mountains and streams'—in other words, improved their terracing and irrigation systems, so as to grow grain on an additional hundred-odd acres.

But the most significant development (in Yangyi as elsewhere in the Chinese countryside) was the drive for bigger crops through carrying out the 'Eight Point Charter'. This condensation of the forty point National Program for Agricultural Development brought together eight of the key elements of intensive farming. While based on the age-long experience of Chinese peasants it incorporated the findings of recent years.

The eight points were:

1. Deep ploughing and soil improvement;
2. Rational use of fertilizer;
3. Water conservancy;
4. Seed selection;
5. Rational close planting;
6. Plant protection;
7. Field management;
8. Improvement of farm tools.

These eight points taken singly were far from new. What was new was their co-ordination into a single system. This, though applicable to the whole of China, had to be flexibly carried out, with consideration to local variations in soil, weather, manpower and so on—each region, county and even commune having to work things out for itself. Thus operating the charter meant overcoming hidebound ideas about farming and called for scientific investigation, primarily through the running of experimental plots.

Experimental plots were not new either. It was often through

50

5 and 6. Actors and actresses of one of the county drama troupes on tour in Yangyi Commune, on stage and off. Plate 6 also shows author Isabel Crook.

7. Cooks in the courtyard of a work-team canteen.

8. "Aunties" and toddlers in a work-team nursery.

them that labour heroes in the past had succeeded in convincing their fellow-villagers of the efficacy of new measures. As Little Yetao brigade's Labour Hero, Ren Qing-mei put it: 'Farmers are practical people. Talk alone won't convince them. They want to see with their own eyes.'

Back in 1952 Ren himself, while busy piloting one of the first co-operatives in the area, cultivated an experimental plot of millet on which he achieved a yield of nearly two and a half tons an acre— a local record. And that same year, in Liezhang, one of the poorest mountain villages of the whole Yangyi area, Labour Hero Liu Wan-fu set a national record. On a small plot he produced 1,520 *jin* of maize to the *mu*—about five tons an acre.

In 1958 the running of experimental plots spread, in the form of a movement, among cadres and Party members in general. And now, in January 1959, Youth Experimental Stations were set up, generally by members of the Communist Youth League. The triple goal of these experimental stations was: to get bumper harvests in 1959, to train a corps of agricultural technicians, and to set an example in applying the Eight Point Charter.

Commune, brigade, and work team cadres, Party members and youth shock teams thus became the spearhead of a movement to spread the Eight Point Charter style of farming throughout Shexian county, with rational close planting as the key to increasing yields and the other seven points as supporting measures. (The eight points were not to be given equal weight at once. At different places and times different points were chosen as the key.) Leading the work personally were Wang De-hen, Shexian County Head and Duan Peng-xiang, First Secretary of the County Party Committee.

There were good reasons for having young people undertake these tasks for it was urgently necessary, at this time, to shatter accepted norms and the youth, lacking the experience of the older farmers, were less wedded to old ways. Besides, they had plenty of energy and imagination which could be called on in the face of difficulties. County leadership, on the other hand, was necessary in order to provide an overall approach: to take local conditions into account as well as to absorb ideas from elsewhere and to make the most of the energy of youth without neglecting the experience of age.

One youth team, for instance, full of zest for experiments, sowed 200 *jin* of wheat seed to the *mu* (over 13 cwt to the acre). The older farmers said this was madness. They were proved right. And when the wheat came up they said, 'You see, you wouldn't listen to us. Now look at the mess that plot is in. It's more like a horse's mane than a field of wheat.'

In another brigade, on the other hand, too much attention was paid to the older farmers' warning and the wheat was planted too sparsely, with only three or four hundred clumps to a *mu*.

E

Clearly an answer was needed to the question: What were the specific figures for 'rational close planting' for each of Shexian's major staples—wheat, maize, millet and sweet potatoes?

County Party Secretary Duan Peng-xiang himself took a hand in finding the figures for wheat—by running an experimental plot, together with the head of a commune and the Party Secretary of one of its brigades. Secretary Duan was an experienced farmer, who had spent his youth as a farmhand and poor peasant.[1] He and his teammates ploughed their 2·3 *mu* experimental plot to a depth of twenty inches, mixing in over ten tons of coarse fertilizer. Then they planted 30 *jin* of previously soaked selected seed to the *mu*, spacing the furrows six inches and the plants four inches apart, and carefully timing the watering and the use of chemical fertilizer. Their total harvest amounted to 6,355,000 ears of wheat or 1,460 *jin* per *mu* (nearly 5 tons an acre). This was a six- or seven-fold increase over average yields for this mountain region.

With the aid of this experiment and others throughout the county, figures were finally determined for the rational close planting of wheat in Shexian. They were:

	jin of seed per *mu*
On unirrigated land	15 to 20
On irrigated land	20 to 25
On high yield plots	up to 30

Similar experiments were conducted with sweet potatoes, a high yield crop rather new to Shexian. One of these was carried out by Liu Bao-an—an 'Education Hero', who had just started to study agronomy.

'We ploughed to a depth of three feet,' he said, 'mixing in plenty of fertilizer, layer by layer. Then we put in 30,000 slips to the *mu*—ten times as many as was usually done. They came up all right and everything went well until it started to rain. Then you should have seen them grow! We were afraid they'd become all leaves and stalk and no root. So we held meetings to decide what to do. We'd been reading everything we could lay our hands on about how to raise sweet potatoes, and we found that down in Kweichow' (two thousand miles away in the south-west) 'they'd run into the same problem. So we followed their example and put up trellises for the vines to let the sun and air in. In fact we went one better and used bellows to blow air through. In the end, through trying out all sorts of things like that we got a yield of 30,000 *jin* to the *mu*' (99 tons an acre).

The main supporting measures for close planting were deep ploughing and soil improvement. These were in a sense the same, for the purpose of deep ploughing was the improving of the lower layers

[1] For a biographical sketch, see Chapter XVIII.

of the soil. One method tried successfully on experimental plots was to work the soil in three layers. First the plough was run over the land, loosening the soil to a certain depth. This loosened soil was then shovelled out on one side of the furrow, which was then ploughed again. This time the loosened soil was thrown up on the other side of the furrow. The third time the loosened soil was not removed, but fertilizer was mixed in with it. Then each of the layers which had been removed was mixed with coarse fertilizer and replaced at its original level.

Though at this time close planting, supported by deep ploughing and soil improvement, received special attention, other points were not neglected particularly seed selection and the introducing of improved strains.

In Guxin Commune, close to Yangyi, seed of a high-yield strain of maize was available; but it had to be planted two weeks earlier than the ordinary strains grown in the area. It seemed impossible to do this, however, for maize, it was thought, could not be planted until the wheat was harvested. The first to tackle this problem was a youth 'shock team' led by a lively and attractive twenty-two year old girl named He Guei-qing. Their plan was to plant the high-yield strain of maize in a nursery and then transplant it after the wheat had been harvested. This, of course, involved much labour, but the youth team proved that it was feasible. But, as often happened with successful experiments, this was superseded by another—involving far less work. The latter was carried out by the commune's Labour Hero, Ma Zhan-yuan, who planted the high-yield maize among the ripening wheat. With careful cultivation the maize came up, without affecting or being affected by the wheat, and the output was double that of the old strain.

In plant protection there were two main advances. The first was routine spraying of insecticide as a preventive measure, instead of resorting to it only when the fields were directly threatened by pests. This had an unexpected result. High winds—one of Shexian county's hazards—had always been a menace to the maize, for they swept through the fields snapping the stalks. But it was found that the fields which had been sprayed went unscathed. Investigation showed that the stalks in the unsprayed fields were weak and brittle because they were riddled with insect holes, while those in the fields that had been sprayed were strong and pliant.

The second advance was in the development of 'home-made' insecticides.

When 'field scouts' of Guxin Commune reported the appearance of red spiders in the cotton fields, the Commune Party Branch Committee called on the youth shock team to make insecticide out of local products. The young folk, who had set up their own 36-member Scientific Research Centre to deal with problems posed by the Eight Point Charter, first consulted the most skilful older farmers. Despite turning the problem over in their minds and delving into their long experience, all the old folk could say was that there were certain herbs up in the hills which tasted very bitter and were possibly poisonous. The eleven women members of the Research Centre, under He Guei-qing, volunteered to look into this. First they pored over the farm journals and reference books in the Commune Centre reading room; then they went up the hills, picking and tasting as they went. Everything bitter they gathered. Altogether they collected 117 different kinds of plants. And after more reading and more discussion with the old farmers they concocted a number of brews. After much trial and error they produced a spray lethal enough, they claimed, to kill 93 per cent of the spiders and to keep ten other kinds of insect pests under control.

Fertilizer was a two-fold problem. The first difficulty was getting enough of it; the second, getting it to where it was needed.

In the past, when land was individually owned, a well-to-do middle peasant owning a draught animal might manage to spread as much as two and a half tons of coarse compost on an acre. By 1959, with the vastly increased resources of the commune and with the mass movement for carrying out the Eight Point Charter the figure claimed was twenty-five tons an acre on the more accessible fields. To achieve this ten-fold increase a variety of sources were drawn on.

In Guxin Commune young He Guei-qing played a leading role. Early in 1959 the Guxin Party Branch called on the commune members to go all out in collecting manure for the corn fields, including that from the cesspools. The Communist Youth League Committee urged League members not to be afraid of getting right into the cesspools to scrape out every bit of fertilizer.

At first most of the women held back. But He Guei-qing, putting on her oldest clothes, waded in and soon others followed. The job done, He Guei-qing led the young people to the tops of the mountains. There they lowered themselves over the cliffs to scrape pigeon droppings off the ledges. The haul was a big one for it was the accumulation of centuries. From the heights and the depths they collected over 260 tons of organic fertilizer.

This, of course, could be only a stop-gap measure, remarkable mainly for showing the spirit of the young people. This was displayed too in their major effort in solving the fertilizer problem—the setting up of an improvised chemical fertilizer plant. He Guei-qing and other young women and men worked for twelve hours in a heavy downpour to put up a rainproof canopy of thatch. Then they dug a pit underneath it in which to mix their home-made brand of fertilizer —a combination of lime, powdered earth, bones, ashes and other locally available ingredients.

The Eight Point Charter

The two chief measures for increasing the supply of fertilizer were the setting up of many small local plants such as this and the raising of pigs, which were nicknamed 'mobile fertilizer factories'. Yangyi Commune itself had no tradition of pig-raising, so there the popularizing of these 'mobile fertilizer factories' was not easy. Though model brigades, like Little Yetao soon set about mastering the new technique, some other brigades held back, feeling that even if the problems involved were not insurmountable, the returns would not be worth the trouble.

Getting fertilizer to the fields in a non-mechanized economy, where the main means of transport was still man and animal power, was no easy job. One of the measures taken was moving pigsties and sheepfolds close to the more distant fields so that barnyard fertilizer was available on the spot.

Application of the Charter was not easy and it took time to get under way. This was not due simply to inertia or conservatism but to shortage of labour. Commune Party Committees, however, made the Charter the focal point of their work and called on youth teams in the different brigades to lead the way in carrying it out. By the end of 1959 they reported that the eight points were in effect on 80 per cent of the fields.

In Yangyi Commune itself, with the aid of the Charter, the output of grain rose from 313 *jin* per *mu* in 1958 to 404 *jin* per *mu* in 1959, while that of cotton reached 91 *jin* (unginned) per *mu*, in spite of a spring drought.

By reaching such yields the commune had gone well beyond the requirements of the National Program for Agricultural Development. This program divided China, with its vast area and wide variations in climate and soil, into three main belts: the first, north of the Yellow River (this took in Yangyi); the second, between the Yellow and Yangtze Rivers; the third, south of the Yangtze. The main targets set for these areas were: 400, 500 and 800 *jin* per *mu* for grain and 40, 60 and 80 to 100 *jin* per *mu* for unginned cotton. These targets were for 1967. Yangyi surpassed them in 1959, thanks largely to the Eight Point Charter and to soil and water conservation work.

THE BUILDING OF THE NORTH ZHANG CHANNEL

In Shexian the weather was notoriously unstable. Describing it County Head Wang De-hen said, 'We generally have a very dry winter. The spring is dry, too, with high winds. And in summer we often get hailstorms and torrential downpours of rain.' To deal with this climate the county, by the summer of 1959, was maintaining a regular labour force of 5–6,000, rising to as much as 20,000 for certain irrigation projects.

55

Two Years' History of Yangyi Commune

The most important of these was the North Zhang Channel.

The Zhang River, the biggest in Shexian, flows deep in the mountains in the west of the county. Close to its source, which is just across the provincial border in the highlands of Shansi, four channels were cut, to lead the water in a roundabout route through the mountains at a very gradual drop, instead of allowing it to fall sharply, as it had done, down to the valley bottom. This involved the moving of a million and three quarters cubic metres of stone and earth and the digging of 65 tunnels of a total length of over four miles. Work began in 1958 and by the summer of 1960 two of the channels were in full operation and the other two 80 per cent finished. The completed project would irrigate 15,000 acres, for even when passing through the heart of the county the channels were still high above the valley bottom and water could be tapped for mountain village fields well above the old river-bed. In addition the channels could generate a thousand kilowatts of electricity, prevent floods down in the plains and provide drinking water for twenty villages where 'water was as precious as oil' and where for centuries the women, as they carried their buckets from afar, had poured curses on the matchmakers for bringing them to such parched places.

One important aspect of the work was the 'communist co-operation between people of the mountains and of the plains'. When the plan to build the channel was drawn up and publicized over 11,000 farmers from four neighbouring counties volunteered to help. They streamed in from a hundred miles around, carrying their own tools. The visiting volunteers held a mass meeting at the work-site at which they pledged 'to fight against the Taihang Mountains and tame the Zhang River with the spirit of San Gang Ling,[2] so that the people would lead happy lives for ten thousand years'. Altogether they moved over 300,000 cubic metres of earth and stone—a good sixth of the job. And during their time off they helped the local farmers. The aid was mutual. The farmers put up the visitors in their best rooms; the women washed and mended their clothes and the men taught them 'to swing the sledge-hammer forehand and backhand, like the Volunteers' who honeycombed the hills in Korea. The visitors worked for seven weeks. When they left they were given a rousing send-off, with gifts of cloth shoes made by women of the whole county, and five lorry loads of sweet potato shoots which the Shexian farmers went along to plant out for them.

The digging of the channel was celebrated in verse by a local bard, who wrote:

The North Zhang Channel is winding and long.
It draws the Zhang River up the Taihang.

[2] 'Mutton Chop Ridge'—scene of an outstanding victory of the Chinese and North Korean forces during the Korean War.

56

The Eight Point Charter

For sixty miles it flows on and on,
Through the blue mountains like a drifting song.
It waters broad acres of land once barren,
Till the mounds of grain reach up to heaven.
Though the river swells, it does not overflow—
The channel saves the plains from woe.
A score of villages stricken long with drought
Can drink and wash at last, they shout.
Electric power lines form a heavenly skein;
Factories spring up like bamboo shoots in rain.
Fruit trees grow thick on every side;
The scent of spice is wafted far and wide.
The people's spirits soar to the sky,
As they see the waters flowing by.
To the Communist Party they sing songs of praise
For the joys of countless future days.

GIVING THE POORER BRIGADES A HELPING HAND

Some brigades were advancing faster than others. The 404 *jin* per *mu* yield of grain, for instance, was the average for Yangyi Commune, but there was a wide range in the average output of different brigades. In Little Yetao, a model brigade, it was 471 *jin* per *mu*; in Ten Mile Inn, an ordinary brigade, it was 401 *jin* per *mu*; and in Yungan, one of the poorer brigades, it was 272 *jin* per *mu*.

The April check-up had put an end to treating the brigades as if they were equal. Now each of them reaped the fruits of its own efforts and accepted the advantages or disadvantages of its own natural conditions. Thus the gap between the better and worse off brigades remained. It was to be bridged by levelling up, not levelling down.

Yangyi Commune Council and the Commune Party Committee took a number of measures to this end. The first was financial aid. Following the April check-up loans from state funds, amounting to 41,000 *yuan* were issued to the one-third or so poorest brigades. Together with the loans a slogan was launched: 'Poor brigades, work with a will! Catch up with and overtake the prosperous brigades!' At the same time the better-off brigades were called on to volunteer aid. Their slogan was: 'Prosperous brigades help poor ones!'

So Little Yetao sent its Labour Hero, Ren Qing-mei, to Liezhang to help introduce sweet potatoes and other high yield crops suited to its poor natural conditions. Yangyi brigade, part of whose prosperity came from carting, volunteered to help remote Lianggou, one-time 8th Route Army arsenal, to transport its fruit and nuts to market. Caozigang, poor partly through not having produced any able local leaders, received help from various sources. Little Yetao released one of its assistant brigade heads to act in the same capacity

57

in Caozigang; prosperous Shidong brigade sent an experienced and reliable accountant; and the commune sent one of its Party Committee members to serve as assistant to the secretary of the Caozigang Party Branch. Altogether the commune released one Party Secretary, six Party Committee members and eight cadres to strengthen the leadership of the poorer brigades. ·

One other measure to help the poorest brigades was re-grouping. The thirty-three high level co-operatives which had merged to form Yangyi Commune had varied considerably in size, degree of consolidation and natural conditions. Now those with the poorest natural conditions and least solid organization were disbanded and merged with their better-favoured neighbours, location of homes and wishes of the people involved being considered in the process. This re-grouping, which brought the number of brigades down from 33 to 29, was intended to 'level up' the poorer brigades; but it still did not bridge the gap between them and the richer ones. (The solution later put forward was not to get rid of the backward brigades by merging, but rather by analysing their particular advantages and disadvantages to set them on the right road of development.[3])

MIXED FEELINGS

The shaping of its administrative set-up and working systems, as well as major large-scale efforts in irrigation, changes in farming technique (which had previously altered little in the course of centuries) all took place in the first year or so of the commune's existence.

These social and technical changes touched almost every aspect of life. Many had proved successful, a few had been failures, some were still debatable. Reactions to the changes were varied. Many commune members tended to judge the developments of the year according to certain limited, specific features with which they came into closest contact and which affected them most personally.

The young people who had 'tempered themselves as they tempered the steel' felt that with the commune behind them and the Party to lead them there was nothing they could not do. It was the same with the youth 'shock teams' who had made bold and successful experiments in carrying out the Eight Point Charter. They were breaking with the traditional hankering of young people to leave the countryside for the cities the moment they became literate. Exciting prospects opened up by the commune stretched before them in the countryside. Inspired by the whitewashed slogan on their own mudbrick walls: 'Three years of bitter struggle! Ten thousand years of joy!' they were prepared to work night and day to bring Communism nearer.

[3] In the winter of 1960–61, the Yangyi leadership criticized itself for continuing tendencies to equalitarianism.

58

This was true not only of the youth. One 75-year-old man said: 'I'd rather lose a pound of my flesh than a pound in the yield of grain.' And he worked with youthful zest.

But others struck a different note. 'All this leaping forward takes it out of you,' one man complained.

Still others stood between these two extremes. They supported the commune on the whole but were critical of some aspect or other of its growth.

Most people, for instance, were proud of the results of the steel campaign. Yet some felt it had its flaws. Almost all the most energetic young people had been drawn into it, they pointed out. As a result, the harvesting had been rather slapdash. With a shortage of field hands at the crucial moment, some fields had been reaped too fast, others too late. So some grain was lost. To those who had suffered from famine in the past, wasting grain was a crime.

The bumper crops of 1958 and the records set on experimental plots had inspired exuberant murals on the village walls, showing sky high piles of golden grain. Now some said: 'We grow more grain all right. But where does it go? The more we grow, the more they take.' This referred to the government's regulation for the planned purchase and supply of grain, aimed at guaranteeing food for the cities, building up reserves and preventing speculation.

As to the community dining-rooms, while one woman exclaimed that it was 'like heaven' to be freed from cooking, some people complained that the canteen food was 'always the same old stuff' and that you could not 'eat what you like and when you like, the way you could at home'. Others worried about waste or extravagance in the running of the canteens.

Many were convinced that the commune would carry them rapidly to industrialization and the material and cultural advantages that went with it. In fact, among the painters of village murals and the composers of the poems on village walls, the favourite symbol for the commune was a railway engine racing across the countryside. Yet at the same time there were people who found the speed unsettling, who would have preferred the spartan 'prosperity' already achieved, to constantly striving for something better. Let well enough alone, they urged. Others, alarmed by the period when the 'winds of communism blew too hard', also favoured putting on the brakes.

The Commune Council and the brigade cadres found that the larger scale and scope of the commune placed heavy responsibilities on them. 'It's harder to lead a brigade than it was to lead a high-level co-op, even though both may have been formed out of the same village,' said one of the commune leaders. 'Cadres who did quite a good job leading a socialist co-op soon find out that it's not enough to rely on their old experience. Something more is called for when you not only go in for farming, but run industry, trade and education and organize defence and social services too.' Some cadres found it hard to measure up to all these tasks and so fell short of the demands of their brigade and work team members.

Mixed feelings about the events of the first year of the commune were not confined to the rank-and-file. Some cadres, carried away by what they saw ahead, made light of problems and difficulties. Their reports to the higher levels stressed successes. Problems and difficulties were hardly mentioned.

In the eyes of other cadres, problems and difficulties loomed large. Mass movements, for instance, had characterized the main events of the year, including the setting up of the commune. But when the winds of communism blew too hard these cadres began to question mass movements in general. Once you launch a mass movement, they reasoned, things get out of hand and mistakes are made. Their conclusion was: the locomotive of socialism should go ahead slowly but surely, with experienced cadres at the controls. Leaving too much to the rank-and-file could cause accidents or even create chaos.

These varied views arose from the changes brought about by the General Line for socialist construction, the Great Leap in steel and farm production and above all by the shaping of the commune itself.

This was how things stood in Yangyi Commune in August 1959, when the Central Committee of the Chinese Communist Party held its Eighth Plenary Session. After reviewing and assessing developments throughout the country the Central Committee reaffirmed the General Line for building socialism and upheld mass movements. It stated:

> The experience of 1958 proved very clearly that the wisdom and strength of the masses is boundless . . . as a mighty, irresistible force under whose impact high mountains bow their heads and broad rivers make way. The great leap forward and the people's communes are new things which have no precedent in the history of our people. In the course of their advance it is naturally inevitable that certain difficulties and shortcomings should arise. But these are of a transient and local nature . . .[4]

The Resolution ended with a call to 'fight for great victories this year and strive to fulfil ahead of time, within the two years 1958–59, the major targets of the Second Five Year Plan'. And as a means to this end to: 'unite more closely, resolutely surmount and correct all shortcomings in our work, overcome Right opportunist sentiments among some unstable elements, strike telling blows against the disruptive activities of anti-socialist elements . . .'

[4] 'Resolution on Developing the Campaign for Increasing Production and Practising Economy', 8th Plenary Session of the 8th Central Committee of the C.C.P., *Documents*, F.L.P., Peking, 1959.

Chapter VI

'RECTIFICATION'
(Winter, 1959-60)

WHEN the autumn harvest had been brought in and the ploughing and sowing of the winter crops was done, there was time to tackle the tasks set by the Central Committee of: 'correcting shortcomings in work, overcoming Right opportunist sentiments among unstable elements, striking telling blows against the disruptive activities of anti-socialist elements.' And in mid-October 1959, a 'Rectification and Socialist Education Campaign' was launched in Yangyi.

The previous 'rectification' had been carried out throughout the Chinese countryside two years before, in the winter of 1957-58. Together with the 'Great Debate' it had played a big part in stimulating the Great Leap Forward and in the forming of the communes. The following two years had been years of great change.

In Yangyi the new rectification was first set in motion in the commune's Party branches, all Party members being called on to look back over the past year, critically examine the key questions which had cropped up, draw lessons from defects in work, improve their style and methods of work as cadres and combat right opportunism. And last but not least to work out, in the light of this examination, how production could be stepped up.

RECTIFICATION AND UPGRADING OF PARTY MEMBERS AND CADRES[1]

The movement combined the study of Marxist theory and current policies with a down-to-earth examination of the leadership each Party Branch had given, of the activities and attitudes of all Party members and cadres. How had they analysed the situation in the commune and the brigade? How had they assessed results?

Each Party member and cadre summed up his actions of the past eventful period. Then his comrades helped him take his understanding a step further by means of criticism and self-criticism based on the principle of 'unity-criticism-unity'. This meant 'starting off with a desire for unity and resolving contradictions through criticism

---

[1] The terms 'Party members' and 'cadres' are frequently coupled in Chinese. See Part Three 'Introduction'.

Two Years' History of Yangyi Commune

and struggle to achieve a new unity on a new basis'.[2] Most time and attention was devoted to those who held posts in the commune or in brigades or work teams. In the case of those holding important positions, the rank-and-file non-Party members were also called on to put forward their views.

The main targets of criticism were 'bureaucracy, sectarianism and subjectivism'.

These high-sounding terms referred to very ordinary, everyday shortcomings. Bureaucracy, which at different times and places has different forms and roots, here was mainly of the type known as 'having-a-hard-time-of-it' bureaucracy. The 'bureaucrats' were as a rule well-intentioned, hard-working, plain-living, self-sacrificing men or women, but they were shouldering jobs they had never done before and for which they had little or no training or experience. Not always knowing how to single out the key problems from among the complex new tasks facing them, they tended to be run off their feet trying to keep up with developments. As a result they found no time to investigate matters carefully enough to make considered judgements. They grappled with many problems but solved few. And some, when distraught, became short-tempered. Thus friction and even antagonism appeared and began to drive a wedge between such cadres and the people.

There was also a second type of bureaucracy to be found, which did not simply reflect a cadre's failure to master his job. It reflected rather the old attitude that those in positions of leadership were above manual work and those who did it. The farmers spoke of such bureaucrats as 'four-armed' cadres—for they went to the fields to give directions, their jackets slung over their shoulders like capes. The limply dangling empty jacket sleeves—the extra arms—were a symbol of their non-participation in field work. A few cadres did not even get as far as the fields. These were described as 'talking a lot but never going to the masses to help them solve their problems'.

Sectarianism, too, has various forms. Here it generally took the form of 'localism'—of being narrowly absorbed in the interests of one's own brigade or work team and determined to make it succeed regardless of how others fared. This might be practised by cadres or rank-and-filers who disregarded their personal interests or ambitions, but when it came to any project involving their brigade or team were calculating in the extreme, working out the balance sheet again and again to make sure that their own group came out best. This was an old problem which in the co-operative period had taken the form of the pulling up a neighbour's sorghum stalks when they threatened the peanuts of one's own co-operative; or in sur-

[2] Mao Tse-tung, *On the Correct Handling of Contradictions Among the People* F.L.P., Peking, 1957.

62

'Rectification'

reptitiously moving a boundary stone to straighten out a furrow. Subjectivism was mainly a matter of jumping to conclusions, of seeing only what fitted one's preconceived ideas, instead of investigating, weighing all the factors or hearing all sides of a case. And with the commune—a more complex social unit than had existed in the countryside before—there were more factors to weigh and more sides to hear than ever.

The Party Secretary of the Shidong District, to which Ten Mile Inn belonged, for instance, was criticized for the way in which time limits were set for the sowing of winter wheat. One brigade had been given seven days. But at the end of that time it had only half finished the job; so its cadres and members were publicly criticized. When the commune leadership looked into the matter, however, it found that the brigade had worked very hard. But they had not enough draught animals and it was unrealistic to expect them to finish in a week without providing any. Once arrangements were made for them to borrow animals from other brigades they soon finished the sowing. The District cadre had not taken the trouble to investigate carefully and weigh things up before setting the targets and meting out criticism. He had been subjective.

Through the thrashing out of such problems and the examination of individual actions it was possible for the Party members and cadres throughout the commune to improve their leadership. Commune leadership was a complex task. It involved keeping close to reality, knowing an immense number of facts and at the same time being able to sort out the major points from the minor ones. It demanded the ability to analyse matters from a class standpoint, instead of being influenced or befuddled by personal relations, the overcoming of any tendency to magnify problems or to underestimate them.

Any of these defects would lead to decisions adversely affecting the lives of the commune members and thereby setting up a barrier between cadres and rank-and-file. Each mistake examined, each weakness overcome removed a barrier and strengthened unity.

This was one of the purposes of the rectification campaign. But in the course of it, in some villages, problems of a deeper nature were brought to light.

THE TWO ROADS

Yuan Tian-fu, a cadre of Liuqu Village, felt dissatisfied with both the commune and the Great Leap. In the course of discussion it became clear that his dissatisfaction was not simply with the speed at which things were moving but also with their direction. 'Life's not as good as it used to be,' he said on more than one occasion.

Such remarks would have been natural enough coming from a former landlord or an ex-Kuomintang official. But Yuan Tian-fu

63

was a Communist. His fellow Party members in Liuqu Village asked him to look into this idea. Just when had life been better? And for whom?

So Yuan, with the aid of the Party Branch, went back over his life. Before the Communists came to the area he had been a farmhand. His whole family of five owned one-twelfth of an acre. In 1940 things were so desperate that he had left home, a beggar, to try his luck in the neighbouring province of Shansi. Life had not been better then.

A few years later came the land reform and Yuan, like others who had been forced to migrate through poverty, went home again. He threw himself into the fight to destroy the old landlord system and became secretary of the village branch of the Youth League and later a Party member. When the fruits of the struggle were distributed Yuan's family received a good-sized house, a mule and an acre and a quarter of land—fifteen times as much as before. Yuan Tian-fu felt that now there was nothing to stop him from building up the family fortunes. He worked with zest and found life good.

In 1954, when the semi-socialist co-operative was set up in Liuqu, Yuan did not choose to join, though as a Communist he was looked to for a lead. He felt he was already getting on well enough; why should he be held back by entangling himself with those who joined the co-op? As far as he could see they were just the ones who could not make a go of it on their own. Yuan himself, young, able and hard-working, was doing well enough even if a few of his neighbours were not.

By 1955, however, the whole village surged into the co-operative and Yuan did not see how he could stay out. But he joined without enthusiasm, accepted no responsibility and even gave up attending Party meetings regularly. With the coming of the commune he grew more dissatisfied than ever. Its more efficient organization of labour struck him as irksome discipline. The planned purchase and supply system, which prevented profiteering, seemed an infringement of his freedom. In short, 'life wasn't as good as it used to be'.

All these facts came out in discussion. And from them questions arose.

Why was it Yuan saw the few short years between land reform and the low level co-op as the 'golden age'? What stopped him from seeing that the capitalist road he was taking—of every man for himself—would have led to a future patteı.'ed on the past, with a handful of exploiters and a mass of exploited; while the socialist road—of one for all and all for one—that he was spurning, led to a life of prosperity for everyone, including himself?

After painful heart-searching Yuan came to accept the criticism levelled at him. He expressed the determination in future to pull his weight in brigade affairs. Instead of 'building his happiness on the

'*Rectification*'

suffering and misfortunes of others,' he said, he would 'take the socialist road of prosperity for everyone.' In this way a new unity was established between Yuan and the rest of the Party Branch, based on the principle: 'unity—criticism—unity.'

Beyond Liuqu, in the mountainous upper reaches of the Min River, is the village of Baicaoping. During the anti-Japanese war this village had been led and inspired by its own Labour Hero, Guo Qing-chun. Its militia had killed altogether 300 Japanese and Guo's two sons and a nephew gave their lives fighting in the 8th Route Army. Baicaoping was now the scene of a less inspiring story.

Guo You-ling, secretary of the village Party branch, was originally a poor peasant. Like Yuan Tian-fu he had thrown himself into the struggle against the landlords and rich peasants, been recruited into the Communist Party and become a village leader.

Guo proved to be one of the ablest farmers in the village, and one of the shrewdest, who could turn his hand to all sorts of profitable ventures. In very short order, following the land reform, he had ceased to be a poor peasant; he had become a middle peasant and was clearly on the way to becoming a new-style rich peasant.

Guo as a leading village Communist should have been a trail-blazer on the road to socialism. Instead, like Yuan, he found each step from individual farming, from private ownership of the means of production and the freedom to buy land and houses, to hire hands or lend money at interest, increasingly distasteful. The one-time revolutionary had become a conservative.

The reasons were not far to seek. The land reform, which destroyed the feudal system of land ownership, though led by the Communist Party, was not in itself a socialist revolution, but only a step towards it. It was part of the 'New Democratic Revolution'. With this, men like Guo felt they had everything to gain and nothing to lose. Following the land reform the Communist Party had started to lead the peasants towards socialism, by way of mutual aid and farming co-operatives. These first took into account the peasants' deeply ingrained sense of property by giving them as big a return on land invested as on labour done. Not until 1955–56 was the land collectivized and payment made solely on the basis of labour. It was only at this time that farming could be considered fully socialist.

During the whole period of the development of farming co-operatives Guo had held back. But all along, the township Party Committee had patiently reasoned with him and tried to convince him. Cadres such as he, steeled in the struggle against the Japanese and the landlords and rich peasants, had courage and experience. They had won the esteem of their fellow villagers and were counted on to lead them forward. They were not carelessly cast aside. So with the organization of Yangyi Commune, Guo, for all his earlier holding back, became secretary of the Baicaoping Brigade Branch. But

65

during the eventful year and a half from the founding of the commune until the winter of 1959–60, there was trouble in the brigade. This came to a head over the running of the canteens. And while the whole record of canteen leadership was being examined, during the rectification, Guo's standing as a Party member came into question.

The task of setting up and running the canteens in Baicaoping had been assigned by the Commune Party Committee to Guo. Under his guidance the canteen cooks simply weighed out one *jin* of cornmeal per person every day, mixed it into dough and steamed it in one big conical cake. This was issued in the morning and had to last all day—though at noon and night boiling water was provided to wash down the remnants. The sizable balance of the canteen grain that was saved, Guo used in a noodle shop which he had set up as a profitable brigade enterprise.

When those eating in the canteen complained that there was not enough food, and that what there was was not palatable, Guo blamed the commune for its 'paltry' allocation of grain, and demanded more. (This being before the check-up, the commune was still the distributing unit.) A commune investigating team was sent to Baicaoping. After listening to the brigade members' complaints the investigators talked with Guo, pointing out the importance of concern for the welfare of the brigade members and urging him to pay more attention to canteen management. They particularly stressed the importance of a varied menu. 'It's no good talking,' protested Guo. 'You can't make bread without flour. All I need to put the canteens on their feet is more grain.'

The commune gave him some, and after a while sent the team back to see how things were going. This time, on entering one dining-room, the investigators were astonished. Some people were eating corn-bread, some had steamed wheat buns; some had pancakes and others doughnuts. Never in all the canteens they had visited had they seen so many kinds of cooking at one meal.

During the rectification the secret of this variety came out. When Guo received the extra allowance of grain he had issued it to the individual families for them to cook at home in any way they liked. When the inspection team was due Guo blew the bugle which was used to give warning of an important announcement. So the brigade members, who were in the midst of eating, went to the central dining-room taking along their bowls containing whatever they happened to be eating.

After thorough study and discussion of this and a number of similar incidents, the Baicaoping Party members came to the conclusion that Guo had no desire to change and that he was an obstacle in the village's advance to socialism. The Commune Party Committee, too, when the case came up to it, saw that the canteen affair was simply the latest of a series of mistakes. These arose, they

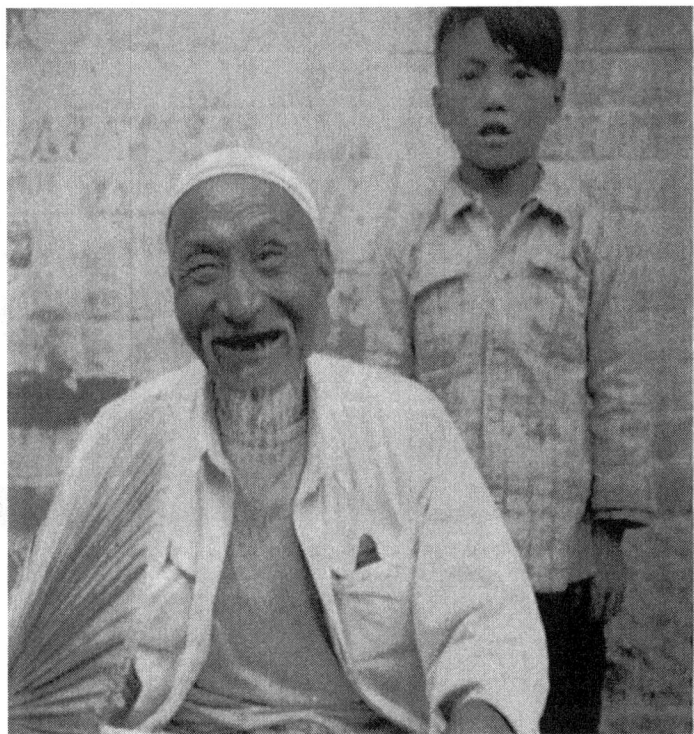

9. In the Bailin old folks' home—old man and adopted "grandson".

10. In one of the Bailin kindergartens.

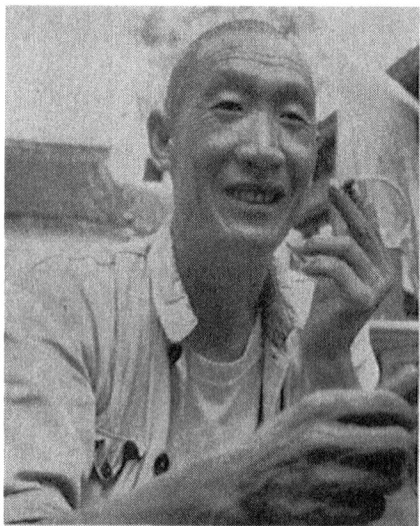

11. County Party Secretary Duan Peng-xiang (see Chapter XVIII, County Cadres).

12. County Head Wang De-hen in his experimental cotton plot (see Chapter XVIII, County Cadres).

13. Commune Party Secretary Jin Han-cheng (see Chapter I, Local Revolutionary Leaders).

14. Young cadres of the Ten Mile Inn Brigade. Li Wei-guo (see Chapter XX, The Communist Youth League) on the left.

said, from Guo's failure to take a working-class stand during this new stage of the socialist revolution; he was no longer loyal to the cause of communism and should be expelled from the Party.

Following Guo's expulsion, the village, which for long had lagged behind, began to make headway.

In the whole county of Shexian there were few Party members like Guo who, in the final analysis, were not in favour of moving forward to socialism. There were, however, a number like Yuan Tian-fu, who after drifting in the direction of capitalism were brought back to the socialist road by the rectification campaign. But the vast majority of cadres and Party members fell into neither of these two categories. For them the rectification meant getting a better grasp of policy and improving their work style and leadership.

Important as this was for individual cadres and Party members, it was of greater importance still for the various Party branches.

RECTIFICATION AND CANTEENS IN TEN MILE INN

In Ten Mile Inn the Party branch made a searching examination of production. Had it gone up as much and as fast as it could? It had certainly gone up, but not as fast as in Little Yetao, for instance. Why not? The branch members went over in detail the records of the various crops and even of the different fields. In certain fields the crops had not been put in early enough to achieve the best results. In others, through late hoeing, not enough rain had been absorbed. With spring and autumn rain so precious, why was it wasted? The answer was: shortage of labour.

Work team records revealed that although there were 480 able-bodied men and women in the village, the average daily working-force had been only 290. A number, of course, had been off on such jobs as railway building; and others were engaged in commune industry or construction. These undertakings were necessary and in the long run would benefit the brigade.

But there were two ways in which much time and labour was being wasted.

Each day some families had already finished their breakfast when others were just starting it. It was the same with the midday meal. By the time all the members of a team had assembled and work had been allocated, valuable time had been lost.

This state of affairs was hardly surprising. Living as they did in a society still in the early stages of industrialization, clocks and watches played little part in their daily life. So long as the household was the unit of production such lack of precision and punctuality had presented no great problem. But with a larger organization, such as the work team, involving the co-ordinated efforts of dozens of people, losses of time were multiplied. Minutes grew to hours and hours to days of work time frittered away.

Housework, too, in such a society, was time-consuming and onerous. Water had to be fetched and carried, often from the outskirts of the village; grain had to be ground at a stone mill turned by a donkey or by the housewife herself; fuel had to be gathered from the hills; clothes and cloth shoes sown by hand; vegetables pickled, or sliced and dried for the long winter months. What with all this on top of daily cooking and washing, few women could be counted on to turn out regularly for work in the fields. Most of those who went at all, arrived late and left early, putting in only about four hours a day.

The solution to this problem, put forward soon after the setting up of the commune, had been canteens. Collectivized cooking made it possible to save much time and energy even before the introduction of running water, power milling, gas or electric stoves; at the same time it paved the way for these improvements. Now, one of the first questions posed in the Ten Mile Inn Party branch during the rectification was: 'Why did we close the canteens?'

In 1959, soon after the April check-up, four canteens had been set up. This was during the summer rush season and 70 per cent of the brigade's families had their meals in the new community dining-rooms. In the autumn, however, the Party branch and village cadres knew that there were complaints such as: 'The food's no good,' 'Always the same old stuff,' and 'You can't eat what you want or when you want to.' They knew, too, that in some other villages in the commune, canteens had already been closed. So the Party branch came to the conclusion that the people of Ten Mile Inn were not yet ready for this step towards collective living, and the canteens were closed (though grain was still issued).

Now the branch considered whether this decision had been correct. Just how widespread was the view that 'the food was no good' and that it was 'always the same old stuff'? An investigation was made. It showed that the former poor peasants and most of the ex-middle peasants, who made up the great majority of the diners, found the food as good as or better than they had at home. One man, called Fu, not only found the food satisfactory but found peace of mind when he ate in the canteen, for his wife was a poor planner, who served such generous meals at the beginning of the month that she had to borrow grain at the end of it. With menu-planning shifted to the shoulders of the dining-room staff, Fu felt freed from this worry. When the canteens closed, back it came. Fu's was not the only case of this sort. Until staple food was abundant nearly every housewife needed to plan consumption to the last grain. Quite a number lacked this ability.

After examining the situation in different households the branch reached the conclusion that it had not looked at things from a class standpoint. The canteens, they decided, had had their defects, due to the inexperience of the managers and the cooks; besides, people could not get used to them immediately. But the former poor and middle peasants who formed the majority had not wanted the canteens closed down, but improved. The well-to-do middle farmers did eat better at home, but with improved management and cooking the canteens would be able to offer better food than the vast majority could provide at home.

Setting up and consolidating canteens, the branch affirmed, was at this stage part of the battle for higher production and better living. With shortage of labour preventing bigger advances in production, canteens could play a key role, both by releasing women for farm work and by helping everyone get to work on time.

In the light of this conclusion the Party and also the Youth League members decided to examine their own attitudes towards eating in community dining-rooms.

Before the canteens were set up, according to custom, people had taken their bowls of cereal, frugally trimmed with vegetable, out to their front doorstep and had stood or squatted eating and chatting with their neighbours. Meals were a free-and-easy affair (except for the housewife) with no fixed time, place or company. The community dining-rooms were different and even a few of the Communist Youth League members found it hard to get used to them.

The Youth League Branch Committee, therefore, posed the question: 'How should a League member look at the dining-rooms?' The conclusion reached was: In the long run the individual way of life is not dependable. It offers no security or worthwhile prospect. Only the collective can bring the people happiness and well-being and accord with the League's aim of fighting for communism. So the old way of eating belongs to the past.

Now that the Party and Youth League members were convinced that running canteens was part of 'the struggle between the two roads', they decided to launch a broad public discussion as a form of socialist education. The questions they put were: 'Are canteens a good thing? Shall we have some in our brigade?'

These questions were discussed throughout the village and the advantages and shortcomings of the defunct canteens were weighed up.

Criticisms fell into two different categories. A large number were the complaints of people unaccustomed to eating in any sort of canteen or at any fixed time and place. They were bound to arise, unless each individual weighed up the disruption of his old habits against the advantages he gained from speeding the advance in general prosperity; in other words against his rising income in terms of food, clothing, thermos flasks, torches, bicycles and so on.

As a result of the discussion most people came to the conclusion that the advantages of the canteens might well outweigh their inconveniences. And they voted to give them another try.

The second main category of criticism concerned defects in management and in cooking. As to cooking, there were complaints of grit in the grain, of flavourless food, of buns not cooked through, of unvarying menus. Defects in management included not keeping the accounts clear, up-to-date and regularly posted where everyone could see them. There were also complaints of some waste and extravagance.

Such criticisms were generally felt to be well founded. The solution proposed was to elect the best possible team of cooks and managers for the canteens, instead of just picking those who could best be spared from field work, as had tended to be the case in the past.

There was, however, a third category of criticism.

In the course of the discussion and the sorting out of the problems, some of the villagers became increasingly indignant with two men who, they suspected, had been consciously undermining the canteens by exaggerating defects that did exist and inventing others that did not. These two men were both former Kuomintang officials who had been 'struggled against' during the land reform, but who later had been admitted on sufferance first into the socialist co-operatives and then into the commune.

One of these was Wang Dian-yuan, son of Ten Mile Inn's once most feared and hated landlord, Wang Ban-yen.[3] The latter had been a Kuomintang official, and a local tyrant guilty of more than one capital crime. He was put to death by the peasants during the land reform. Wang Dian-yuan himself, who had also been a Kuomintang official, had been fined for tax evasion during the land reform and had not qualified for membership in the semi-socialist co-operative.

Of the same type was the former rich peasant Wang Jia-wen. He too had served the Kuomintang and later been penalized for opposing the land reform. He had then left home, returning only in 1949 when he felt things had quietened down.

When the discussion on canteens was being wound up, these two men, in line with the policy of 'striking blows against the disruptive activities of anti-socialist elements', were singled out for public reprimand.

Meanwhile, when everyone had had ample chance to air their views, a summary was made. The consensus was that the canteens had six important advantages—and that they should be given another try. The six advantages of the canteens were:

1. They enable us all to go to the fields and come back from them at

[3] For details of his life, see *Revolution in a Chinese Village*, Routledge & Kegan Paul, London, 1959.

'Rectification'

the same time; to have unified, collective action. Without them it's come and go as you please.

2. They take a great load off the minds of those people who don't know how to plan and budget properly and so are always finding themselves in a fix.
3. They free women from household chores and so bring a big increase to the working force in the fields.
4. They free people living on their own from having to start carrying water, lighting fires and cooking at the end of a hard day's work.
5. They permit a great saving in overhead expenses on fuel, oil, seasoning and so on.
6. They strengthen the spirit of collectivism.

Following this summing-up the Party and Youth League members called on all the teams to set up their own canteens. Eighteen of them were soon established and, though some people later dropped out, in the high tide of enthusiasm which followed this discussion, everyone in Ten Mile Inn applied to join, including the two former Kuomintang officials.

Wang Dian-yuan, in fact, had little choice, since his wife and daughter-in-law both applied and it was they who had always done the cooking at Wang's home. When it came to a choice between cooking for himself and eating in a community dining-room, even he saw the advantages of collectivism. Wang Jia-wen was less fortunate. The members of his work team, angered at what they considered his undermining of the canteen in its early days, refused to accept him. But they did accept the nephew and niece with whom he lived. So Wang Jia-wen had to do his own cooking, day in and day out, after working in the fields. Again and again he went to the brigade office and pleaded with the Party Secretary to intercede for him. But it was a good two months before his team-mates grudgingly permitted him to eat in their new canteen.

The analysing of the canteen problem—first inside the Party, then in broad, public discussion—was only one of the matters dealt with during the campaign for 'rectification and socialist education'. The chief lessons which the Ten Mile Inn Party branch members felt they learnt from it were: the need for finding out all the main facts instead of jumping to conclusions on the basis of a few complaints; and the need to 'subject the facts to a class analysis, not to give equal weight to all views regardless of their origin'. In this case a class analysis meant looking at the canteens with the eyes of the majority—that is, of the poor peasants and most of the former middle peasants—not with the eyes of a handful of well-to-do farmers; still less with those of ex-landlord and rich peasant Kuomintang officials such as Wang Dian-yuan and Wang Jia-wen.[4]

[4] In 1960–61 new problems arose in the running of canteens and (as in many parts of China) they were closed once again, except during rush seasons. See Chapter XIV.

71

LESSONS IN SOCIALIST THINKING

Solving specific problems such as that of the canteens, upgrading the cadres and Party members and strengthening unity between the cadres and the rank-and-file were only part of the 'Rectification and Socialist Education' campaign. Another important aspect of it was the public airing of views and the clarifying of the main lines of Communist policy among the commune members. Was the Great Leap tempo too fast? Were communes a good thing? Did mass movements bring losses as well as gains?

These questions were discussed within the Party and Youth League branches and among the ordinary run of commune members.

The question of tempo was related to the General Line, the Great Leap and mass movements. It was posed in the following context: was there really a choice between 'more, better, faster and more economical' on the one hand, and 'fewer but better' or 'slow but sure' on the other? China did not exist in a vacuum but in a world where war could be averted and socialist construction defended only by the most widespread and strenuous efforts of the masses of the people, by the building of a strong socialist country with modern industry, agriculture, culture and science. So wasn't it rather a question of working intensively now under favourable conditions, and working equally or more intensively later under unfavourable ones? In other words, of working hard of one's own initiative today or equally hard out of dire necessity tomorrow?

To settle the question of gains and losses during mass movements an appraisal was made in each brigade of the campaigns for water conservancy, for steel and for bumper yields. Failures were weighed against successes. The consensus was that losses amounted to only 'one finger out of ten', and that, in the case of steel, for instance, the gains could not be mechanically worked out in terms of cost accounting or prices on the world market. A solid foundation had been laid for a local metal industry, where before there had not even been the notion that farmers could make steel.

But the focal point of the socialist education campaign was the comparison of life today with life in the past.

This was discussed throughout all the brigades of the commune, so that everyone might see his life in perspective. How had he lived in the past? How did he live now? And how would he be living in a few years' time—say towards the end of the sixties? In South Cunjing village the Party branch asked each household to work out its income over the past few years. The figures showed a steady rise. When they had been discussed they were summed up and presented in traditional Chinese style in the following contrasting formulas:

'Rectification'

'The Evil Things of the Old Days'	'The Good Things of Today'
The Chiang Kai-shek government	The leadership of the Communist Party
The corrupt Kuomintang politicians	The policies of the Communist Party and the People's Government
The exploitation and bullying of the landlords	The People's Communes; the improvements in agriculture; the canteens and old folks' homes

Similarly, past worries about food, clothing and shelter were contrasted with present security, and the 'banes of the old society' with the 'boons of the new'.

'The Banes of the Old Society'	'The Boons of the New'
Being poverty-stricken	More income
Being rack-rented	More grain
Eating chaff	More and newer houses
Living in tumble-down houses	More savings and capital
Paying usurious interest on loans	accumulation
Being forced into beggary	More children at school
Being cursed and beaten	More happy homes and better
Being driven to gambling and drugs	family relations

In nearby Yungan village the following table of grain output was drawn up:

	jin per *mu*
Before land reform	120
Just after land reform (1946)	146
Semi-socialist co-operative period (1954)	183
Socialist co-operative period (1957)	230
People's commune period (1959)	272

In Ten Mile Inn the contrasts were posed in a more concrete form. Two village families were chosen, one representing about 30 per cent of the villagers and the other about 70 per cent; and an exhibition was organized at which were displayed their possessions past and present. The rags they once had worn during the day or covered themselves with at night were placed beside their new clothes and their piles of flowered silk and cotton bedding, gaily coloured and thickly padded against the winter cold. Cracked

73

earthenware begging bowls were set near new enamel wash-basins and shiny thermos flasks; tattered cloth shoes and wooden clogs, beside glossy rubber boots.

Similar exhibitions were to be found in every village. In one place, to settle an argument, practically the whole village got together to work out just how many—or how few—people had owned various items which were now becoming an index of the rising standard of living. It was recalled that before the land reform there had been three torches, three pairs of galoshes, four umbrellas, two thermos flasks and so on in the entire village. Now such things were possessed by every family. An exhibition was arranged and it filled several rooms with rows of thermos flasks, torches and other stuff such as only landlords had owned in the past.

Everywhere village artists or local school teachers were called on to paint pictures for village exhibitions. These were normally in three sets. The first one, of life before liberation, showed begging, eviction, rape, torture, famine, disease, death—at the hands of the landlords or the invading Japanese. These pictures were not stereotyped. They were graphic histories of each particular village in which the people portrayed could be recognized. While educating the young they brought back bitter memories to the old and middle-aged. They were followed by a second set reviewing the various reforms initiated by the Communists—distributing the land, mutual aid, co-operation. The third and last set of pictures would show tractors and combine harvesters in the fields, electric power lines overhead, new-style villages with lofty blocks of flats and modern factories, hospitals, schools, theatres and parks—a vision of the future.

RESULTS OF RECTIFICATION

After the campaign for rectification and socialist education had been carried out all over the Chinese countryside, its results were summed up by vice-Premier Li Fu-chun:

> By effective use of the method of rectification campaigns in the Party and among the whole people in the period of national construction we have been able to handle correctly not only class contradictions among the people, but also the contradictions between the advanced and the backward in their ranks. Because of this we have been able continuously to overcome bureaucratic and authoritarian styles of work among leading cadres and constantly to sharpen the people's socialist and communist consciousness. Thus we have made advanced, revolutionary ideology play the part of a powerful propellent in the course of the development of socialist society.[5]

In Shexian as elsewhere the rectification and socialist education

---

[5] Li Fu-chun, *Raise High the Red Banner of the General Line* (pamphlet) F.L.P., Peking, 1960, also in *Peking Review*, No. 34, August 1960.

campaign carried forward the socialist revolution in the ideological and political field—and set the stage for another advance in production. Commenting on how the rectification had helped the cadres to improve their style of work and increased their ability to discover, analyse and solve problems of socialist construction, one of the county leaders said: 'Cadres throughout our county were able to improve their way of working, so that the relations between them and the rank-and-file commune members became closer. Management was improved, too, at commune, brigade and work team level; and we also took a step forward in "the four services and two homes".' (These were: canteens, kindergartens, tailoring centres and mills and the old folks' and maternity homes.)

When the campaign ended in Yangyi itself the Party branches and branch committees of the commune found themselves strengthened and ready to face fresh problems. So did the cadres at the different levels of the commune: the Commune Council, the district committees, and brigades and work teams.

The Commune Party Committee was strengthened by the addition of three new secretaries, which increased the total from four to seven. Altogether, including these seven secretaries, it now had twenty-eight members. These, as preparation for pushing forward the work of the commune, now embarked on a study of Party and Government policies. Their starting point was Mao Tse-tung's statement on the supreme importance of agriculture: 'In developing the national economy agriculture must be taken as the foundation and industry as the dominant factor. The speeding up of agricultural growth is the central link in the rapid and proportionate development of the national economy.'[6]

They went on to call for the carrying out of the four 'izations'— irrigation, mechanization, electrification and 'chemicalization' (use of farm chemicals)—in order to step up agricultural production. In all this the main field of operations was to be *the high yield tract*. Its importance was proclaimed in the slogan: 'Agriculture the base. The high yield tract the battlefield'—the battlefield for a revolution in farming technique.

[6] (Not a verbatim quotation.) This is borne out by the fact that a good harvest is always followed by an increase and a poor one by a decrease in the rate of industrial production, states Liao Lu-yen, Minister of Agriculture. (*Peking Review*, 14 September, 1960.)

Chapter VII

HIGH YIELD TRACTS
(Winter and Spring, 1960)

THE socialist co-operatives had changed the system of ownership and brought some increase in the size of fields, but they retained a system of field management suited to small scale cultivation. Applying the Eight Point Charter even to small fields had brought striking results in 1958; still more so in 1959. But this was only one prong of the revolutionary advance taking place in farming technique. The other prong was the merging of small plots into large one-crop tracts, while keeping up the intensity of farming. This would speed the revolution in technique which the National Program for Agricultural Development demanded, for large tracts would pave the way for machines which would raise the productivity of labour. (Hence the Yangyi Party Committee's drive to make the high yield tract the battlefield for the revolution in farming technique at the beginning of 1960.)

In 1958, during the Great Leap Forward, six farming co-operatives in Tzexian county on the vast North China cotton-growing plain had pooled 500 acres of their land to form a single tract. This pioneering venture ran into difficulties when it came to accounting, for each co-operative had its own way of calculating costs. Nevertheless, its advantages were apparent for the use of machines and for rationalizing the use of labour. With the forming of communes later that year the ground was cleared for the large-scale development of big single-crop tracts. By 1959 these accounted for a quarter of Hopei's cultivated area.

This trend brought in its train another upsurge of capital construction. The big tracts were contoured and served by new irrigation works. Standards were set for fertilizer and specifications for planting. Tractors could now be used to better advantage. And when, in the summer of 1959, some tracts were attacked by insect pests, aeroplanes sprayed them with insecticide. Tzexian county, which had led the way, could by then boast of tracts of 3,000 acres sown to one crop and under single management.

In the Handan Region a series of auxiliary enterprises were set up on the tracts: pig farms—to provide organic fertilizer, chemical fertilizer works, tool repair shops and so on. With unified management it became feasible, too, to organize technical study groups and to set up part time schools for the training of cotton-growing specialists.

When the harvest was gathered in the autumn of 1959, it was estimated that the yield on Hopei's big tracts was generally 30 to 50 per cent higher than that on small plots. A quarter of the province's farm land, cultivated in big tracts, had produced 40 per cent of its total output.

On the basis of these results in 1959, Hopei decided to push this new development in farm management into all areas of the province and all types of farming. There were to be high yield tracts not only for cotton but for wheat, sweet potatoes and maize; not only for field crops but for animal husbandry and orchards; not just in the plain but in the mountains.

So, in mountainous Shexian, too, as the rectification movement drew to a close, a drive to organize big tracts was launched among the ten rural communes of the county.

These tracts were developed under the direct leadership of the commune not of the brigade. This was a natural result of the lie and quality of the land. Each village was the centre of a series of concentric bands of land. The innermost ring was the richest, for the greater part of the peasants' labour had been lavished on it for centuries. It had received the lion's share of fertilizer and, whenever water could be spared, had been irrigated from village wells. Here, too, labour had been at hand for removing stones and levelling.

Beyond this inner ring of rich land lay one of medium quality, to which fertilizer had to be carried by donkey or even on carrying-poles by the farmer himself. Efforts were made to enrich this land, but the cost in labour being greater the quality of the soil remained poorer than that of the inner zone. Finally came the outlying fields. the amount of time and labour needed to cultivate them at all was so great that little could be done to improve them and they received little fertilizer or watering.

From the standpoint of the brigade, based in the village, the problem of converting this outer zone into high yield land seemed well nigh impossible. It was too dispersed and distant. From the standpoint of the commune as a whole, however, it was a compact mass of no-man's-land lying between different brigades. This made it possible for the county leaders to inspire the various commune councils with the vision of consolidating precisely those rather barren areas into high yield tracts; of organizing picked teams to carry out capital construction on them and convert them into top-quality land equal to that immediately surrounding the villages. By going all out and waging a determined struggle, said the county leaders, this could be accomplished within a year or two. The task would not be easy, they acknowledged, but the reward would be great. The result would be a spectacular rise in the output of the communes.

The rectification had given the Commune Councils and Party Committees a view of the road ahead. If farming was to be mechanized and electrified, they knew, the unit of cultivation and field management would have to grow from small plots to big tracts. The former belonged to the era of animal- and man-drawn ploughs and of ownership and management by the brigade; the latter would make possible the widespread use of tractors and other modern equipment, which would usher in the era of ownership and management by the commune.

With this prospect in view steps were taken to merge 60 per cent of the arable land of the county into tracts averaging 100 acres apiece. In Yangyi Commune, which is rather less mountainous than the county as a whole, plans were put forward to amalgamate plots into single-crop tracts averaging three hundred acres each. These plans were placed before the various brigades for discussion and volunteers were called for to take up the task of 'changing poor land into rich'.

At the same time the commune leadership, concerned about the gap between the poorer and better-off brigades, proposed that the eight smallest brigades should be merged into three, in order to concentrate their resources. (This meant reducing the number of brigades in the commune from 29 to 24.) This proposal being acted upon, the ground was further cleared for organizing big single-crop tracts.

SETTING-UP A HIGH YIELD TRACT IN YANGYI

Parched, flat uplands, gashed by deep ravines which drained away the summer downpours, stretched between Bailin and North and South Cunjing. The farmers of these three villages had done what they could to make this land produce crops, but hundreds of acres of it lay at a distance of two or three miles from their homes—and they had no means of getting to it except on foot. Besides there was no water at hand but that which fell from the unpredictable heavens. So each year some crops were put in, but the returns fell far short of those obtained from fields closer to the village, while the trouble involved was greater.

Now the commune leadership proposed to the three brigades that this very area, amounting to 670 acres in all, should be converted into high yield land through the forming of one large single-crop tract. The proposal provoked the remark from one farmer: 'That's no place to raise bumper crops. It's so bleak a dog wouldn't lift his leg there.' Others, too, felt the land was too poor and too far away from the villages. Some suggested that the experiment with big single-crop fields was worth trying, but that it should be carried out on better soil closer to home. The commune leaders, however, pointed out that the purpose was precisely to 'turn poor and distant land into land that was rich and near'. These fields had been neglected just because they were dry and hard to get to. Such drawbacks could not be overcome in the past, even by the socialist cooperatives. But the commune, with its greater resources in labour power, and its more collective way of life, would be able to take both water and labour where there had been none before. How was this to be done?

Leading from the uplands to the bottom land beside the dry bed of the River Min was one gully broader and deeper than the others. If this were dammed a reservoir with a capacity of 50,000 cubic metres would be formed to trap the summer rains. Once it was filled it would make up for the shortage of water on the uplands. Then a new idea took shape. Though the bottom land was beside the river it was far from well watered, for the Min River was usually dry. Besides, there were no villages along the road from Yangyi to Ten Mile Inn and to get at the land lying half-way between them meant a two-and-a-half-mile walk. What about turning the whole five mile stretch into a long narrow tract? Then part of that, too, could be watered by the newly-planned reservoir. This prospect of two high yield tracts linked by a reservoir caught the imagination of the keenest members of all the brigades concerned, especially of the youth. As to the labour force having to walk to and fro—if canteens could be set up in a village, then why not in a tract? In fact why should not sleeping quarters be built there as well?

A discussion of the triple project was launched among all the brigades concerned. Some of the older and more conservative-minded had their doubts about it. One old man scoffed: 'Your earth dam will never hold back the water. You wait till the big summer rains come. The Dragon King will only have to stretch out his leg—and down the dam will fall.' (The Dragon King, the mythical god of the waters, is still used as a figure of speech.) Nevertheless, agreement was finally reached to undertake the project.

The reservoir being the guarantee of the success of both tracts, it was decided that work on an earth dam should begin first. Volunteers were called for, to be paid in work points by their respective brigades. Ten Mile Inn, the brigade nearest the dam site, could expect to irrigate much of its own land from the reservoir; so there was no demurring when its cadres proposed that eighty men might be spared from the brigade and this number of volunteers was soon forthcoming.

The dam builders set to in the winter, pushed vigorously ahead and with Party members from all over the commune putting in voluntary work on their days off, finished the job within a month.

Next came the organizing of the working force for the tracts, first of all that on the uplands, which was to be planted to cotton. For this it was decided to form three teams, one from each of the three nearest villages, Bailin and North and South Cunjing. These teams were placed under the direct leadership of the commune, represented by Commune Party Secretary Jin Han-cheng; and all three were headed by Party members, provided by their respective brigade branches.

The volunteers included both veteran guerilla fighters of the 8th Route Army and young people who were not even born when the Communists first came to the area. Teen-aged boy and girl members of the Communist Youth League were among the most eager to sign up, and those who could not be accepted felt aggrieved. A rash of quarrels broke out, between mothers telling their daughters that this was no job for them, and daughters who insisted that they lived in a new age; between young people demanding to join, and brigade leaders pointing out that there was still important work to be done in the ordinary teams and that some of the young folk must be left to get on with it.

But at last 220 people, 80 of them women, were enrolled in the three teams. Their first task was to build themselves living quarters out in the bleak, barren tract.

It was the time of year when 'you dare not stretch your hand out in front of you, for fear of freezing it', when they started on the first settlement. First they hollowed two rows of caves out of a mound, working in shifts day and night to prevent the freshly-turned earth from freezing. When they sprinkled lime to mark the layout of the hall and other buildings, just enough snow fell to cover it up. But with the Party branch stressing the importance of the tract, they stuck at it; and in seven days and nights three settlements were established.

Once the buildings were up, some were for calling a halt before levelling the land. The ground was too hard, they said, better wait till the weather was warmer. But the Party branch called a meeting to discuss the meaning of 'continuous revolution', and then launched the slogan:

> The wind is cold, but it cannot chill our ardour.
> The earth is frozen, but it cannot freeze our will.
> The howling gale can never blow down our conviction.
> The drifting snow can never cover up our courage.

In response to this appeal they set to work, in the teeth of the winds which swept across the uplands, to fill in five gullies and level over 350 acres. With little but simple hand tools this was a test of stamina and will. And as the days went by, though most persevered, some found it hard to face. They were not used to such close collective life; the weather was cold and the caves were damp; in short, they wanted to go home.

The thirty-one members of the tract's Party branch met to

discuss this problem under the guidance of stocky Secretary Tian, once a farm-hand for the landlords, later a coal miner, and gaunt Vice-Secretary Fei, an old 8th Route Army man. The branch adopted three measures:

First the Party members themselves made sure that they grasped the importance of high yield tracts for increasing the output of agriculture, for paving the way for mechanization, electrification and 'chemicalization' and more efficient irrigation. They agreed that for the time being living conditions were hard, but how were they to be improved except by increasing production? And how was production to be increased except by enduring hard conditions? 'Today's hardships are for tomorrow's happiness,' said Zhu Xu-mei, a young woman of twenty-two, one of the vice-heads of the tract.

This first measure was followed by an airing of views among all of the tract workers, revolving around three questions: the significance of high yield tracts, their practical advantages, and the proper attitude to living and working in them. 1,500 *dazibao*[1] were posted up and altogether 2,300 ideas and suggestions put forward. On this basis the branch summed up the following advantages of high yield tracts:

1. The single crop makes management easier. It also permits rational division of labour, specialization and high efficiency.
2. Living and eating on the spot 'brings distant land close at hand'; it saves time and energy from being wasted walking to and fro, permits more rest and thus makes for better work.
3. Living and studying together and facing the same problems makes for a close-knit collective.
4. The joining together of small strips and plots paves the way for mechanization and water conservancy projects.
5. The tract, with its concentrated labour force, facilitates not only technical training but general education and the training of cadres.
6. The tract lends itself to the full application of the Eight Point Charter and thereby to increasing production.

The pointing out of these advantages stiffened determination. This was further strengthened by a course of study of the three philosophical works of Mao Tse-tung[2] aimed directly at achieving 'the proper attitude to living and working in the high yield tract'. One man, looking back on his own recent thoughts, said during a discussion of the essays: 'I used to think that the work on the tract was too hard and that there was too much of it. Several times I thought of packing it in and going home, though I never quite got

[1] Posters written in large characters—in this case putting forward views on the three questions posed, together with criticisms and suggestions for improving the work on the tract.

[2] *On Practice, On Contradiction*, and *On the Correct Handling of Contradictions Among the People*. See Chapter XXI.

81

to the point of doing it. Now I realize that I wasn't looking at things in an all-round way. I was just thinking of one side of the matter—of myself and having the good things of life here and now. Being self-centred like that is a bourgeois way of looking at things; and seizing on only one side of a problem is a metaphysical way of thinking. Now I've made up my mind to make the tract my home and I'm going to work as hard as I can, like a Communist, so that before long everyone can be having the good things of life.'

The Party branch did not stop at organizing study and discussion. It set about improving living conditions.

'The greater the working enthusiasm of the masses, the more attention the Party should pay to their well-being. The more attention the Party pays to the living conditions of the masses, the greater their enthusiasm in work.'[3]

In line with this Party principle, the Branch Committee decided that 'politics must enter the dining-room and Party secretaries go into the kitchen' and be personally responsible for the providing of good food. The seven members of the Branch Committee took turns working in the cookhouse and three Party and five Youth League members were assigned to regular work there to show the staff the political importance attached to their work.

Branch Committee member and work team leader Guo Chen-tai was not feeling well when his turn came round to act as cook. But he kept it to himself and tackled the task of turning 35 *jin* of flour into noodles, a tough job in a kitchen with no modern equipment, involving kneading, rolling, chopping and stretching, all by hand. When he finished he was tired out, but his heart was warmed by the praise of the diners. When a traditional holiday of the lunar calendar came round everyone was looking forward to a day off, except the cooks. For them holidays meant more work, not less, and they accepted the fact stoically. But the members of the Party Branch Committee took over the kitchens and gave the cooks a holiday. This unexpected turn of events caused one cook to remark: 'Our Party secretaries can even read our minds.'

Over a third of those at the tract were women. Some of them found themselves worrying about how they could manage to make cloth shoes for the family. The Committee took up the question and it was arranged that women should have an extra half day off each week. This gave them altogether five free days a month, instead of the normal three.[4]

All these measures—the airing of views, the study of Mao Tse-tung's essays, the Branch Committee's welfare work—strengthened the determination of those who had wanted to go home. As a result, within twenty days 'the face of the uplands was changed'. Except

[3] 'Resolution on Some Questions Concerning the People's Communes.'
[4] For more on this subject see p. 96.

15. Village militia training.

6. Labour Hero Ren Qing-mei of Little Yetao
see Chapter I, Local Revolutionary Leaders).

17. Labour Heroine Guo Heng-de of
Bailin, with three of her four children
(see Chapter I, Local Revolutionary
Leaders).

18. Ten Mile Inn School—playground scene.

19. Science class in Ten Mile Inn School. The characters on the blackboard read: "Science is no mystery. There's no need to look down on yourself" (see Chapter XV, The Ten Mile Inn Primary School).

for a fringe of standing wheat planted the previous autumn, the whole 670 acres had been ploughed and lay 'straight as a ruler, smooth as glass and soft as flour'. It was at this time that the poetically-minded County-Head, surveying the scene and foreseeing the time when the entire expanse would be covered with cotton bolls, christened it the 'Silver Sea Tract'.

(Meanwhile work had been going ahead on the five mile stretch beside the Min, which was to be planted with maize. This was christened the 'Long March Tract', after the Red Army's epic 8,000 mile fighting trek in 1934–35. The reservoir in between the two tracts, taking a word from the name of each, became known as 'The Long Sea'.)

The lunar new year was now approaching and with it the traditional spring festival. To celebrate it the County Head suggested they build a tower right in the centre of the tract—'not just for show, but to spur on production'—and call it the Tower of Heroic Ambition. The proposal was adopted by acclaim and the tower was built in ten days—before the first full moon of the New Year. It had an arched, battlemented base, like an ancient city gate, forming an entrance to the biggest of the newly-built settlements. From this pedestal, on whose parapet fluttered a score of coloured silk banners, rose the square tower. It could be seen for miles around.

When the tower was finished, there was a ceremony to celebrate the opening of the tract. An estimated 10,000 people attended, from babes-in-arms to old men of eighty, among them visitors from other communes, workers and soldiers on leave. The mass meeting was topped off by entertainment and a banquet for the team members which lasted until midnight.

THE LAYOUT AND ORGANIZATION OF A COTTON-GROWING FACTORY

The Silver Sea Cotton Tract was now a reality. At its centre lay eight acres of experimental plots worked by different Party secretaries and other members of the tract leadership.[5] Beside each plot stood a board bearing particulars of the area, planned yield, special measures adopted (generally some variation of the Eight Point Charter) and the name of the person or group responsible. Most of the plots had a planned output of 1,500 *jin* of unginned cotton per *mu*—about five times the final target of the National Program for Agricultural Development (1956–67). These experimental plots formed the innermost kernel of the tract. Immediately around them was the main central area of some 350 acres, worked by the crack teams of volunteers living in the three settlements. Finally there was

[5] This included county, commune and brigade cadres. See Chapter XVII for this system of multi-level leadership.

the outer rim of land, nearest the villages, worked by the ordinary teams of the three surrounding village brigades. Their planned yield, though the lowest on the tract, was well above the average target for the ordinary cotton fields in the commune.

The 220 people living in the three settlements worked roughly half of the tract. They were divided into three 'companies', one from each of the villages to which the tract belonged. Each company consisted of three teams, which in turn were split into groups.

Perhaps the main difference between the tract force and the teams of the village brigades was that they had left the ways of the old-style peasant even further behind than had the ordinary commune farmers. They considered themselves agricultural workers rather than farmers and they worked, in their own words, 'as in a factory'.

The tempo of work on the tract was certainly fast by rural standards.

Competitions or 'emulation drives' and the election of model workers or teams were a spur to production. During every stage of work competitions were arranged between companies, work teams, groups and individuals. There was also a 'mobile red flag' awarded every month to one of the companies. As to the model workers, their photos—taken by the commune photographer—were posted up at the foot of the Tower of Heroic Ambition, with a brief account of their accomplishments in work, study and physical training; and all were called on to follow their example.

Sport was recognized as important for both relaxation and physical fitness; and basket-ball, volley-ball, gymnastics and running, hardly known in the villages until very recently, were gaining popularity. To promote them, during the wheat harvest in the spring, the Party Committee of the tract called on the workers to 'win a basket-ball court from the wheatfields'[6]—in other words, from gleaning. The tract workers spent their spare time going over every inch of the ground and gleaned enough to pay for a basket-ball, a volley-ball net and parallel and horizontal bars. For the courts and posts they drew on their own resources. All that was needed was to gain proficiency in these new sports, so different from the traditional wrestling and sword-play. Commune Secretary Jin, who had gone in for sport during his years as a teacher, and the other Party secretaries, even the middle-aged ex-coal-miner Tian, all turned out. One of the work groups, made up of five girls each with the character 'Mei' (meaning 'Flowering Plum') in her name, formed a team on their own, led by twenty-two-year-old Zhu Xu-mei. The 'Five Plums' soon gained a reputation as basket-ball players, standing up against teams of men on the tract and challenging the girls of Yangyi Middle School.

6 These were fields already sown to winter wheat when the tract was first planned. They were not planted to cotton until after the wheat harvest.

84

High Yield Tracts

The basic militia, formed of those up to the age of twenty-five, had regular drill and shooting practice. Of the 47 who took part in a shooting contest in May, 6 were rated as crack shots, 9 as excellent, and 32 good. The result of all this sport and training was an improvement in general health. Sick list figures went down and the workers declared themselves 'so full of life and energy that we hoed the cotton three times more than was done on the ordinary cotton fields last year'. On top of this they found time for study five evenings a week. Monday and Tuesday evenings were set aside for political study in the tract's 'Red and Expert College'.[7] (It was here that Mao Tse-tung's philosophical works were taken up.) Wednesday and Thursday evenings were for general education and Friday for technical subjects. Saturday night team members went home for the week-end —something new in the lives of Yangyi farmers. Sunday evening was for Communist Party and Youth League meetings, often followed or preceded by sing-songs and amateur dramatics.

AN ASSESSMENT

Pioneering high yield tracts, like the Silver Sea, caught the imagination and aroused the enthusiasm of those eager to break free from the old ways of farming. For they did indeed 'bring distant land close at hand' and 'make poor land rich'. Together with improvements in management and technique they brought higher yields to the once relatively neglected outer rims of village land than the ordinary work teams obtained on their more favoured fields. They showed that the record yields achieved in 1958 on tiny experimental plots could in time be extended to large areas. Their paving the way for tractors by levelling the land was as significant for mechanization as the building of reservoirs and channels was for irrigation.

Taking high yield tracts as the battlefield meant giving priority to advances in technique. Actually, in the course of 1960 it became clear that there were still urgent problems remaining in the management of ordinary brigades and work teams. These problems had to be sorted out before great strides could be taken in the technical revolution in farming.[8]

The resultant policy, eventually adopted in Yangyi Commune as elsewhere, was: High-yield tracts might be run by brigades or by the commune, but not at the expense of work teams. The teams, on

---

[7] See Chapter XV.

[8] According to a summary made in the winter of 1960–61, the work team must be guaranteed by the brigade its land, labour, animals and tools; and these might not be withdrawn or re-allocated (though minor adjustments might be made if notice was given well in advance and the team's consent freely granted). See Chapter XI for examples of these problems of management.

the other hand, should be drawn into cultivating whatever part of their land might be made part of high yield tracts.

This did not lessen the achievements of the tracts. But it did make clear that the work team was still the basic unit of production. The high yield tract was, for this stage at least, a glimpse of the shape of things to come. Not yet the main battlefield but an outpost in the fight for higher production.

Chapter VIII

COMMUNE AGAINST CLIMATE
(Spring and Summer, 1960)

THE BATTLE AGAINST THE DROUGHT

THE climatic conditions in 1959 throughout China were the worst for decades. Those of 1960 proved to be the worst in over a century.

In Shexian county all through the winter and early spring the sun rose and set in a cloudless sky. The drought soon approached emergency proportions. Everything had to make way for the war against the elements. Over 520 Party secretaries and 2,000 cadres threw themselves into the fight. The County Head and vice-heads, the secretaries of the County Party Committee dispersed themselves among the communes to give leadership on the front line. County Head Wang De-hen took charge in the eastern part of Shexian which included Yangyi.

There the task was to find sources of water beneath the surface and use them to the greatest effect, for there the underground Min had its course.

The Min River, the third biggest in the county, flows from near Lianggou, in the northern tip of the commune, past Little Yetao to Yangyi. But most of the year it is underground even before reaching Little Yetao. All that remains on the surface are the stones, washed down by the floods of centuries. In 1960 the river-bed was drier than ever and the wind blew eddies of sand among the boulders. But the commune members, determined to tap the water which they were sure flowed wastefully below, sunk wells in the river-bed at Ten Mile Inn, but without success. The river had evidently changed its course.

Still the search for it continued and finally, a few miles down the river-bed, in the neighbouring commune of Gujeng, it was found and water was struck. But wells were no sooner sunk than the walls caved in. At last, after a number of experiments, a new type of well was devised—the 'big socialist well'. This was 40 to 50 feet deep and was spanned in the middle by a buttress. It had a surface area of one *mu* (about 800 square yards) of clear, blue-green water.

In Yangyi Commune other solutions were found.

Of all the Yangyi brigades, Bailin's plight was among the worst. It was a village of over 1,000 families, with a stretch of high, rolling

87

loess fields, good land provided there was rain. Skilfully placed rain catchment tanks were its main method of coping with its situation. But this year, with the long, rainless winter and spring, they were useless.

Attempts to sink wells, even to a depth of 300 feet, had yielded no result.

It happened that at this time a young accountant from the regional government in Handan, was doing a few months manual work in Bailin.[1] He was struck on the one hand by the vigour of the work carried on under the guidance of Guo Heng-de,[2] who managed to be everywhere at once on her tiny bound feet; and on the other, by the magnitude of the task of growing crops with no sure source of water. On a trip back to Handan the young accountant reported on the brigade's acute need for water and its strenuous but fruitless efforts to obtain it. The case was examined and found to be both urgent and deserving. An immediate decision was made to include Bailin among the limited number of regional projects for sinking deep wells with power equipment, and by the early summer of 1960 a derrick with a tractor-driven borer appeared in the village. Drilling went ahead rapidly until under the blanket of loess soil a layer of rock was struck. Progress was slowed down but not stopped, and by the middle of the summer the borer was approaching its mark, a depth of 750 feet. It was estimated that the resultant flow of water would be enough to irrigate well over a thousand acres, about half of Bailin's arable land.

Such solutions as this, however, were the exception not the rule, for power drills were few and the demands on them throughout the province great. For other brigades the most promising source of water seemed to be the hills above Little Yetao.

County Head Wang De-hen set out to scour these hills for new springs. First he questioned the old shepherds. Then, following their leads he three times led prospecting parties mile after mile over rocky mountain paths, goat-tracks and no tracks at all. At last a cluster of nine springs was found, their water seeping into porous earth. Conferences were called at which the cadres drew on the knowledge of the old shepherds and farmers as well as on that of the commune's irrigation experts and electricians. Equipment was made or borrowed from local reservoirs and from Little Yetao's power station. Working round the clock, with the County Head on

---

[1] The systematic transfer of city office personnel and other 'intellectuals' to the countryside for a spell of manual labour or other work at grass-roots level, had been instituted in 1957. Its aim was to keep bureaucracy out of government offices. (See Chapter XVIII.) In the summer of 1960, the Mayor of Handan, senior administrative officer of the region, was trundling a wheelbarrow at a reservoir construction site, returning to Handan only for occasional key meetings.

[2] See Chapter I, 'Local Revolutionary Leaders'.

the job all through the night, commune members cleared away the earth until a pool was formed. Then they set up a pumping system to conduct the water to an irrigation channel higher up. When the pressure of the water sank too low, much still being lost in soakage, Wang De-hen was the first to wade in with his spade to deepen and widen the trench in which the spring water accumulated. After two days of hard digging, during which six more springs were tapped, the flow of water was quadrupled. In this way thousands of *mu* of newly sown dried-out crops were irrigated.

But up on the Silver Sea Tract the ground was still so dry that 'even the weeds wouldn't grow'. The whole spring sowing was in danger. Then the Tract Party Committee launched the slogan: 'Beat the Drought.'

'We'd been studying *On Contradiction* at the time,' said Zhu Xu-mei, the 22-year-old vice-head of the tract, 'so although we had a hundred and one things to do, we could see quite clearly that the major contradiction at that stage was between the dryness of the ground and the cotton seeds' need for moist soil. Of course, if you can solve the major contradiction, everything can be managed all right. So we decided that we'd have to muster our whole force for one job: seeing that every hole for every seed was filled with water.'

But little water had accumulated in the Long Sea reservoir during its brief existence. In fact it was so low that not a drop could be wasted in transit. Whatever there was must safely reach each separate cotton plant. First they pumped it up to the level of the tract, twenty metres above, with the aid of tractor-engines. Then they carried it to every single plant on the tract, in every sort of vessel, from buckets to saucepans—even chamber-pots! For twenty days and nights this went on, till each plant on the tract had been separately watered. Towards the end the Long Sea was so shallow that the pump would not work; so three Party and two Youth League members stood in the water and dug a deep hole from which almost the last drop could be sucked up.

Later in the spring a high wind swept the plateau, snapping many of the young cotton stalks. Some people were disheartened. It seemed as if all the fruits of their toil in the battle against the drought were to be blown away. But when the wind at last died down the Party branch started a re-planting movement to ensure that every damaged plant was replaced. This battle was short and sharp and in two days it was won.

AFTER THE DROUGHT, THE DELUGE

Early in the summer the weather broke. The Long Sea filled at last and next year's harvest seemed guaranteed. Meanwhile the crops already in the fields, kept alive at such cost during the drought, now began to pick up, promising a reward for the months of arduous toil. The cotton on the Silver Sea Tract flourished, and the sight of it inspired one of the tract farmers to compose the verse:

> As far as the eye can see is a stretch of green.
> When the breeze blows the cotton plants nod their heads,
> Promising us a bumper harvest—
> The first of the new decade.

But neither on the tract nor elsewhere in Yangyi Commune was a good harvest yet assured. On July 8th hail-clouds swept across the sky towards the commune. As news was urgently telephoned along the course of their advance, Yangyi prepared to ward off the blow—with rockets.

Rockets and other fireworks had long been made in nearly all parts of China, to be set off during the lunar new year celebrations and on other festive occasions. But a new use had been proposed for them. Bigger and better rockets, it was suggested, might go high enough to scatter hail-clouds. So a group of firework-makers in the coastal city of Tientsin started experimenting. News of their efforts reached Yangyi and the commune sent some of its own firework-makers to investigate. In Tientsin they were shown rockets so big that they needed a wooden launching platform. They were said to reach a height of 1,500 metres.

On returning to Yangyi the investigators set up a workshop in an old temple courtyard on the outskirts of the townlet. And there, in the shade of a walnut tree, they started making outsize rockets.

On July 8th these rockets were fired into the concentrated hail-clouds above Yangyi, and no hail fell in the vicinity. The rocket-firers claimed victory and followed up this first engagement with a drive to increase their output. The Party Committee encouraged them, but took a more cautious view. Had the rockets really broken up the hail formations? Or had they merely shifted them from one place to another? In fact had they affected the clouds at all? A lively discussion sprang up, but it was still too early to draw conclusions. Nevertheless, the Committee and the Commune Council saw this as the dawn of a new day in the age-long struggle with the elements, as an inspiring refusal to 'bow to the heavens'.

One thing was certain. The hail which had not struck the fields of Yangyi brigade, wrought havoc elsewhere in the commune. It bombarded the cotton on the Silver Sea Tract and the damage it did brought tears to the eyes of 8th Route Army veteran, Party Secretary Fei. It not only battered the cotton on the Silver Sea; it lashed the young maize on a high yield tract at the model brigade of Little Yetao.

These two projects were focal points in the whole of the commune. Good crops here meant more than just a few extra tons of cotton and corn. They meant the vindication of certain policies being pushed by the Party leadership. These were test cases intended to inspire the farmers of all 24 brigades with confidence in the infinite possibilities of increasing output and winning prosperity for every household in the commune.

The Commune Party Committee met at once and launched the slogan: 'Hail or no hail, no loss in output.'

On the Silver Sea Tract the heads of the teams held an emergency meeting to decide on measures for restoring the crops. The decision was: extra hoeing and fertilizing. The teams were soon engaged in these tasks over the whole expanse of the tract.

At Little Yetao, when the hailstorm stopped, the fields were a sorry sight. The maize stalks were bent almost to breaking point and the tender leaves torn to tatters. Weeks of hard work seemed to lie in ruins.

What was to be done? Should the crops be pulled up by the roots and sown again—or could they in some way be salvaged?

Ren Qing-mei went round 'consulting the masses', asking especially the oldest and most experienced farmers which would be the best. 'Too late to start sowing again now,' was the general opinion. 'If there's any hope at all it's in putting life back into those bedraggled crops.' So the five Party branches of the brigade held a joint meeting and made restoration of the corn their 'general line'. Everyone was called on to go all out at watering every single plant and feeding it with fertilizer. After one application of fertilizer and two hoeings each stalk put out two or three new leaves. Within five days the face of the cornfields was changed.

The worst effects of the hail had hardly been tackled before more trouble came, in the form of a torrential downpour of summer rain. Vegetable seeds just planted, at the urging of the Party Committee, to provide more varied menus in the canteens, were washed out. Then came news that water was seeping through the Long Sea Dam.

Commune Party Secretaries, members of the Commune Council, County Head Wang De-hen all rushed to the spot to help the tract workers save the dam. As the word got round Party and Youth League members, ordinary brigade members dropped whatever they were doing, grabbed reed mats, sacks, anything they could lay their hands on and ran to the site. One boy from Ten Mile Inn, Li Wei-guo, Communist Youth League secretary for the district, tried to plug the biggest leak with his own body. It was no use. The water broke through and young Li was only just pulled to safety. The dam was breached and those who came to help could only stand and stare.

The breaching of the dam was another staggering blow. Even the buoyant Secretary Jin was cast down by it at first. From the day the dam had been built, whenever he was going from Yangyi townlet to Ten Mile Inn he had left the broad dirt highway for the narrow paths which ran beside the reservoir. It had warmed his heart to see it. After the dam was breached he stuck to the highway.

To make matters worse, those who had scoffed that the Dragon King had only to stretch his leg to knock the dam down, now hardly hid their satisfaction. They had always thought the building of the dam an impractical scheme, a waste of precious labour. Now they felt more than ever that they were right. They talked so much about how right they were that they 'blew up a little typhoon'.

In the long run this little typhoon blew some good. It helped crystallize the determination not to bow to the heavens, but to rebuild the dam at once.

But it was the height of the busy season in field management.

The commune leaders called meetings to work out how to provide labour to repair the dam in time to trap the remaining summer rains. Offers of help came in from the different brigades, but they were turned down. Field management demands were too pressing. It was decided that a few dozen cadres should form the kernel of the labour force, under the direct leadership of County Head Wang De-hen, aided by four of the commune Party secretaries. The two tracts sent crack teams of young workers, 80 from the Silver Sea, 50 from the Long March. 180 school-teachers from all over the county, who were at Yangyi on a refresher course during the summer holidays, volunteered to help. This combined force, working round the clock in shifts for four days and nights moved 4,160 cubic metres of earth and packed it into the breach.

'The work went with more of a swing than when we first built the dam seven months before,' said Secretary Jin, 'because from the very start we put politics in command.' When the workers saw County Head Wang pushing barrow after barrow-load of earth and staying on the job till four o'clock in the morning, it spurred them on. So did the work of us Party secretaries. There were 67 of us Party members altogether and we volunteered for all the hardest work. When the commune inspection team came down and saw all this, they rolled up their sleeves and put in a whole night shift. We organized competitions, too. We split up into teams and had races to see which could finish a one and a half foot layer first.

'Another thing was mechanization. This time we used more up-to-date equipment. Instead of hurricane lamps for night work, we rigged up electric lights. And instead of carrying the earth in baskets on poles, we used barrows and push-carts. But the biggest advance was in the pounding. When we first built the dam we used the old method of half a dozen men heaving a great flat stone up and down.' (The stone was tossed up and down by means of ropes held by a ring of men, chanting rhythmically as the weight rose and fell.)

Commune Against Climate

'This time we ran a tractor back and forth on top of each layer as it was completed. That packed the earth tighter and took much less time and effort.'

When the job was completed, the dam was six feet higher than before.

*   *   *

Yangyi was able to substantiate the claim that the commune had 'great power to resist natural calamities'.³ In spite of 200 days of drought followed by hailstorms and torrential rain, farm yields had been maintained at the level of 1958. Every one of the 24 brigades had succeeded in fulfilling its quotas.

This achievement was due above all to the unprecedented scale of soil and water conservation made possible by the concentration of resources brought about by the organization of the commune.

The year 1960 showed once again the instability of an agriculture so dependent on natural conditions.⁴ At the same time it proved the value of the irrigation work already undertaken throughout the county of Shexian and emphasized the need to press on with more. The commune members realized that much remained to be done before they could be free from the ravages of the weather. Their determination to become so was summed up in a couplet by a commune poet:

> The hills are high, but not so high as our ambition.
> The rocks are hard, but not so hard as our resolve.

Throughout the county, from the summer of 1959 to that of 1960, 480 large and small water conservation and irrigation projects were carried out. In addition to the four Zhang channels, 9 reservoirs (including Yangyi's Long Sea) and over 900 ponds were dug, as well as 7,546 storage tanks to trap rain water. Many gulleys were dammed —at intervals, from top to bottom—to form giant, widening staircases. 1,930,000 'fish-scale pits' were made for fruit trees and general afforestation. The number of power pumps rose from 38 to 93, and

³ 'The power of the people's communes to transform nature and resist natural calamities is great indeed. In the battle against serious droughts and other natural calamities . . . in 1959 and 1960 . . . they showed a heroic spirit, which worked countless miracles in refusing to bow to the heavens.' (Liao Lu-yen, Minister of Agriculture, 'The Whole Party and the Whole People Go in for Agriculture in a Big Way', *Peking Review*, No. 37, 1960.)

⁴ 2,000 years of Chinese government statistics demonstrate this instability, meteorological records showing that from the third century B.C. until the fourth decade of the twentieth century there were over a thousand major floods and over a thousand droughts—an average of almost one major natural disaster a year.

The People's Government set about ending this historical record by transforming nature. When it came to power in 1949 only 40 million acres of land were irrigated. Within ten years the figure had been raised to 167 million acres.

93

in 45 places the old-style water-wheels were set up in series, one above the other, to raise water uphill from 30 to 60 metres.

The result of all this activity was that the proportion of irrigated land in the county was increased by over 69 per cent and altogether 88 per cent of the erosion area was estimated to have been brought under control.

This capital construction made it possible for Shexian communes to achieve creditable cotton and grain harvests despite the worst weather in a century.

But the victory was costly. From the point of view of labour expenditure Yangyi itself had never reaped such a costly harvest before. Yet however high the costs, such a harvest was an achievement. With calamities ravaging vast areas of the country, every kernel of grain was precious.

1961, however, was to have ushered in the first of 'ten thousand years of joy' following 'three years of bitter struggle'. The weather rolled back this time-table. Yangyi Commune, which had been pressing ahead with capital construction, local industry, high yield tracts—to advance from brigade to commune-level ownership— now had to take stock of the situation and re-assess its task.

Chapter IX

TWO MAJOR CONTRADICTIONS
(Summer, 1960)

THE Commune Party Committee was always on the alert for 'major contradictions', the solving of which would speed-up the commune's advance. In the summer of 1960 Commune Party Secretary Jin listed these under two headings: those to do with the allocation of labour and those concerning distribution. Both types were 'contradictions among the people', to be dealt with by discussion, education and adjustment; but they involved various levels all the way from the state to the individual farmer, the focus of attention varying at the different levels.

Between the state and the commune these contradictions had to do with the allocation of labour and grain. Between the commune and its brigades they were over the labour force and accumulation. Between the brigade and its members they centred on accumulation.

YANGYI COMMUNE'S ACUTE LABOUR SHORTAGE

Allocation of labour had in fact become a problem throughout China, the countryside having shifted, with the Great Leap Forward of 1958, from a situation of chronic under-employment to one of acute labour shortage. In the Taihang Mountains, before the anti-Japanese War and the setting-up of a communist-led Liberated Area, the average able-bodied man put in at the most 104 days of work a year.[1] This was partly because capital was too limited and the economy in general too undeveloped to provide more employment; partly because during the lean winter months food was so scarce for the mass of peasants that they were forced to rest much and eat little. The peasant's comment on this state of enforced semi-hibernation was: 'One half of the year you sweat your guts out, the other half you sit on your backside.' After land reform, with systematic, long-term mutual aid (but before the setting up of co-operatives), farmers were working an additional twenty-odd days a year. With the co-operatives employment rose steeply. This trend was contrary to some people's expectations. 'There's a surplus of labour already,' they had said. 'With co-operatives it'll get bigger.' The opposite

[1] *Socialist Upsurge in China's Countryside*, F.L.P., Peking, 1957, p. 89.

95

proved to be true. For with each advance in social relations from the semi-feudal system of land-ownership, went an increase in economic activity—more meticulous cultivation of the soil, diversification of farming, development of trade-and-transport and other farm sidelines and finally large-scale soil and water conservation, including the building of dams, digging of channels, terracing and afforestation.

After 1955 the employment of women, which had previously been limited and sporadic, also rose. With the commune and its widespread activities—diversified farming, local industry, welfare services and above all its onslaught against nature—the Taihang area had its first experience of an actual shortage of labour. This was intensified by the demands of fast expanding urban industry and by the need of both workers and farmers for time to improve their general, technical and political education—without which they could not cope with modern industry and agriculture. Somehow these contradictory demands must be met, for they were bound up with the mechanization of agriculture—which alone could end the labour shortage.

Meanwhile pressure of work brought to the countryside two novel problems: the need for regular days off and for limited working hours.

The week, to say nothing of the week-end, had never been part of Chinese culture or custom. The month, divided into ten-day periods (*xun*) was the important unit according to the ancient lunar calendar. Though this might be broken by periodical market days (at intervals of anywhere from three to fifteen days depending on local conditions) regular days off were unknown and the sole holiday was the lunar new year's festival. This arrangement was suited to an era of chronic under-employment, when work-days not holidays were the pressing need of the overwhelming majority.

In the early days of the commune the tendency was not merely to continue, under the unprecedented conditions of labour shortage, the traditional month without a holiday and the unlimited working day. It was to carry on for longish periods at 'shock-task tempo'—relieved only by normal work. The Central Committee, however, in December 1958 (some three months after Yangyi Commune was formed) pointed out that the way to deal with the shortage of labour lay in improved tools and management, not in longer working hours. Its Resolution went on:

> Our intensive work at present is precisely to create conditions for a six-hour workday and even shorter working hours in future. At present the system of eight hours actual work and two hours of study should be put into effect in both city and countryside. During the busy farming season or when other work in the rural areas is particularly heavy, working hours may be appropriately extended. But

whatever happens, eight hours for sleep and four hours for meals and recreation . . . must be guaranteed . . .²

In Yangyi Commune, by the summer of 1960, a system of limited working hours and regular days off had been most fully developed on the Silver Sea High Yield Tract. Here above all, such a system was both possible and necessary, the tract workers' morale being particularly high and their tempo of work correspondingly fast. The tract workers started and stopped work to the sound of their 'factory' whistle, carried out the Central Committee's instructions on working hours and had regular days off—three days a month for men and five days for women.

But though on the tract a solution was found for this particular aspect of the labour shortage problem, the problem as a whole remained. In fact with the natural calamities of 1960 it took on new and critical dimensions, bringing strains and stresses which set some commune enterprises and activities at cross purposes. Both quantity and quality of labour were involved.

'When we were starting the new commune mine last year,' said Secretary Jin, to illustrate this point, 'we knew we had a tough job ahead of us. So we wanted a really good working force—hardy lads who weren't afraid of difficulties or of trying something new. Preferably members of the Communist Youth League. But of course people like that are the backbone of every team. As a matter of fact the work teams and brigades found it hard to spare any hands at all, let alone the best they had. So some of the people they sent us were lame, others were night-blind or had something else wrong with them. Anyway, they were no good for mining.

'Of course we understood how the brigades felt. We'd been up against the same sort of thing ourselves when the Regional or Provincial Government were recruiting workers for the big state factories or mines. But that still didn't solve our labour problem.'

The difficulty was not peculiar to Yangyi. With agriculture 'the base of the economy', efforts to increase farm output were being stepped up everywhere. But the application of the Eight Point Charter, the opening up of high yield tracts, the many-sided activities of the commune—all required immense expenditure of labour. To these were suddenly added the battle against the elements. Labour was needed everywhere. How should it be allocated? Should it be concentrated in the fields? Should more be diverted to the workshops to make labour-saving farm tools and machines? Should farmers working in commune mines continue to extract the ore needed to make these tools and machines? Or should they go back to the land?

With state and commune, commune and brigade, agriculture and

² 'Resolution on Some Questions Concerning the People's Communes.'

industry all competing for labour, a national policy for labour allocation was clearly essential.

In April 1960 such a policy was laid down at a Communist Party
Conference in Shanghai. The tenor of its decisions was: agriculture
—particularly grain production—must be guaranteed the labour
force needed to consolidate the base of the economy and to fight
against the natural calamities striking vast areas of the country.
The state was accordingly to recruit no more workers for factories
or mines; any shortage of industrial labour was to be dealt with by
means of technical innovations, improved tools and machinery
and better management.

In the light of these decisions the Hopei Provincial Government
instructed the province's communes that 70 per cent of their labour
force should be directly engaged in field work. Furthermore, this
70 per cent was to be a representative cross-section of the force, not
largely women, old men and boys as was tending to become the case.

In Yangyi the management and Party committees made an
investigation of labour allocation in the commune. This showed
that the total labour force was 13,352 and that it was employed as
follows:

	%
Doing field work	65·4
Caring for animals	4·6
In side occupations (mainly short-haul transport)	9·9
In community dining-rooms	6·6
Milling (only Little Yetao had a power-driven mill)	6·1
In commune or brigade industry	4·7
Working outside the commune	2·7

Thus measures had to be taken to ensure that field work should be
given an additional 4·6 per cent of the total labour force.

Laying down regulations for the proportion of people to be
engaged in field work was only part of the solution. Matters were
complicated by fluctuations in the need for labour in the fields.
While it had long been customary to talk of busy and slack seasons
in farming, the pattern was in fact more complex. In North China
there were during the year roughly four months of slack (December,
January, February and March), four months of rush (May, July,
August and September), and four months of neither rush nor slack
(April, June, October and November).

Experience was now showing that the commune's trend towards
specialization (with separate labour forces for industrial enterprises,
animal husbandry, afforestation and so on) though it helped improve
the quality of work in these various lines, brought about an acute
shortage of labour in the fields during the four months of the rush

season. To protect agriculture, therefore, the commune had to oppose the formation of special, non-agricultural working forces and a regulation was drawn up to the effect that: 'No commune activities must be allowed to interfere with field work.' This meant that in the slack farming season there was scope for a wide variety of work; in the intermediate season this scope should be suitably narrowed to release labour for the fields; and in the rush season, supplementary production should come almost to a halt to allow concentration on field work.

For this reason, in the summer of 1960, brigade industries throughout Yangyi Commune were closed. And in the commune centre only the Farm Tool Manufacture and Repair Shop was still hard at work, making and mending implements for the teams in the fields.

Another complication was: which level was to control and use the labour force? One of the advantages of the commune was its ability to make a rational, overall allocation of labour and to increase its mobility. It was this which had made possible the lengthening of the Republic Channel, the building of the Long Sea Dam and the digging of the Ten Mile Inn pond. But the intricacies of Eight Point Charter farming required detailed long- and short-term planning by the work team itself. This was out of the question if the team did not control its own labour force. It was essential, therefore, not only to guarantee that those available for work in the fields should be sufficiently numerous but that they should belong to a well-knit, permanent team.[3]

THE CONTRADICTION BETWEEN
LONG AND SHORT-TERM INTERESTS

As to the second set of contradictions—those dealing with distribu-

---

[3] In the winter of 1960–61, when the efficacy of the measures taken to deal with labour shortage was examined and improvements were worked out, the following percentages were issued to the communes:
1. The labour force of the village (including both the weak and the strong) should comprise 40 per cent of the total population; and of this force two thirds (i.e. approximately 27 per cent of the village population) should be strong. This meant that of the able-bodied men who had been recruited into factories, mines, transport and so on, a sufficient number should return home to make up the required 27 per cent.
2. Of this augmented labour force 95 per cent should be in work teams and only 5 per cent under the jurisdiction of either the commune or the brigade. In other words, 95 per cent should be in field work, animal husbandry, carting for work teams and so on.
3. The Hopei Province decision that 70 per cent of the labour force should be directly engaged in field work was now modified to fit the different seasons. At the busiest time 80 per cent were to be in field work and only 20 per cent in industry, trade, social services, animal husbandry, short-haul transport and so on; at other times of the year 60 per cent was enough.

tion—the main issue was disposal of grain and pay of commune members.

In relations between commune and state the question was, how much of the output was each to receive? In 1960 the arrangement was: under normal circumstances (that is, so long as no disaster threatened), first the commune members' needs in food, fodder and seed were to be satisfied; at the same time 7 per cent of the total grain output was to be paid to the government as one, overall tax. After this, 90 per cent of what was left was to be sold to the state at controlled prices; the rest being kept by the commune.

On the surface the arrangement was clear-cut. But how was the commune to estimate its needs in food, fodder and seed? It might be far-sighted and frugal in order to help the state accumulate more capital for industrialization. On the other hand, the commune members might 'loosen their belts and eat their fill'.

The matter was not an easy one for the cadres to deal with. Some of them tended to set the interests of the commune members against those of the state, thinking that the less they handed over and the more they kept back the better they were 'serving the masses'. This made them inclined to submit low estimates even when production prospects were bright, and to appeal for a reduction of tax even though the amount due was unprecedentedly low.

Others with a more long-range view pointed out that the state's gain was not the commune members' loss, that strengthening the state economy speeded up industrialization, which would increase the supply of farming and irrigation machinery and farm chemicals, and that these in turn would enable the commune members to raise production and their own living standards. They maintained, in other words, that in a socialist state there was an identity not a conflict of interests between the Government and the people; that the Government's gain was in the long run the people's gain, and that sacrificing the commune members' long-term to their short-term interests was harming not serving the masses.

Between the commune and the brigade the main contradiction was over accumulation.

The amounts to be handed over by the brigade to the commune had been fixed by the Yangyi Commune Congress in line with national policy. According to this, accumulation for expanding production and funds for welfare services were to amount to 10 per cent of the commune's gross income. Of the sum earmarked for accumulation 40 per cent should be kept by the brigade for its own accumulation, 60 per cent should be handed over to the commune. Of the funds for welfare, 20 per cent should be handed to the commune for its services, while 80 per cent was to be used by the brigades. The total amount payable to the commune was to be between 5 and 7 per cent of the brigade's net income.

Two Major Contradictions

Certain of the brigades, however, tried to keep more grain than they were entitled to. Their chief way of doing this was under-reporting their income. Altogether 13 out of 33 brigades did this to some extent.

In the winter of 1959–60, for instance, after the annual accounting, Guantao (a mountain brigade above Little Yetao) was found to have under-reported. A commune inspection team discovered that in 1959 this brigade had actually achieved an increase of 34,271 *yuan* over its 1958 income. But in handing in the figures to the commune it had shown an increase of only about 4,000 *yuan* or so, leaving over 30,000 *yuan* of its income unreported. As the amount payable into commune funds was 5·7 per cent of income, this under-reporting secured the brigade 1,700 *yuan* at the expense of the commune.

When the investigators reported their findings, the joint commune leadership (the Commune Council and the Commune Party Committee) decided that the case should be dealt with by the Party Committee.

'We handle this sort of problem,' said Party Secretary Jin Han-cheng, 'by raising political consciousness. So this time we gave the Guantao cadres a lesson in socialism, driving home the importance of taking both long- and short-term interests into account.

'Here are the figures we worked out together with them:

Year	Gross Income of Brigade	Commune's Share	Brigade's Balance
	yuan	*yuan*	*yuan*
1958	189,729	10,867	178,862
1959	224,000	12,776	211,224

Increase to brigade in 1959 over 1958: 32,362 *yuan*.

'This showed them that though they handed the commune more they still had over 32,000 *yuan* more for themselves in 1959 than in 1958. That's an increase of over 18 per cent in a single year. How had they done it? By being part of the commune. We hammered home this point—that it was only through the commune that the brigades could achieve such an increase; so they should give the commune full support and not hold anything back.

'As a matter of fact, once brigade cadres have grasped the whole picture and can see their long-term as well as their short-term interests, they don't under-report.'

Besides carrying on such political education, the commune leadership took two organizational steps to discourage under-reporting of income. One was to strengthen accounting, the other was to introduce a system of written contracts.

101

Two Years' History of Yangyi Commune

The main contradiction between the brigade and the individual farmers took the form of a tussle between pay and accumulation. One extreme would have meant paying out the whole of the brigade's income to the members and not leaving any funds for expansion of activities; the other, holding back such a large percentage as to allow little or no yearly increase in the member's cash incomes.

This problem had existed ever since the setting up of co-operatives. At that time the formula for solving it had been: 60 to 70 per cent of a co-operative's total income should be set aside for wages and efforts should be made to ensure that at least 90 per cent of the members received an income higher than that of the year before;[4] what was left should be used for expanding production. Applying this formula called for thinking along socialist lines. Accumulation had to be seen as the long-term interest of the individual, personal income as his short-term interest. So the hazards of the individualist way of life and the security and steady improvement of the collective way, were constantly contrasted.

In the philosophical terms current among members of the Commune Party Committee, these contradictions over labour and distribution differed from those of feudal or capitalist society, for they were 'contradictions among the people'. They could be resolved and 'need not become antagonistic'. This was because they arose on a basis of unity—the interests of the people. The two aspects of each of these contradictions were the people's long-term and short-term interests; and the contradiction between them arose when the people could not see their own interests in perspective, or when the leadership was so concerned about the future that it neglected the immediate welfare of the people.

This latter aspect was a danger in Yangyi, because of its long record as a revolutionary base. With this tradition behind them some members, cadres and, above all, Youth League members felt not merely that the advance to communism should be swift; but that the careful waiting for and educating of the rank-and-file advocated by the national Party leadership was not necessary in a place with such a revolutionary background.

According to the Commune Party Committee the solution to both sets of problems (those of allocation of labour and those of distribution) was: accurate gauging of the people's political consciousness, measures appropriate to it and then education to raise it step by step. For the short-sighted it was a matter of placing things in perspective and seeing them from a socialist standpoint—of putting politics in command. For the Party and Youth League members

⁴ Teng Tse-hui, 'The Peasant Movement and the Worker-Peasant Alliance', Speech at The 8th National Congress of the C.C.P., *Documents*, Vol. II, F.L.P., Peking, 1956.

and cadres in a rush to reach communism, it was a matter of improving their style of work, of gaining closer understanding of the thoughts and feelings of the mass of commune members.

These were the main contradictions singled out by the Commune Party Committee during the summer of 1960.

INTERLUDE:

A FIRST survey of Yangyi Commune late in the summer of 1960 revealed no sign of 200 days of drought followed by hailstorms which tore maize leaves to tatters and rain that breached a newly-built dam. The crops were flourishing and there seemed every prospect of a good autumn harvest.

About two-thirds of the commune's 16,000 acres had been sown to grain (mostly wheat and maize) and sweet potatoes; another fifth to cotton. Close to the villages were vegetable gardens, larger than ever before, of carrots and cucumbers, turnips and radishes, onions and aubergines, chives and leeks. Between the villages were single-crop tracts sown to maize, cotton or sweet potatoes, the biggest of them 660-odd acres in area. These contrasted sharply with the patchwork pattern of tiny holdings existing after the land reform only a dozen years before. In a gully between two of those tracts was the newly-built Long Sea dam, forming a reservoir with a capacity of 50,000 cubic metres.

On the outskirts of the villages were sties for altogether 27,000 pigs, and on the hillsides grazed 14,000 sheep and goats. Some of the hills, set aside for afforestation and orchards, were dotted with hundreds of thousands of 'fish-scale' pits, trapping water for their saplings.

Down in the valleys repair and maintenance squads, supplied by the different brigades, worked on the dirt roads, along which flowed a traffic of carts. And on the tamped-earth threshing-floors, early in the morning, young militia men—and women—drilled and had firing practice.

Commune industry being geared to agriculture, most of the 47 brigade oil-presses, lime and brick kilns and other industrial plants were closed for the time being to free labour for field manage-ment—weeding, hoeing, spreading fertilizer, spraying insecticide. But the commune's iron mine had already turned out 5,000 tons of ore. And its Farm Implement Manufacture and Repair Shop, next to the tractor station on the outskirts of Yangyi townlet, had made or repaired 20,000 tools and devised improved models of several implements.

Interlude

The middle school beside the tractor station was closed for the holidays and the pupils were helping in the fields or gathering fuel or fodder from the hills; but the buildings were being used for a summer session to up-grade 180 teachers from different parts of the county.

The Yangyi shops displayed not only improved ploughs, harrows and seeders, but a variety of consumers' goods almost unknown before the commune, ranging from bicycles to flowered cloth, galoshes, torches, thermos flasks, fountain-pens and face-cream.

Scattered throughout the different villages of the commune were the social services—canteens, kindergartens, nurseries, old folks' homes, maternity homes, tailoring and dress-making centres—which had already freed 5,000 of the commune's women from the greater part of their housework.

Half-way up the main street of Yangyi townlet was a massive, black, lacquered doorway guarded by two lions carved in stone, the entrance to what had once been the home of a well-to-do landlord-trader. Inside was a chain of courtyards, ending in one with vines and cassia trees, latticed windows and tiled roofs. At its north end, up a short flight of stone steps, was the innermost hall, once the sanctum of the patriarch, now the Commune Council's meeting hall. In place of the old ancestral tablets there were now red banners fringed in gold, awards from the region and county for outstanding achievements in the varied activities of a commune.

The meeting hall like the offices round the courtyards leading to it, was generally deserted. For most of the time the commune leaders were out 'at the production front'. On only two days out of seven did they attend meetings and hold study sessions or discussions, summing-up experiences, singling out problems, working out systems of organization, drawing up plans.

There was plenty for the Council members to do, both in and out of the office, responsible as they were for a variety of brigades—ranging from two model brigades (Little Yetao and Bailin),[1] through several ordinary ones (like Ten Mile Inn) to a few (such as Caozigang and Liezhang) with more than their share of difficulties. The Committee had to lead 24 of them—good, average and poor—in their many-sided activities.

[1] See Chapters X and XIV.

105

PART TWO

*Yangyi Commune's
Many-sidedness*

Chapter X

FIVE-SIDED FARMING IN THE MOUNTAINS

BROAD lines for the development of commune farming had been laid down in the 'Resolution on Some Questions Concerning the People's Communes'. First was the carrying out of the Eight Point Charter, making for intensive, garden-style farming. Second, mechanization and electrification were called for. This was a long-term project. Third, of similar importance but more immediate realization was diversified or 'five-sided' farming, the five sides being: field cultivation, forestry and fruit farming, animal husbandry, farm sidelines and fisheries. In mountainous areas such as Yangyi, the starting-point for all these was soil and water conservancy.

In the summer of 1960 Yangyi Commune already had an example of what five-sided farming meant in the Taihang Mountains at the current stage of development. This was Little Yetao brigade, consisting of ten tiny mountain villages, its nucleus being Little Yetao village once 'one-tenth farmland, two-tenths water and seven-tenths mountains—bald as a monk's pate'. When the brigade was formed in 1958 Little Yetao village itself had a population of just under 700. The brigade as a whole had over 4,600 people, divided into 34 work teams, and some 1,250 acres of farmland.

A Little Yetao ballad-monger had summed up the brigade's many-sided activities in a jingle which ran:

A HARVEST EVERY MONTH

In January[1] we raise chicks, gather winter fuel and carry on other sidelines;
In February, when the earth thaws we dig up wild herbs;
In March, when the peach trees blossom, we shear the sheep;
In April, when the wild flowers bloom, we take sweet apricots to market;
In May we gather in the golden wheat;
In June the millet ripens and potatoes are ready to harvest;
In July it is time to pick the apples and pears;
In August the maize is ripe and we fill our bins;
In September the fields are harvested, but there are walnuts and persimmons to gather;
In October we bring in the carrots and cabbages;

[1] The months are according to the traditional lunar calendar, which starts a month or so later than the solar.

In November, when there's little to do in the fields, we climb the
mountains to cut grass and withies;
In December, as New Year draws near, we butcher pigs and sheep
to sell.

The jingle made no mention of fish-breeding, which was introduced after it was composed. But by 1960 all five sides of farming,
were being practised in Little Yetao.

Little Yetao's flourishing diversified farming had not sprung suddenly into being. It had a history going back some twenty years.
The struggle for success had been hard, above all at the start, for
few of the villagers then believed that such a place as theirs could
ever prosper. Their dream, like that of their fathers, had been to go
down to the plains to escape the poverty and rigours of life on these
stony slopes; for every village in the Taihang Mountains had to
contend with two difficulties: bare, eroded hills with outcroppings
of rock, and valleys with unstable, loess soil. The more favoured
villages, down where the Min River valley opened out towards the
Hopei plain, had a few broad, rolling fields covered with thick layers
of loess. But though this fine, yellow-brown earth was rich, during
the long windy winter and spring it dried to powder and much was
swirled away. During the hot summers with their sudden downpours
it was easily carved into gulches. And the water which poured down
the hillsides into the river-bed was brown with silt. Villages with
fields on the banks of the Min could lose 100 acres of land in one
flood, for the overflowing torrent churned up and swept away the
fine powdery soil leaving nothing but bare rocks. In 1917 Ten Mile
Inn lost nearly 170 acres of valley land in one flood alone.

While some of the villages in the area had a few rich valley
bottom fields, all of them owned stretches of rocky mountainside.
Some had little but hills with scattered plots of thin soil. Little Yetao
itself was one of these less-favoured villages. Its 670-odd people had
some 650 acres in all; but in the old days only 150 acres of it could
be described as farmland. The remaining 500-odd acres was made
up of rocky slopes and dry stony river-bed. There were no trees on
the hillsides or along the river; and with grass and shrubs being
scoured from the slopes for fuel, there was little good pasturage
either. The loss of soil and water was extreme and Little Yetao,
despite its 'two tenths water', before liberation had only a fraction
of an acre of irrigated land. The water which rushed down the
mountain rills and gullies, washing away soil and damaging crops,
was rarely referred to without a curse—as if the phrase 'damned-
water' was a hyphenated word.

110

Five-sided Farming in the Mountains

When the Communists came to Little Yetao in the late thirties, 70 per cent of what farmland there was belonged to landlords and rich peasants, who made up 10 per cent of the households. The remaining households had between them 3 draught oxen, 6 sheep and no pigs (or even chickens) at all. Thus there was next to no animal manure for enriching the soil. The villagers had only 5 ploughs between them. Nearly all the land was tilled with a hoe.

In those days, relate the old folk of Little Yetao, the people of their village had four ways of escaping starvation: 'Praying for rain, cutting brushwood to sell, working for the landlords, and fleeing to other parts.' In 1943, the second year of a drought which brought famine in its train, 130 households fled. When the famine was over they returned—what was left of them.

The Communists led the villagers in this area in struggle not only against the Japanese but against their rocks and torrents. First they launched a movement to reclaim wasteland. Terraces were built, higher and higher up the mountains. New crops were introduced. The first wheat to be grown in the area was sown by Ren Qing-mei[2] in the early forties with seed smuggled in from the plains occupied by the Japanese. Cotton, too, was introduced at this time, to counteract the Japanese blockade and make the guerilla base self-sufficient.

When land reform threw the landlords and rich peasants off the farmers' backs, the drives for increased production, launched each year by the Communists, went with a greater swing. Winters were spent collecting all possible forms of fertilizer, in repairing terraces and in the old standby of cutting brushwood to sell in the market of Yangyi. Production loans from the Border Region Government enabled mutual aid groups to buy goats to graze on the thin grass of the mountains.

As the war against Chiang Kai-shek's troops advancing further south the Border Region Government was able to do more to help villages like Little Yetao by popularizing new strains of seed and improved techniques. But what was needed above all was to convince the peasants that a good life could be won from their stony hillsides and unstable valley land. Until this time Ren Qing-mei himself was influenced by the old belief that 'without ten thousand *mu* of land you can't get ten thousand *dan* of grain'. Then, soon after the Central People's Government was set up in 1949, he went to a provincial conference of labour heroes. There, after hearing other delegates' reports, he threw off these doubts. It was then that he saw the film about Michurin and determined by following in his footsteps to make a poor mountain area prosperous.

Once the People's Government was established it became

[2] See Chapter I.

111

possible to draw on Soviet agricultural experience not only through the medium of films. Model farmers from various parts of China went to visit collective and state farms in the Soviet Union. Among them was Li Shun-ta, a nationally known Labour Hero from the Shansi side of the Taihang Range. On his return to China, in 1952, he told how farmers in the Siberian uplands, as part of a vast plan to re-make nature, were planting great numbers of trees; and how in the mountains of Georgia they were using machinery and power and combining agriculture, forestry and animal husbandry.

These facts had special significance for such areas as the Taihang, where natural conditions were not favourable for field cultivation. As one Taihang farmer put it: 'There are gullies and bare rock everywhere! How can you think of tilling land by machinery and marching towards socialism when you can't even find a plot big enough for a tractor to turn round on? We've pooled our labour and draught animals and tried every feasible technical improvement. There just isn't any way of getting bigger yields—there's not a dog's chance.'[3]

If this were true, there was still no hope but the age-old expedient of leaving the mountains for the plains. The Communist Party emphasized that this was not the socialist solution. For mountains covered two-thirds of China, and they had great untapped resources. The question was how to exploit them. The policy put forward was the development of a three-sided economy—a blend of agriculture, afforestation (including orchards) and animal husbandry.

It was in this context that Ren Qing-mei set up in Little Yetao the first semi-socialist farming co-operative in the Yangyi area. Between 1952 and 1955 he led its members in developing a three-sided mountain economy, at the same time reclaiming waste land and doing soil and water conservancy. This last activity ran into difficulties at the start, for Little Yetao lacked explosives. So the co-operative farmers had to choose between putting off the work until they could get some from elsewhere, or manufacturing their own. They decided on the latter and after some experimenting, with the aid of farmers from Lianggou who had worked in the 8th Route Army arsenal there, they succeeded in making what they needed. During these years the co-operative members terraced 12 acres of wasteland on the slopes above the village, where they planted 5,000 apple trees. It was during this period, too, that they planted their 'Green Great Wall' of 70,000 willows on 40 acres of land reclaimed from the dry river-bed. Their final aim was to plant two-thirds of their mountain land to trees. The other third was set aside for grazing.

Gradually the herds of sheep and goats grew. Pigs were raised

[3] Quoted in *The Socialist Upsurge in China's Countryside*, F.L.P., Peking, 1957, p. 84.

for the first time. Families which had only recently begun to keep chickens now raised more and more. New crops were introduced. In 1953 sweet potatoes were brought in and in 1955 cabbages and carrots. These were dried, pickled or salted for the long winter months. Never had the people of Little Yetao, long used to famine and begging, enjoyed such a varied menu. Yet still the village was short of grain. In 1954 the Government sent in 10 tons of relief grain to make up the deficit. In the words of one villager the four old ways of keeping alive had given way to three new ones: 'Government relief grain, Government grants or loans and bank loans.' 'It's because of Government help that we're so much better off than we were,' said another man. This was only partly true, for the farmers themselves had worked hard. But it was a fact that the fruits of their capital construction could only be reaped with time. Meanwhile government aid tided them over.

In 1956–57, with Little Yetao and several small neighbouring villages combined into a socialist farming co-operative, still greater forces could be concentrated for capital construction. 800 people set to work on reconstructing a watercourse which drained 73 slopes and was fed from over 100 gullies. Here every year when the rains came, water poured down 1,500 acres of hillside to damage crops and wash away topsoil. On this area new terraces were now constructed and old ones repaired; a small reservoir was constructed and 350-odd miniature dams were built in the gullies to arrest the torrents and retain the topsoil. In addition 210,000 fish-scale pits were dug and planted with trees: apricots, peaches, walnuts and mulberries for silkworm breeding, a newly-developing sideline. From the lower slopes 16 acres of vegetable plots were carved and cucumbers, tomatoes, aubergines, chives and other vegetables made their first appearance. In the sheltered courtyard of village houses melons and grapes were planted.

The new undertaking not only conserved soil and water. It made possible the generation of power—though only in the face of some scepticism. One old farmer named Yuan scoffed as he watched the power station going up. 'Whoever heard of lamps without oil and mill-wheels that turned without donkeys?' he asked. He stayed sceptical to the last, even when the bulbs were being screwed into their sockets. Suddenly the lights flashed on. Then, the story goes, the old man was so carried away that he shouted, 'Long live the Communist Party!' This incident not only won a place in village history for old Yuan—who had never been known to shout a slogan before; it marked a turning-point in the thinking of many of the older and more conservative farmers. With the building of the power plant, enthusiasm for capital construction rose.

At the same time advances were made in animal husbandry. Not only was the number of livestock increased but great efforts were made to improve the strains. In 1956 the Little Yetao Co-operative Breeding Station was set up. This procured Sinkiang rams with heavy, silky fleeces to breed with the light and coarse-fleeced local sheep. Ukrainian and Berkshire hogs were brought in to improve the quality of the local pigs, and tough, swift little Mongolian stallions for breeding horses and mules. Leghorn poultry was introduced and fine silkworms were brought in from Kiangsu province in south-east China.

Although Little Yetao now considered itself a farming, forestry and livestock co-operative, it went in for sidelines as well. The farmers had never given up climbing the mountains to cut brushwood for sale. The traditional gathering of medicinal herbs from the mountain tops and crags now became better organized. Throughout the year it was the task of the shepherds, but early in the spring when it was still too cold for field cultivation other villagers joined in. In late autumn, when all the crops were in, withies were cut for the weaving of bins and baskets.

A climax to all these efforts was reached in 1958. That year, for the first time in its history, Little Yetao had a surplus of grain. After setting aside what was needed to feed the people and the livestock, as well as the next year's seed, there was almost 75 tons left for sale to the state. Vegetable production amounted to an average of half a ton per person and the villagers boasted: 'Now we have vegetables to eat with our grain every day of the year.' The fruit trees, too, planted some years before, began to bring in a cash income. In 1958 this amounted to 15 *yuan* per head (out of a total cash income of just over 74 *yuan* per person). For Little Yetao this was a new peak of prosperity.

TABLE 3: *Use of Fields of Little Yetao Village in 1958* [4]

Type of grain	Area sown	Yield per *mu*
	mu	*jin*
Wheat	275	272
Maize	302	411
Millet	308	302
Sweet potatoes (at 1:4 ratio)	150·9	480
Coarse fodder grain	5·5	215
Total sown area:	1041·4	

With the 47 kilowatt hydro-electric power station and a 15 horse-power generator to do the milling and pumping, a considerable

[4] Some fields were double-cropped.

amount of labour was released. This made possible, among other things, the launching of a drive to improve village housing. A check showed that there were 950 rooms in Little Yetao village homes, but many of these were dilapidated. During the drive new houses or extensions to old ones amounting to 135 rooms were built, while 235 rooms were repaired. The village's 200 families (678 people) now lived in 1,085 rooms, an average of 1·6 rooms per person.

But what changed the atmosphere of the village most of all was the glow of electric light through the latticed paper window-panes and the strains of local opera or news echoing along the narrow, flag-stoned streets from the loudspeakers slung above the village gates.

In September 1958, when Yangyi Commune was set up, Little Yetao Socialist Farming Co-operative, with its 10 small mountain villages, 4,600-odd people and 1,250 acres became Little Yetao Brigade.

With the commune the scope of soil and water conservation increased. A bald, bare hill a mile up the valley was terraced, irrigated, afforested, stocked with farm animals—and re-named 'The Mount of Ten Thousand Treasures'. During the winter of 1958–59, 380,000 more fish-scale pits were dug and over 250 acres of terraces made or repaired, which increased the area of the brigade's arable land by nearly 100 acres. A reservoir with a capacity of 15,000 cubic metres was built, with 21 small dams above it and 5 channels below, to water 300 acres. 50 feet above the reservoir was another channel, a mile long, into which water was pumped to irrigate a further 50 acres. The brigade members summed up all this work in the words: 'We have rearranged the mountains and streams.'

With the setting up of the commune, too, 30,000 fish fry were brought in to stock the newly-dug fishpond. These were the first fish to be bred in the area. Thus Little Yetao was the first of Yangyi's brigades to go in for all five sides of diversified farming.

At the same time a new advance was made in animal husbandry: artificial insemination was introduced. White-smocked and hospital-masked technicians appeared in the breeding station, in the person of two local teen-aged girls and a boy who had finished primary school. These village 'intellectuals' handled test-tubes and kept pedigree records. The first year they achieved only 13 per cent success, but by 1960 they claimed 100 per cent efficiency. The number of pigs (improved by Berkshire and Ukrainian stock) was fast approaching the first of three goals—a pig for every household. (The subsequent targets, as throughout China, were first, one pig per person, then one pig for each *mu* of farmland. Such increases would not have been possible without vigorous land reclamation, for a pig needed, on an average, 100 to 200 *jin* of grain and over

3,000 *jin* of coarse and green fodder during the 10 to 12 months it took to reach a (gross) weight of 150 *jin*.[5]

Progress was also made in farm-sidelines. A poultry farm was set up in a ruined temple on the Mount of Ten Thousand Treasures (this was in addition to the earlier practice of each household keeping two or three hens). The poultry were in the charge of a teen-aged girl who had succeeded in using a *kang* (heated brick bed) as an incubator and in 1960 hatched 3,000 Leghorn chicks. (She had also, to the village children's delight, trained her charges to respond to a whistle, so that they not only came clucking up at meal times, but followed her down the hill to eat insects in the cornfields.)

Medicinal herbs were now transplanted from the mountain tops onto six acres of brigade fields. By 1960 there were 6,500 clumps (25 varieties in all) and brigade members, quoting traditional figures of Chinese medical lore, said: 'Now we produce all the ingredients for the 880 medicines that cure the 440 diseases.' The brigade did in fact provide its members with free medicine, either of its own cultivation or received in exchange for its home-grown herbs.

With these advances in old sidelines came the introduction of two new ones—bee-keeping and Angora rabbit raising. The bees had not only the wild flowers of the pastures and the blossoms of the fruit trees to suck, but the flowering shrubs which had been planted along the edges of the irrigation ditches; for in answer to the Government's call to beautify the countryside with flowers (one of the 40 points of the National Plan for Agricultural Development) the farmers had planted thousands of flowering shrubs.

Comparing 1960 with 1958, brigade members pointed out: 'In 1958 we had electricity, but it didn't run machines for us; we had water but there were no fish in it; we had woodland but it hadn't started to bring in much income; we used good stock for breeding, but the efficiency was low.' By 1960 electrically-run mills and fodder-choppers relieved brigade members of thousands of hours of heavy labour; the fish fry had already grown to a fair size; income from trees (fruit, nut, spice and timber) had risen to 35,000 *yuan*; in place of only nine fine-fleeced Sinkiang sheep there were flocks of sheep of improved breed.

There were similar advances in field crops. The first greenhouses were built. These gave the vegetables an early start in the spring, when frosts prevented their being sown outside. This made possible double and even triple cropping. Sprayers were purchased to extend the use of insecticide.

But the centre of all farmwork in Little Yetao was raising the output of grain.

Acting on the principle that 'agriculture is the base of the econ-

[5] See Liao Lu-yen, *Agriculture—Foundation of the National Economy*, F.L.P., Peking, 1960, p. 7.

116

Five-sided Farming in the Mountains

omy and grain the key lever', each year the brigade sowed more wheat, maize, millet and sorghum as well as sweet potatoes (counted as grain at a ratio of 4 *jin* of sweet potatoes to 1 *jin* of cereals). By applying the Eight Point Charter and by increasing the rate of double-cropping it pushed up the yield per *mu* from 382 *jin* in 1958 to 471 in 1959. In the summer of 1960 it forecast, on the basis of standing crops, a yield of over 500 *jin* per *mu*. Since according to the National Program for Agricultural Development this was the 1967 target for the area between the Yellow and the Yangtze rivers, the brigade members boasted that they were about to 'cross the Yellow River', as the People's Liberation Army had done a dozen years before in its victorious southward offensive.

In 1960 Ren Qing-mei was chosen as one of six 'standard bearers' in the whole county for outstanding efforts to raise grain output.[6] His achievement had been restoring the ravages of two natural calamities—hail and flood.

RESULTS OF LITTLE YETAO'S EFFORT

The villages now forming Little Yetao Brigade, which until 1954 had received relief grain from the Government, in 1959 had a surplus of some 500 tons of grain (including sweet potatoes). By the late summer of 1960, on the basis of summer crops already in and of an estimate of the standing autumn crops, the brigade was anticipating the record annual net income of 1,170 *jin* of grain and 155 *yuan* for each of its members. It would thus be among the first of Yangyi's brigades entitled to go over to free food and the payment of wages (the provincial pre-requisities for this step being a net income of 1,000 *jin* of grain and 150 *yuan* per person).

Higher living standards in Little Yetao Brigade had first been shown in the members' diet. In 1958 they had boasted, 'We now have vegetables to eat with our meals every day of the year.' That year, too, housing had received attention. By 1959 higher living standards were spreading over to clothing and a trend towards store-bought garments appeared.

TABLE 4: *Money Income of Little Yetao Brigade*

Year	Income per Member
1949	36 *yuan*
1952	41 *yuan*
1958	74·27 *yuan* (53% of which came from side-lines)
1959	92·50 *yuan*
1960	155 *yuan* (estimate)

[6] See Chapter XVIII, p. 236.

117

So far as clothing and bedding were concerned every adult had at least one summer suit of trousers and jacket. Most had two complete suits. Every adult also had a warm padded quilt and nearly all had a cotton-padded jacket and trousers for winter. The few exceptions were families with many mouths to feed but few hands to work. Knitted vests were common among the men and children. A few had woollen sweaters and raincapes, but these were still rather a luxury. Sets of heavy cotton fleece underwear were a common index of prosperity.

Brigade members saw their advances against the background of pre-land reform days when the poorest families had one tattered quilt between them and husband and wife might even share one pair of trousers, and when in one year of famine, 130 of Little Yetao village's 162 families had fled from home to go begging.

The record of this one brigade was of more than local significance. First, in bringing under control an area of erosion in this part of China, it played a part in a project of nation-wide significance: control of the Yellow River.[7] When all brigades in its middle reaches had 'rearranged' their share of mountains and streams, the Yellow River could be tamed.

Second, Little Yetao's success showed the soundness of the policy of diversified farming in the mountains, proving that emigration to the plains was not the only solution for mountain dwellers, as many had previously thought. From the record of villages like Little Yetao some general conclusions were drawn which appeared in *The People's Daily*.[8]

Mountain areas have great resources which can be rapidly developed. Watered plains have certain natural advantages . . . But mountain areas have advantages of their own—an extensive area with grassy slopes for grazing and plenty of wild products.

These areas lend themselves to the development of forestry, livestock raising and secondary occupations. Some of them have rich ore deposits . . . But the main thing, of course, is the people. We all know that 'the poorer people are, the greater their urge for change'. As mountain folk are poorer than plains people, their urge for change is especially strong. This is a powerful driving force for the transformation of the mountains. The key lies with the leadership. Their job is to arouse, inspire and organize the people to throw themselves into the struggle to transform the mountain areas.

Finally, Little Yetao provided a wealth of practical experience

[7] Part of the silt which gave the Yellow River its name, and the highest sedimentation rate in the world, was washed down from this region. As the river started to flow more gently on reaching the broad north China plain, the silt began to settle, raising the river-bed above the adjacent fields. For generations the dykes were built higher and higher only to be breached every few years by floods which brought disaster to millions of people on the plains.
[8] *The People's Daily*, 25 January, 1960.

118

in how to put policies for mountain farming into effect. Many Yangyi brigades were still far behind it. Perhaps the biggest obstacle to their catching up was the soil and water conservation that was needed for bringing prosperity. This took hard work without giving immediate results. It demanded willingness to sacrifice immediate interests to long-term ones. For brigade members to do this demanded skilled leadership and good all-round political work. 'You need to know how to lead people, how to convince them,' said Ren Qing-mei, 'to get them to overcome their doubts and to work enthusiastically.'

Chapter XI

FARM MANAGEMENT

CO-OPERATIVES had made way for communes because they were too small and too narrow in scope to permit the most rapid progress in production. Capital construction in the countryside in the form of soil and water conservation and the development of industry to spur on the mechanization of agriculture and the raising of rural living standards, both required a larger and more comprehensive unit. Yet in one way the co-operatives had been not too small but too big, for with the long tradition of intensive, small-scale, non-mechanized farming and shortage of educated personnel, planning and management were easier in small units. The co-operatives had solved some of the problems arising from the increased size of the farming unit. But others remained.

The problem of combining centralized leadership with de-centralized management was still unsolved. First there was the matter of planning what crops to raise. How could this be done with a view both to meeting the needs of the country and to growing what was suited to local conditions such as soil, climate and methods of farming? Another question concerned the organization of labour. What was the best size for a work unit? How should it be organized to bring the best results? How should it plan its daily work? What sort of checking and supervision was necessary? Still another question was that of distribution. Here the guiding principle was clear: 'To each according to his work.' But how was this broad principle to be concretely applied? By regular wages? By a work point system? By daily appraisals of work done? By the rate for the job?

As time went on it became increasingly clear that the crucial task was to raise the efficiency of the brigades and work teams through evolving good systems and procedures, through attending to a mass of details. Success in handling these would call forth the energy and enthusiasm of rank-and-file commune members, which in turn would bring bigger yields; failure to deal with them would make for apathy and discouragement—and smaller yields.

First among the problems to be solved was that of planning.

THE PLANNING OF CROPS AND OUTPUT

To achieve the best results each brigade had to grow the crops best suited to its soil and other conditions. At the same time it had to meet the broader needs of the state. The state plan, in its turn, had to adapt national needs to the potentialities of the brigades—taking into account soil, water resources, raw materials and communications. The system devised for ensuring this co-ordination was for the brigades to submit tentative plans for kinds of crops and total yields. These various brigade plans then went into the making of commune plans (after adjustment, if necessary, by mutual consent). The commune plans in turn were submitted to the county for inclusion in its plan. The process was continued by way of the region and province until at last it reached Peking. There it was taken into account in the drawing-up of the national plan. Then the whole process was reversed, again with certain adjustments in the light of overall national needs, until the plan finally filtered back to the brigades where it was to be carried out. (This state plan applied to only 90 per cent of the brigade's land; of the remaining 10 per cent, half belonged to individual households as private allotments, half was to be used by the brigade as it wished.)

With the state plan arrived at in this way, theoretically no serious discrepancies could arise. Yet problems did crop up.

The Ten Mile Inn brigade leadership, including the heads of the various work teams, when drafting its 1959 plan submitted output figures which would have meant an average yield for grain of 600 *jin* per *mu*. This figure was a product of the confidence which came from the Great Leap Forward of 1958 and of determination to 'continue to oppose conservatism' as called for by the Central Committee of the Communist Party.[1] But it was based on the early, exaggerated figures for the previous year. When the actual grain yields for all the brigade's fields had been carefully worked out, instead of simply being estimated, the average output proved to be 316 *jin* per *mu*. This was a striking increase, but it was well below the exaggerated figures which had been largely based on estimates of the most successful plots.

When this corrected figure was announced a feeling of pessimism began to grow among the rank-and-file brigade members. Targets were the basis for both bonuses for overfulfilment and penalties for underfulfilment, and some had thought 600 *jin* too high at the outset; now this feeling spread. It was reflected in listlessness in the fields and dissatisfaction with the brigade and work team leaders who had been carried away by enthusiasm and by determination to reach communism as fast as possible.

Meanwhile, in accordance with a decision of the April check-up (based on a Central Committee directive), the Commune Party Committee re-opened the whole question of quotas to see if the

[1] 'Communique of the 6th Plenary Session of the 8th Central Committee of the C.C.P.', *Documents*, F.L.P., Peking, December 1958.

targets set were realistic. As a result a new series of meetings was called, and after discussion the figures were changed. Ten Mile Inn's quota was now set at 370 *jin* per *mu*. This was a big drop from 600, but it was still 17 per cent above the peak yield of 1958. This revised figure raised the spirits of the brigade members. They were convinced that the new quota could not only be achieved but surpassed and went to work with an eye on the bonuses they now felt confident of winning. In the autumn when the crops were brought in and the figures worked out, Ten Mile Inn was found to have produced 400 *iin* per *mu*—8 per cent above the harvest aimed at and 26 per cent above that of the previous year. As a result of experiences of this sort, the system of fixing quotas was improved, the verified figure of the previous year being made the quota of the year to come.[2]

Other problems remained, among them the kind of crops to raise. Some, from long-standing tradition and because of the rationing made necessary by natural calamities, wished to cut down on industrial crops, such as cotton, and produce more grain. This was one of the matters that had to be thrashed out during the setting-up of the Silver Sea Tract, when some were pressing for a maize or sweet potato tract rather than one for cotton. According to Party policy, they argued, grain was the key lever. Yes, acknowledged others, but the country needed cotton, as county directives made clear.

Another question was how to reconcile the general need, both national and local, for wheat, maize, sweet potatoes and cotton, with more specialized and limited local demands. These last included glutinous millet (used in traditional festival dishes), soya beans for cheese-like curd products and for sauce, sesame for oil and for sprinkling on wheat-cakes, sorghum for vinegar. In the drive to raise the output of staple cereals, these smaller, diverse crops had tended to be squeezed out. Some provision had therefore to be made for growing them again. How to do this while concentrating on the more general demand for staples, had still to be worked out.

Planning involved questions of still another type. Should the brigade concentrate more labour on the best fields or should it expend some on distant and scattered mountain plots which could hardly be expected to yield more than 50 to 80 *jin* per *mu*. To discover the point at which diminishing returns on the best fields would make tilling of the poor and distant ones worth while required a good system of cost accounting. Few brigades as yet had accountants able to deal with such problems.

Even without cost accounting, one important advantage of extending the area sown to grain did emerge. Widely dispersed fields gave some insurance against natural calamities. If the low fields

[2] Thus the Ten Mile Inn quota for 1960 was fixed at 400 *jin*. The figure for Yangyi Commune as a whole came to 404 *jin* per *mu*.

Farm Management

were flooded, the higher ones might escape; if frost nipped the crops in the higher fields, the lower ones might still go unscathed; if hail struck the eastern slopes, the western ones might be safe. It was a question of not having all one's eggs in one basket.

The summing-up of experience throughout the country led to a decision that two courses should be followed simultaneously in the drive to increase grain output. The average yield per *mu* should be raised and the sown area expanded.[3]

OWNERSHIP AND MANAGEMENT IN
THE BRIGADES

The April check-up had placed ownership of farmland, of the chief farm implements (ploughs, harrows, seeders, etc.), and of draught animals in the hands of the brigades. But the farming itself was done by the work teams. So good farm management revolved largely around relations between the brigade and its work teams.

In 1960 some systems had already been devised for establishing the brigade's leadership over the teams. First and foremost were the 'three quotas and one bonus', introduced during the period of the socialist co-operatives.

These quotas were based on a detailed assessment of the land made at that time. In Ten Mile Inn, for instance, in 1956 the committee of the newly-formed socialist co-operative spent ten days going over every piece of land in the village and putting it into one of three grades. The grading took three factors into account: first, the fertility of each plot; second, its distance from the village (which affected the time taken walking to and fro, the amount of labour needed for carrying fertilizer, etc.); the shape, size and contours of the field (uneven lie of the land making some fields harder to work than others). All this was done according to the 'mass line',[4] the committee's findings being posted up, discussed by the co-operative members and modified where necessary. The resulting figures, with minor adjustments made during the following years, formed the basis for the 'three quotas and one bonus'.

The output quota was simply each work team's share of the brigade target, worked out according to the area and grade of the fields it cultivated.

The costs quota covered fertilizer and insecticide, maintenance and replacement of implements, fodder for draught animals and such things. If these expenses exceeded the amount allotted by the

[3] What had been advocated in 1958 was raising the yield per *mu* but reducing the area sown to field crops, in order to save labour, water and fertilizer. Two years of disastrous weather, however, showed that in a period when man was still not in command of the elements, extending the sown area was a necessary form of crop insurance.
[4] See Introduction to Part Three.

123

brigade, the team had to make up the difference; if the team spent less than its allotment, it kept the balance.

As for the labour quota, the brigade drew up long- and short-term plans, for the year and for the season, listing the various tasks—ploughing, sowing, hoeing, applying fertilizer, reaping, threshing—and the total number of work points for each. (Ten work points corresponded to a normal day's work for an able-bodied man.) Then appropriate targets were set for each team in accordance with its labour force.

The 'bonus' consisted of everything produced above the output quota. It was divided equally between brigade and work team, according to the decision passed by the Yangyi Commune Congress.

Material incentives such as fixed targets, quotas and bonuses were not the only ones adopted by the brigade to spur production. The tempo of work was further stepped up by 'socialist emulation campaigns'.

These campaigns, described by the Central Committee of the Communist Party as 'the noblest task of the workers, farmers and revolutionary intellectuals throughout the country, at the present time',[5] were a regular feature of village life. In Ten Mile Inn Brigade every ten days a 'mobile red flag' was awarded to the work team with the best record in carrying out the current task. For the cotton hoeing in May 1960, for instance, a hundred points was the target. Four factors were considered: the plants were to be evenly spaced, without any gaps where shoots had not come up (40 points); they must all be growing well, none being sickly or yellow (30 points); all the fields must be hoed once (20 points); there must be no weeds (10 points). Work Team 8 won, with full marks. Team 7, the previous holder, got only 86 points and handed over the flag at a meeting of the whole brigade.

After the handing over, standards were set for the tasks of the next ten days: harvesting the wheat (40 points); sowing corn and millet (40 points); planting one-fifth of the sweet potatoes (20 points). The defeated Team 7 was determined to wrest the flag back from Team 8 and issued it a challenge. Some members of Team 7 proposed that during this ten-day 'battle' they should shorten their noon rest. This was agreed and Work Team 7 finished the three jobs in eight days instead of ten and won back the red flag.

RIGHT TO USE—AND LABOUR MANAGEMENT
IN THE WORK TEAMS

The planning of day-to-day work in the fields—which day to plough

[5] 'Resolution on Developing the Campaign for Increasing Production and Practising Economy', 8th Plenary Session of the 8th Central Committee of the C.C.P., 16 August, 1959.

or sow, which fields to weed or hoe first, which to irrigate, how much fertilizer to spread on this field or that, how many hands to assign to a job, when and where draught animals were needed—all this was left to the work teams.

Within the teams a system of checking on work had been evolved, known as 'the five set standards'.

There were standards for quantity and quality of work, for time and work points allotted, and finally for awards and penalties for good work and bad. The setting of these standards was the task of the work team leadership. If a certain field was to be hoed, for instance, the stipulations might be: no weeds to be left; the job to be finished in five days; number of work points: 50. If a check showed that weeds had been left in the field, the job had to be done again until the quality of work was up to standard, without any extra points being given. If the job was finished in four days instead of five, a bonus of five points might be awarded; if it took six days, a similar number might be deducted.

In spite of such developments in methods of management that came with the organizing of the commune, there were still problems left over from the high level co-operatives which had not been thoroughly solved. The vesting of ownership of land once more in the brigade (which was the equivalent to the socialist co-operative) after correcting the mistake of vesting it in the commune, left problems that had existed earlier. For instance while the co-operative had been too small to carry on the capital construction and planning for developing modern agriculture, it had been too big for the most efficient field management. This problem remained. With the brigade now confirmed as the basic level of the commune, owning the means of production and holding the right to allocate labour, there was uneasiness in the work teams. It was hard for them to plan on more than a day-to-day basis, for the brigade could withdraw their land or hands. It would do so, in theory at least, only in the overall, long-term interests of the brigade. Yet short-term work team projects could not be set aside without affecting day-to-day field work.[6]

In addition to this long-standing difficulty, there was another which was quite new. This was the planning of work for women team members. The canteens and other social services had made possible an increase in the number of women taking part in field work. This brought new power to production; but women's work could not be handled like men's. Personal circumstances had to be taken into fuller account. Nursing mothers needed to be given work

[6] This problem was solved in the winter of 1960–61 with the vesting in the work teams of rights to use. This meant that no land could be withdrawn or labour re-allocated without the work team's approval, and without sufficient advance notice to make necessary re-arrangements of work.

near home so that they could get back easily at feeding times. There had to be constant adjustment of work assignments to suit the state of health of each woman. All this had, in fact, been dealt with by the Central Committee of the Communist Party and summed-up in the form of 'Three Musts and Three Must Nots' in assigning work to women:

When pregnant they must be given light work, not heavy.
When nursing they must be given work close by, not far away.
During monthly periods they must be given dry work, not wet.

Attending to all this involved a mass of intimate details which the men team leaders found hard to handle.

The problem was widespread and accordingly was reviewed throughout the commune. Thus in the summer of 1960 the decision was made that every work team should have a woman vice-team leader (unless the leader was a woman, in which case the vice-team leader might be a man). This would have two big advantages. First, women would be better able to cope with the complicated question of women's work assignments; second, they would learn the art of leadership by taking part in it. For except in such model brigades as Little Yetao and Bailin, women still played only a small part in leadership.

'TO EACH ACCORDING TO HIS WORK'

Smooth running of the teams also demanded a system of payment which would call forth the best efforts of the team members. The guiding principle, put forward by the Central Committee, was the socialist one of: 'From each according to his ability, to each according to his work.'[7]

At this time each team member's work was measured in terms of points, and it was these that determined an individual's income. In Yangyi the work point system already had a history of ten to fifteen years, having first come into being with mutual aid in the forties The earliest system was a rough-and-ready one reached by agreement between two families. One family might agree to lend another a donkey for a day and receive in return two days' work by an able-bodied man. Once permanent mutual aid groups replaced casual mutual aid between individual families, a more systematic procedure had to be worked out. It was at this period that the custom arose of rating a whole day's work of an ordinary able-bodied man at 10 points. With this as a starting-point, a man known for exceptional strength or skill might come to have an assessment of 12 points, while teen-aged boys just starting work might rate 7. The normal assessment for a woman was 8 points.

[7] See also Chapter XVIII, under 'Putting Politics in Command'.

Even in those early days the question of assessment was a vexed one, for there were certain farm tasks, such as weeding, which women did as fast as men or even faster. So when, as quite often happened, a woman did more in a day than a man it was obvious discrimination to give her fewer points. In 1944 the Ten Mile Inn leader of production had organized a competition between a team of women and a team of men, to prove that the women deserved a new rating. The women won—but no change was forthcoming, the majority of men feeling that the competition had little bearing on the main problem. The overall picture, they maintained, was that men bore the brunt of the farmwork, while women merely did casual work in the fields. In fact at this time the majority of women, being engaged in housework, spinning and weaving, did no field work at all and were inclined to support their menfolk rather than the few members of their own sex who worked in the fields.

In 1953, however, in its decisions on the development of semi-socialist agricultural producers' co-operatives, the Central Committee of the Communist Party stated: 'Equal pay for equal work should be the rule for both men and women, based on the quantity and quality of their work.'[8] Two years later, when the need for more labour power was keenly felt in the fast rising socialist co-operatives, Mao Tse-tung himself more than once underlined the importance of the rate for the job in drawing women into production.

Nevertheless, in 1960 the traditional assessment of women's work still prevailed in Yangyi. But the setting up of the Silver Sea Tract made women's rates once more the focus of attention. It became clear to the tract leadership that women were quicker and better than men at a number of tasks connected with cotton-growing. The crucial and highly-skilled job of pruning the young plants was one of them, the women on the whole pruning faster and with better judgement. Commune Secretary Jin Han-cheng, who gave political guidance to the tract, himself raised the question of equal rates for women. The subject was debated with some heat by the tract members and Secretary Jin's proposal met with strong opposition. Some of the men argued: 'We're the main breadwinners of the family, not these teen-aged girls. They'll soon be leaving home to get married, anyway. No household is run mainly on the earnings of its teen-aged daughters. If they bring in a bit of pin-money that's enough. They're earning plenty as it is.'

There was another factor. Work points had no fixed value. Only an estimate of their worth could be made beforehand, on which advances of pay were given. The actual rate could not be worked out till the harvest was in, the accounts were done and tax and accumulation payments had been made to the commune and the brigade.

[8] 'Decisions on the Development of Agricultural Producers' Co-operatives', adopted by the Central Committee of the C.C.P., December 1953.

Then the total number of work points earned by all the members would be divided into the total income of the brigade and the value of a point be established. If the women received a higher rating for their work the total number of points would rise and the value of each point would fall. This the men thought would affect their pay. They did not take their deductions a step further—that with better pay the women might work harder and produce more, thus increasing the total income and raising, not lowering the value of the points.

Men who opposed raising women's rates agreed that women were better not only at pruning but at certain other jobs as well; but, they argued, men were better at heavier work, such as ploughing and contouring. So they proposed that some jobs should be assigned to women only—and paid at women's rates; others to men only—and paid at men's rates. This, they said, could be called 'the rate for the job!' And while avoiding comparisons between men and women it would still get the best out of each. At the same time it would maintain the solid basis of the household economy by keeping the man as the main breadwinner. So ran the argument.

And here it was agreed to let the matter rest for a while, though Secretary Jin and others who felt that women were not getting a fair deal did not consider it closed. Actually on the Silver Sea Tract the issue was not a burning one, for the girls who had broken most records and who might logically have been most dissatisfied, belonged to the 'Five Plums' team. They would go all out whatever happened, for they saw themselves as 'builders of communism' and were quite ready to be patient with those whose vision was as yet less broad.

This temporary arrangement had simply changed the problem from one of women's rates versus men's into one of rating jobs according to the skill they called for. The latter was perhaps at this time the more pressing problem. How, for instance, should one differentiate between tasks which required judgement, skill and experience and those demanding mainly physical strength? Of this the Central Committee had said in its Resolution of 1958, that in the rural areas existing differences in skill were not such as to warrant wide differences in pay.[9]

In interpreting this in Yangyi there was a tendency at this time towards evening things out. As a result, strong and hardworking young fellows might be given the same rating as old farmers with a lifetime of experience behind them.

With mechanization still in its infancy, much did indeed depend on physical strength, and the existing work points rating was such as to encourage team members to put forth what they had unstintingly. But setting an ideal ratio between strength and experience

[9] 'Resolution on Some Questions Concerning the People's Communes'.

128

was difficult. The old farmers' experience was actually of a high order, representing perhaps the highest technical level that could be reached under the old conditions of small-scale intensive farming without large-scale water and soil conservation, mechanical equipment, chemical fertilizers or insecticide; but it did not encompass the new possibilities created by collective farming. So though its rating deserved to be high, it ought not to be so high as to discourage the spirit of enterprise and innovation. Thus the setting of rates for the skilled and the unskilled, for men and women, was no mere matter of payment to individuals. It had broad implications for increasing output.

Implementing the principle 'to each according to his work', did not end with the fixing of rates, but included the daily assessing of work done by each member of a team. Most team members had their ups and downs, so a person's normal work rate was one thing and the amount of work he did on any particular day might be another. Work teams with good leaders dealt with this by means of encouragement, criticism and public opinion. But still a good system was considered necessary to prevent unfairness and discourage slacking. In Yangyi slackers were rare; but they existed. And one might affect a whole team. 'If old Wang's going to get ten points for working like that,' was a natural reaction, 'why should I strain myself?' For in most teams, whoever turned out for work was credited at his assessed rate regardless of how much he did. For this reason, as far back as the time of the socialist co-operatives, individual daily assessments had been advocated. This meant that points were added to or subtracted from each member's rating depending on how he had worked, the appraisal being made at the end of the day by the worker himself together with his team-mates.

Some co-operatives had accepted this system in principle but had not put it into practice. It was the same now in many of the work teams. They simply stuck to the rating. Not without reason. In the first place, with the fixed rating, all that was needed was to note presence or absence and every so often (in some teams every five days, in others every ten or twenty) to multiply the total attendance by the rating. Assessing and entering points at the end of the day meant extra work. Secondly, when it came to making an appraisal, most team members hesitated to point out to a neighbour, an old friend or close relative—much less the parent of a sweetheart! —that he had not done a good day's work and should receive less than his rating. And few liked to suggest to a well-meaning team-leader that he had wasted time running around instead of getting on with the job. They felt that broaching such subjects would only cause unpleasantness, bring disunity and thereby harm the work. So the less said, the better.

Nevertheless there were teams which did put the system into

practice and found it effective. Much depended on the team leaders. They might on occasion spend more time than necessary going round to see how things were progressing. But if they took the lead in making an accurate self-appraisal, giving a modest and realistic assessment of their day's work, others followed suit. This made it easier for the team as a whole to bring into the open any cases of slacking or point-padding.

One team which had applied the appraisal system unsuccessfully and abandoned it during the period of socialist co-operatives, tried it again in 1960. This time the team leaders showed the way. Formerly a handful who took things easy had affected the tempo of the whole team; with realistic appraisals the slacking of one or two individuals no longer had an effect on the rest. There were no 'injustices' to rankle and to lower spirits. Those who worked harder earned more; those who slacked got less.

Such experiences convinced the commune leadership that while work ratings were important, they were not enough in themselves. With the prevailing 'level of consciousness' of many farmers, democratic appraisals of the day's work were also necessary to operate the principle 'to each according to his work' most effectively.

RECORDS AND ACCOUNTS

Besides assessing work points correctly it was necessary to keep accurate records. If this was not done clearly and efficiently when accounts were presented some would feel, rightly or wrongly that they had done more work than they were credited with. They would blame the registrar for mixing-up records, for failing to make entries, for faulty arithmetic. If actual mistakes came to light the whole team might become unsettled.

To this there was no easy solution, for despite advances in literacy, it was still hard to find competent book-keepers and work-point registrars. In many teams it fell to some teen-age boy fresh from school. Yet the work of a registrar demanded more than a legible hand and a head for figures. It called for judgement, initiative, tact—for ability to deal with people as well as with numbers.

Record-keeping was so important that it was made the subject of special study, not only in Yangyi but in communes all over the country.

According to one report studied in Yangyi, questions commonly arose in the case of housewives who could not turn out regularly for a day's work but put in half a day as a rule and a whole day now and then. One case cited was of an older woman who did milling for a work team canteen and who devised a book-keeping system of her own, despite being illiterate. On the wall by the donkey-driven mill she would scratch a long stroke for a whole day's work and a short

130

20. Part of the North Zhang Channel, blasted from the rock-·
face. Right, leader of one of the women's teams that helped
dig the channel (see Chapters V and XXI).

21. A section of the North Zhang Channel, halfway up the hillside.

22. Young woman tractor driver at the Yangyi Tractor Station.

23. Wang Jin-lin and son—
with traditional local hair-
cut (see Chapter XX, The
Contradictions of Youth).

one for half a day. At the end of one month she had 8 long scratches and 14 short ones, amounting to 15 work days. With her rating, as an older woman, of 7 points a day, this worked out at something over 10 standard work days. But when the accounts were posted, she was down for only 6. She took the matter up with the registrar, showing him her carefully scratched entries; and though she was unable to convince him that they were accurate a compromise was reached and she was credited with an extra three days.

The solution to such problems urged in the report was a double entry system, with regular entries in the books of the team and of the individual team members. One team devised the system of issuing tickets to each member at the end of the day's work. These were recalled, together with individual member's books, every five days so that the registrar could enter the points.

All in all the registrar played a vital part in the work team. If he was painstaking and thoughtful he could bring problems to light and get them solved. One registrar, in preparing for the public posting of his monthly records, noticed that one of the best workers of the team had three work days less than the previous month. Yet this had been a busier month in the fields and all the other team members had earned more points. The registrar felt there must be some mistake and called in the man's personal points book together with all the daily tickets. He found that he had misread a figure on one of them.

On another occasion this same registrar, on entering the daily appraisals, found that a young man named Niu, not known as an outstandingly hard worker, had carried 50 loads of fertilizer to the fields; while one of the hardest workers had carried only 43. At supper in the canteen that evening the registrar took his bowl and went to eat and chat with some women who worked with Niu to find out what had brought about his transformation. It turned out that there was no transformation at all, Niu had simply been using smaller baskets than the others. Realising that when the news of this got round the morale of the hard workers would be affected, the registrar spoke to the team leader about standardizing the size of the baskets. He also took the matter up with Niu himself, explaining that such practices meant inflating work points and bringing a drop in their value. Eventually the young man himself proposed that the day's work should be reassessed and the whole team was satisfied.

Again, during the wheat harvest some team members were assigned to reap, others to thresh. On the threshing floor certain jobs required greater strength, skill and experience than others. After a couple of days the farmers assigned to these tasks asked to be transferred. The registrar guessed that they must be dissatisfied with the points rating. Visiting them for a smoke during the lunch hour he found that this was so. A flat rate had been set for all work on the

threshing floor, although the tasks were not equally skilled or
arduous. When the registrar brought this matter up it was set right.
In short, just as a rational system of work points acted as a spur
to production, a competent work points registrar could contribute
much to the smooth running of a work team.

BUSINESS MANAGEMENT

The recording of work points was, of course, only one aspect of
business management. This also included accounting, handling of
cash (placed in different hands to prevent graft), looking after public
property and financial planning.

The last of these involved estimates for the brigade's gross
income, its expenditure, total labour requirements, amounts for
accumulation and distribution, the estimated value of work points,
and the average incomes of working members, and so on.

North Cunjing, for instance, (one of the villages which provided
a team for the Silver Sea Tract) worked out its financial plan for the
whole of 1960. The brigade's planned gross income was 316,499
yuan. From this was to be deducted 142,345 *yuan*—or 44·9 per cent
—to cover expenditure. The sum left for distribution was 174,154
yuan. As the brigade had a total of 1,200 labour hands (including
both full- and part-time workers) this meant an average income of
145 *yuan* for the year. (There was, of course, a big difference between
the lowest part-time and the highest full-time worker's income.)
Of the amount distributed to members, 70 per cent was to be in cash
or kind, 30 per cent in the form of free grain. The number of work
days planned for the whole year was 110,000, so rates of pay worked
out at just over one *yuan* per standard work day.

With the setting up of the commune in 1958, the tasks of business
management and accounting in the countryside grew bigger than
ever. The need for reliable, conscientious and competent accountants
and registrars became so pressing that a national call went out for
Young Communists in the villages to learn accounting, and special
training courses were set up.

In the earliest stage of the commune the main centre of accounting was commune headquarters and in the course of a year commune
accountants found themselves handling millions of *yuan*. Their
difficulties were great. These were largely overcome by the check-up
of April 1959, with its introduction of 'three-level accounting'. At
that time the brigade became the chief level of accounting, though
the commune continued to handle a small percentage of the funds.[10]

[10] The percentage was to increase with time, for it was mainly the commune
that ran industry, the income from which was to grow more rapidly than that
from farming, which was mainly in the hands of the brigades. See Chapter XII,
'Industry in the Service of Agriculture'.

Part of the accounting, too, such as that for canteens, went down to the work teams. These were the lowest level for accounting and the level for recording work points.

In the summer of 1960, to help communes improve their business management, various summaries were made and useful experiences were publicized. The first aim in doing this was to dispel the idea that accounting was a mystery. The gist of one report ran:

> Business accounting is no mystery. It is a matter of keeping records of people's daily economic activities and adding them up, of comparing this year with last year and one unit with another, to find out which is advanced, which backward, which economical, which extravagant; and on the basis of these findings of pushing forward the work all along the line.
>
> In the trade and industrial enterprises of the commune, accounting is not so much of a problem, for we can draw on the experience of state enterprises. As to accounting connected with farming (i.e. in the brigades), the methods used must be simple, economical and easy to demonstrate and understand.

The report went on to make the following proposals:

> Apart from the day-to-day financial work of the accountants, it is important to have two mass movements a year (one after the summer and one after the autumn harvest) to check on the work and audit the accounts. These movements are not simply to guarantee accurate accounting but to give everyone an overall picture of the sequence of farmwork in a whole season, of lessons in actual production, of the nature of management and of the work style of cadres. They serve as a school of management for the mass of brigade members. In addition, such movements can disclose and deal with problems which are hard to discover in the course of day-to-day work. Consequently they can raise the level of financial work, accounting and management.

The goal set for the whole countryside was to set up in each commune, within two to three years starting from the summer of 1960, a scientific system of financial work and economic management.

DEMOCRATIC MANAGEMENT

'There are four aspects to management,' said Commune Party Secretary Jin, 'production, labour, finance and finally, how to do it all democratically.'

To guarantee democracy the commune constitution laid down that a Commune Congress should be held every six months to fix overall plans and targets, to sanction purchases, such as those for machinery, and to determine how much grain was to be sold to the state. Within the brigade, democratic procedure called for membership meetings to decide all important issues.

Over the years a set of democratic procedures had been devised.

Nevertheless there were still practical problems to be solved. First, time being precious, there was a contradiction between holding meetings and getting on with the job. (This had emerged soon after the Communists assumed leadership in the Yangyi area. At that time a local bard, more accustomed to extortion than discussion, had composed the couplet:

> With the Kuomintang 'twas more taxes to pay!
> With the Communist Party it's meetings all day!)

Second, meetings were effective only if they brought to light what the participants were thinking, and not all people could express themselves well in public. This applied in the first place to poor peasants, farmhands and women, who in the past had had no say in public affairs. One procedure which the Communists evolved early on to help them out was 'fermentation'. This was used at any meeting of more than fifteen or twenty people. After a report had been presented or some subject been put to the meeting for discussion, following the first exchange of views the chairman would suggest: 'Now let's "ferment" a bit.' Those present would then split up into groups of four or five, stools and benches being shuffled around to form little knots and circles and people moving about to join groups of friends or neighbours. As the informal exchange of views got under way a buzz or murmur would arise—the sound of 'fermentation'. Meanwhile members of the steering committee would circulate among the groups to catch the trend of the discussion and to find out when people felt they had sorted out their ideas. Then the chairman would call the meeting together again and throw it open to discussion. There were no official spokesmen, but generally someone from each of the groups would voice the various views expressed. Group members knew if there were any ideas which were not brought out and would indicate it to the chairman or nudge the person until he spoke for himself or got someone else to speak for him.

In 1960 the contradiction between full expression of opinion and not spending too much time on meetings was receiving considerable attention. This was evident from the articles on the subject in the local and national press. The gist of one of these (in the *People's Daily*) ran:

> It is not necessary to have too many meetings. The chief thing is to run them well and to really solve the problems of the commune members.
> Their views on the matter in hand should be sought in advance. On this basis a plan should be drafted and put to the meeting for thorough discussion.
> There is no need to fear that if there are a lot of people there will be too many views. Different views give rise to lively discussion and this can bring out the main problems in all their aspects. In this way problems can be solved in a deep and overall manner.

Farm Management

In Yangyi, cadres of the commune's 24 brigades and 300-odd work teams were still working out how to put such advice into practice, deciding which matters should be discussed at which level; who should attend which meeting; what should be settled through broad discussion, what by prompt decision of the leaders of the unit concerned; how many matters should be tackled at any one meeting; who need and need not be present. For while everyone liked to have his say, no one wished to spend more time than necessary at meetings.

* * *

Working out an efficient system of democratic management was especially difficult in so new and many-sided an undertaking as the commune. Yangyi Commune's leadership was aware of the challenge confronting it. 'There is a gap between the demands of the times and the actual level of leadership,' said Commune Secretary Jin. 'Some brigades are still relying on experience gained in the days of the socialist co-operatives. This is not enough to guide us in the period of the communes.'[11]

---

[11] Improving systems of management in the communes became a key task in the face of the natural disasters of the next two years.

135

Chapter XII

INDUSTRY IN THE SERVICE OF AGRICULTURE

SELF-HELP IN MECHANIZING FARMING

IN 1958 industry accounted for 4·2 per cent of Yangyi Commune's income. By the first half of 1960 the proportion was four times as big. Animal-powered pumps for the battle against the drought, a rotary cultivator which brought about a twenty-fold increase in efficiency at hoeing time, a treadle-thresher which could handle four tons of grain a day, an animal-drawn drill which raised maize-planting efficiency ten-fold, labour-saving gadgets for canteen kitchens, rockets to disperse hail-clouds—all these were products of commune industry.

The commune and brigade farm tool plants were the key not only to raising farm production, but to developing commune industry itself. Shortage of labour in the fields being one of the commune's most pressing problems, the productivity of this labour had to be raised. Until this was achieved commune industry could not hope to recruit an adequate labour force or to expand to any great extent. Yet it was partly on just such an expansion that an increase in labour productivity depended.

Mechanization of agriculture was therefore urgently necessary.

This advance from the hoe to the tractor was not being put off until state tractor plants could provide machines for the whole of the Chinese countryside. Like the general advance of China's economy it was being made by 'walking on two legs'. One leg consisted of large, modern state implement works such as the giant Loyang Tractor Plant;[1] the other of medium-sized plants and the decentralized, small-scale industry of the twenty-odd thousand communes. Here, day in and day out, small workshops grappled with the problem of mechanizing agriculture, starting with whatever tools were in use, improving them step by step, and taking them through various stages from man and animal power to semi- and full mechanization.

One advantage of this step-by-step advance was that it allowed the farmers to gain new skills to match the new machines and workers in the workshops to become more and more technically proficient. As a new saying had it:

[1] China's first modern tractor plant, completed in 1959, with an output capacity of 30,000 tractors a year.

136

Industry in the Service of Agriculture

Machines are good, we all say so;
But without technique they just won't go.

In Yangyi Commune the linchpin of the mechanization process was the Farm Implement Manufacture and Repair Shop next to the tractor station on the outskirts of Yangyi townlet. Here, roofed-over but open-fronted workshops lined two sides of a fenced-in field. In one section were the blacksmiths with their small open furnaces and ringing anvils; in another the carpenters; and in a third the metal-workers, with their casting paraphernalia, blow-torches, electric lathes and a 24 horse-power diesel generator.

The shop's motto was that industry should serve agriculture; so during the 1960 spring sowing the workers formed themselves into small groups and scattered among teams working in the fields. In this short period they repaired over 20,000 tools on the spot.

They were not concerned with repairs alone. With field-work going on all round them the workers could see which jobs consumed most time and labour. And by observing work processes closely they could get ideas for more efficient tools. At the same time they could check on these ideas with the farmers and obtain new suggestions. It was in this way that the animal-drawn drill was devised for planting maize on the seven-mile Long March Tract. Later, when the tract teams were having difficulty in keeping up with the hoeing, the workshop mechanics invented the animal-drawn rotary cultivator, which they named the 'leap-forward hoe'. By way of tribute to the workers for this labour-saver, a group of young farmers composed a ditty. This they wrote out in bold brush strokes on a sheet of red paper three feet square. Then with a fanfare of drums and a clashing of cymbals they paraded to the works where they posted their poem on the wall. It ran:

Our worker brothers are politically alive,
They invent new tools with terrific drive.
Their leap-forward hoes are a genuine boon;
They help us push on and end the job soon.
So come on lads, let's work with a will!
And pledge our target to overfulfil!

Altogether, by the summer of 1960 the Farm Implements Manufacture and Repair Shop had to its credit 56 inventions or innovations (so far as Yangyi was concerned, at least), involving 6,500 implements.

Providing raw materials for the commune workshops was also a matter of 'walking on two legs', for Yangyi Commune did not depend on allocations of iron and steel from the big state mills, nor on coal and iron ore from state mines. In 1960 a small iron mine was opened in the commune itself and by the summer had already produced 5,000 tons of ore. A small commune iron and steel works

137

was also under construction and due to go into operation in the latter half of 1960. This together with the iron mine and the farm implement workshop was to provide the commune with a miniature industrial complex as the nucleus of its industry. Other industrial units were the rocket and explosive plant, the hydro-electric plant at Little Yetao, a number of pottery and brick kilns and a print shop.

In some of these industries—notably pottery and iron-mining, as well as in brick-making—there was a long-standing tradition in the area. But the steel, electricity, and printing industries were entirely new. One of the tasks of the Shexian county government, therefore, was to give technical advice and assistance to Yangyi and to the other ten communes under its jurisdiction.

To raise the technical level of Yangyi Commune's industrial enterprises, the County Government sent it six experienced workers on a long-term basis and thirty more for a short period. In addition to this, the county seat accepted a hundred commune members for short-term training.

As a result of all these measures and developments Yangyi Commune, starting in 1958 with one industry employing 102 workers and bringing in 4·2 per cent of the commune's annual income, by the summer of 1960 had seven industrial enterprises (including workshops and a mine) with 420 workers, bringing in 17 per cent of its income. By the end of the year, according to the commune plan, the figure was to reach 24 per cent.

TABLE 5: *Rate of Development of Commune Industry*

	Number of Enterprises	Number of Workers	Percentage of Commune Income
			%
1958	1	102	4·2
1959	4	310	12·3
1960	7	420	24·0 (planned)

While in the narrowest sense 'commune industry' in 1960 involved only seven enterprises employing 420 workers, taken in the broader sense it included brigade-run industries. This brought the total figures up to 54 enterprises employing 845 workers.

Brigade enterprises, like those owned by the commune, were directly geared to agriculture. The commonest were tool manufacture and repair works, farm chemicals plants, presses for extracting oil from local products (such as walnuts, cotton seeds, sesame and rape), brick and lime kilns for local construction.

Little Yetao Brigade was one of the most active in developing local industry. It had a grain processing plant with three electrically

138

powered mills run by eight workers. This handled all the grain required in the brigade and was able to take state orders for milling as well. In addition it had an electric fodder chopping plant, the first of its kind in the commune. These two electrically-powered operations alone saved the brigade thousands of man-hours.

TABLE 6: *Commune Industrial Enterprise*, *(1960)*

Level of Ownership	Number of Enterprises	Number of Workers
Commune	7	420
Brigade	47	425
Total	54	845

Little Yetao's tool shop was a centre for mechanical innovations. One group of young brigade members rigged up a two-car overhead cable railway from the pigsties at the foot of the Mount of Ten Thousand Treasures to the first series of terraced fields some 150 feet above. The weight of fresh earth loaded into the downward car brought up the other, loaded with manure from the pig-pens.

BACKGROUND OF LOCAL INDUSTRY

Some local industries had come into being quite recently; others had been started in the co-operative and mutual aid group periods. Only a few had a history going back to pre-land reform days, for the landlords and rich peasants had increased their wealth mainly by the closely-linked processes of usury, land-grabbing and grain speculation. Failing scope for this they would simply hoard silver dollars. Consequently landlord and rich peasant owned industry had been small and undeveloped.

In the immediate area of Yangyi there had been some lime-burning and brick and tile making, but this was only seasonal. A landlord or rich peasant wishing to have a new house or courtyard built, would set aside a site on his own land for brick-makers to dig clay and build a kiln. To cut overhead costs and make a profit the land-owner would contract for more bricks than he needed, the surplus being sold on the market. The brick and tile makers of the Yangyi area were known far and wide for their skill, some of them venturing as far as the north-eastern provinces (Manchuria) and to Mongolia in the north-west during the slack winter months.

Shortly before the land reform there was an advance in industry. This was brought about by the Communists as part of their struggle against the Japanese invaders. Here and there arsenals were set up,

139

such as that in the mountain caves of Lianggou. But more widespread were the cottage industries of spinning and weaving which were organized all over the Border Region to counter the Japanese economic blockade and make the region self-sufficient in cloth. These crafts, which had all but died out in the area before the arrival of the Communists, were so effectively restored during the late thirties and early forties, that they were able to meet the basic needs of the peasants for clothes and to supply the 8th Route Army with uniforms and quilts.

During the land reform what landlord and rich peasant industry there was, was protected by communist policy, which called for 'a sharp distinction . . . between the feudal exploitation practised by landlords and rich peasants, which must be abolished, and their industrial and commercial enterprises, which must be protected'.[2]

In the late forties, when the land reform was completed, handicraft industry took another step forward, with the post-land reform mutual aid groups taking it up. In Ten Mile Inn, for instance, in the winter of 1947–48, one mutual aid group ran a press for extracting oil from cotton seeds, walnuts, sesame, rape and other local crops. The press was a primitive and picturesque contraption, power being supplied by a man-propelled pendulum-like battering-ram consisting of a tree-trunk suspended horizontally from the ceiling. Another group ran a lime kiln, and still another, a plant for dyeing home-spun cloth with local vegetable dyes.

During the co-operative period of the early and middle fifties there was a growing emphasis on making improved farm tools. At the same time, with the rapid development of a modern textile industry in the sub-province capital of Handan, hand spinning and weaving, revived during the war against Japan, began to die out once again. The hard-wearing but coarse home-spun cloth which was once the village women's pride was displaced by machine-made products.

Then in 1958 came the Great Leap Forward and the mass movement for smelting iron and steel in makeshift furnaces. This was the time when Ten Mile Inn farmers who 'hardly knew what iron and steel looked like before', turned it out by the ton. What was done in Ten Mile Inn was equalled or surpassed elsewhere in the Yangyi area. The basis of the new commune industry was laid.

CURRENT INDUSTRIAL PROBLEMS

The most important industry in Yangyi was the making and repair of farm implements in both commune and brigade workshops. The bringing together of carpenters, blacksmiths and other craftsmen

[2] Mao Tse-tung, 'On the Policy Concerning Industry and Commerce' *Selected Works*, Vol. IV, F.L.P., Peking, 1961.

from various villages into the commune Farm Implement Manufacture and Repair Shop in Yangyi townlet, was a step towards rationalizing production and increasing its all-round efficiency. But certain individual craftsmen and small handicraft co-operatives had a good reputation locally and their trademark was a guarantee of quality. When these craftsmen joined the commune workshop, their trademarks were given up. Besides, with the larger-scale production of the new workshops the quality of their tools was not always up to that of the best which had been turned out by the older, smaller shops. The result was that some farmers would treasure an old tool and have it repaired again and again, rather than buy a new one without a well-known trademark. Besides, designs which were very popular with farmers in one locality did not always find favour in another. Even with a hoe there were small but significant differences in design which made one suitable for light, sandy soil, another for heavy clinging clay. So rationalizing production was not simply a matter of standardizing design. These were two of the problems which emerged with larger-scale production of traditional tools. They could be solved by improving management.

But farm implement workshops also had the task of helping commune farming to advance step by step to semi- and then full mechanization. This involved a second type of problem connected with innovations.

The Yangyi Farm Implement Manufacture and Repair Shop had a good record, as did a number of the brigade tool shops such as that in Little Yetao. Their innovations were usually the product of collaboration between worker and farmer. Even then, they still needed a trial period to bring to light flaws or the need for modification. However, farmers easily became impatient with an improved but unfamiliar and unperfected implement and would lay it aside, fearing that delays for adjustment would interfere with quota fulfilment. Thus an innovation might be rejected simply because the last step in the re-designing process had not been worked out. Little Yetao's newly-designed cable car for carrying manure, for example, had not yet been perfected in the summer of 1960, and had a tendency to tip over and strew the hillside with its cargo, so some of the brigade members maintained that it would be less wasteful and troublesome to carry the manure up on their backs as before.

Such problems as these were taken up when the nation-wide movement for innovations was summarized. It was then pointed out that new and improved tools should not be thrown aside because of initial shortcomings; they should be perfected step by step. Also, they should not immediately be put into large-scale production, but time should be allowed to test the tool and win the farmer's acceptance.

Another hazard with innovations was obsolescence. An individual or group of innovators might work hard and long devising some new gadget, only to have it superseded in a matter of months by something better. This was the case with the improved chaser mill. Four traditional chaser mills were ingeniously hitched up by a system of wheels and belts so that they could be worked all at once by one donkey. But soon after the new contraption had proved its worth, an electric mill was installed.

Industries other than tool-making faced other problems, above all, that of shortage of manpower. They therefore found it necessary to adjust themselves to the rhythm of agriculture. This meant many of them functioned only in the winter, or else closed down as soon as current needs had been met. Thus in August 1960, the only brigade industry operating in Ten Mile Inn was the Farm Implement Manufacture and Repair Shop. The oil press had already finished handling the local oil-bearing crops and the farm chemicals plant had met current needs. The brick and lime kilns had no orders since no building could be done until the winter. Labour was so urgently needed for field management that no one but the tool-makers could be spared for industry.

At the end of the first year or so of their existence, an estimate of commune industries was made by Vice-Premier Li Fu-chun who defined them as a 'starting-point for changing the poverty-stricken and backward face of China's vast countryside'.[3] He went on to sum up their advantages as follows:

1. Set up in the countryside they directly serve the needs of the farmers, who can see the advantages of such industries themselves; and relatively little money is needed to set them up. These factors help to call forth the farmers' initiative in accumulating funds for running industry.
2. They can easily make use of China's somewhat scattered local mineral and agricultural resources and gear production more closely to the specific needs of the local farmers.
3. They help carry out technical transformation in the countryside and raise labour productivity in agriculture.
4. They can make use of the old equipment of large and medium-sized enterprises that has been replaced, thus prolonging its life and saving public funds.
5. They can provide technical reserve forces for socialist industrialization and the modernization of agriculture.[4]

[3] Li Fu-chun, 'On the Big Leap Forward in China's Socialist Construction', reprinted in *Ten Glorious Years*, F.L.P., Peking, 1959.
[4] Ibid.

Chapter XIII

COMMUNE COMMERCE

'INCREASE PRODUCTION AND SERVE THE PEOPLE'

VILLAGE stores, which in land reform days sold little but salt, oil, tobacco and matches, in the summer of 1960 carried radio sets, sewing machines, alarm clocks and acetylene lamps. This, however, was far from revealing the scope of trade in the Yangyi area or its growth during the two years since the commune was set up.

With the slogan 'Increase production and serve the people', Yangyi's trade department at commune, district and brigade levels had been active in the battle against the drought. In Shidong district with its 8 brigades, the district trade centre sold, installed and maintained 120 bucket-chain pumps in 1960, as compared with only two in 1959. (These pumps were easy to handle, an old woman or teen-aged child being able to keep an eye on the blindfolded donkey turning the cogwheel which raised the endless chain of buckets. Without them a good proportion of the work force was kept busy doing nothing but watering the fields.) Even with these 120 new pumps, a good deal of water was still carried on shoulder-poles, of which the trade centre sold a couple of thousand in the first half of 1960. Among the disadvantages of this primitive method of water transport was the weight and cost of the big wooden buckets. To offset this, the Yangyi trade department started a pottery kiln to make light crocks. These were not as strong as the buckets but they were much cheaper and only about one-tenth the weight. This saved a good deal of labour and the crocks became very popular.

Another way in which the trade department served production was in acting as the link between farmers and the state processing plants. It collected unginned cotton from the brigades, for instance, and delivered it to the state ginning plant in Handan. There the seeds were extracted and returned to the brigades for processing in the brigade oil-pressing industries. Again, when canteens in Shidong district wanted to raise more vegetables, the trade centre secured seeds for them down in the plains (a special favourite being a peppery turnip); and when they produced a surplus of vegetables, the trade centre marketed it for them in a mining centre in the next county.

These activities had to do with 'increasing production'. 'Serving the people' consisted mainly of providing commune members with the consumer goods they needed. For this type of work the department slogan was 'Take the goods where the people are!' This meant opening new shops (the number increased from 52 in 1959 to 66 in 1960) and sending travelling salesmen with supplies loaded on to carrying-poles to out-of-the-way hamlets and even to set up shop in the fields.

A marked rise in purchasing power was evident throughout the commune. The shop on the Silver Sea Tract had a turnover of 100 *yuan* a day. In Shidong district the sale of consumer goods had risen from 200,000 *yuan* for the whole of 1959 to 190,000 *yuan* for the first seven months alone of 1960. The head of the district trade department said, 'Nowadays we're selling articles we'd never even heard of a couple of years ago. Even after the land reform when things started to get better, all people did at first was to put more cotton padding in their clothes; then they switched from home-spun to machine-made cloth. Now they're beginning to get factory-made clothing. Last year we sold nearly a thousand sets of machine-knit heavy cotton fleece jerseys and long pants. This year, just before the new year festival, we sold 4,000-odd sets in a few days.'

It was the same with footwear. Rubber-soled canvas shoes, hardly known in the area a year before, were now in great demand. This followed a similar spurt in the popularity of rubber boots a few years earlier.

People had more money to spend than ever before.[1]

This was reflected in banking, loans to individuals being down and savings up. In 1958, commune members had borrowed 230,000 *yuan*; in 1959 the figure had dropped to 140,000 *yuan*; while in the first half of 1960 it was only 40,000 *yuan*, a drop of 122 per cent over the corresponding period in 1959.

Savings, on the other hand, were mounting. In 1958, 7,000-odd households made deposits amounting to 740,000 *yuan* in round figures; in 1959, 8,600 households deposited 820,000 *yuan*. For the first half of 1960, savings deposits came to 440,000 *yuan*.

BACKGROUND OF RURAL TRADE AND TRADERS

Typical of trade in the Yangyi area before land reform was that of Ten Mile Inn. There the biggest trader was a rich peasant named Fu Pei-yin, whose capital was borrowed from landlord kinsmen. His shop displayed salt, matches and oil, but his main business was in heroin and money, lent at a rate of 100 per cent for every 20 days. The money-lending and drug traffic were closely connected, addicts

---

[1] This rise in purchasing power in the countryside was the continuation of a trend. National figures showed that in 1957 purchasing power had risen by more than 50 per cent compared with 1952, and more than 10 per cent compared with 1955. See Teng Tse-hui, 'The Socialist Transformation of Agriculture in China', in *Ten Glorious Years*, F.L.P., Peking, 1959.

TABLE 7: *An investigation made in 1959 into the clothing of four sample families of Little Yetao Brigade*

	Home Made			Store Bought			
	Quilts	Un-lined	Clothes Lined or padded	Fleece pants or shirt	Vests (cotton knitted)	Wool jerseys	Rain-capes
Li Mao-ling 3 members (2 working)	3	12	6	6	2	0	0
Ren Wan-he 3 members (2 working)	4	19	4	8	4	1	1
Ren Nan-kan 7 members (1 working)	3	16	2	8	0	0	0
Liu Ji-fu 5 members (3 working)	6	16	10	10	4	1	2
Total 18 people (8 working)	16	62	22	32	10	2	3
Average per person	0·88	3·44	1·22	1·77	0·5		

being encouraged to take goods on credit, provided they offered land as security. Fu was able to collect his interest or make his foreclosures by using his office as ward head, which gave him command of a force of armed toughs and influence with the Kuomintang courts and government machinery. The feudal trader Fu Pei-yin was one of the most hated men in the village.[2]

In this same period non-feudal trade also existed. This was capitalist in nature. Though by no means free from profiteering, hoarding, speculation, adulteration and such practices, it was not characterized, as feudal trade had been, by the tight combination of usury, force and officialdom. This capitalist trade, even when conducted by landlords and rich peasants, was protected by Communist policy throughout the land reform period and later.

In the late thirties and in the forties, supply, marketing and credit co-operatives were set up in the Yangyi area. Their aims were

[2] For further details on Fu Pei-yin, see Chapter XVI, p. 189. Also, *Revolution in a Chinese Village*.

to bolster the struggle against the Japanese by increasing production; and to improve the lot of the people by making available such necessities as salt, oil, matches and, above all, cloth.

The local communist-led government did propaganda for the new co-operatives and gave them all-round support. To secure salt for them it organized daring bands of armed smugglers to steal or break through the enemy blockade at night. To increase the supply of cloth it first launched a drive to increase the output of cotton by freeing cotton fields from tax, and by buying the crop at a fair price. These measures greatly increased the supply of cotton, which was issued to the village co-operatives. These in turn advanced it to the peasants for spinning and weaving, a good price again being paid by the government for yarn and cloth.

Later in the forties, when mutual aid groups were formed, another type of co-operative commerce developed—the 'trade-and-transport expedition'.[3] For such undertakings long lines of pole-carriers or caravans of donkeys and mules were organized. This was done mainly during the slack season, but it was made possible largely through the saving of man and animal labour brought about by mutual aid. Capital for these ventures was advanced by the co-operatives' credit departments.

Co-operative enterprise of various types made headway—but not without a struggle. Overcoming the peasants' initial doubts, raising capital, mastering management and accounting were part of the problem. So was competition with private trade and private trade mentality.

In Ten Mile Inn, for instance, before land reform the rich peasant drug-trader-usurer and ward-head, Fu Pei-yin, became a major shareholder in the consumers' co-operative. And in 1947 Fu Xin, formerly a landlord with a cloth shop in Yangyi, was made manager of the village co-operative store because of his business ability. Fu Xin ran the co-operative as he had run his own shop—strictly on the principle that business is business. He approved loans only to the better-off middle peasants, who had business experience and were 'good risks', not to the poor peasants who most needed money for tools, seed and animals to promote production on their under-capitalized farms. Before long he had changed th co-operative from an enterprise 'serving production and the people' into a profitable joint-stock company. He was replaced in one of the land reform campaigns. His successors, themselves poor peasants, carried out the policy of increasing production by giving loans to those who had been forced into semi-unemployment by lack of capital. But having no experience in accounting or business management they ran the co-operative into near bankruptcy.

The root of such difficulties in village co-operative stores lay not

[3] See p. 7 f.n.

24. The Ten Mile Inn pond, built during the great leap forward of 1958.

25. Yangyi firework makers with their anti-hail rockets.

26. An imaginative view of the period from 1960-69. Commune industrialization, the "chemicalization", mechanization and electrification of agriculture, all-round water conservancy and irrigation, advancing at the speed of rockets.

only in lack of experienced personnel but also in shortage of capital. So in 1949 all such stores in the county were federated and placed under county leadership. In this way their needs for capital could be more easily dealt with.

Credit and marketing co-operatives held key positions in the struggle between the two roads; for with the polarization of classes following the land reform, they could help keep poor peasants out of the clutches of those with a surplus, who were eager to lend money or buy land. An effort was therefore made to enlist and train good socialist cadres in the field of rural trade.

One of those enlisted at this time was Wang Xi-tang, a popular township cadre who came from Ten Mile Inn. As a youngster Wang Xi-tang had seen his father, a skilled peasant tilewright, driven by misery into taking heroin. Wang Xi-tang like his father was both a farmer and a craftsman. When the Communists came to Ten Mile Inn he set his heart on becoming a Labour Hero. But before realizing this ambition he was swept into the struggle first against the Japanese, then against the landlords.

He was soon chosen chairman of the peasant association of Ten Mile Inn. As such his life was in constant danger. For long periods during the forties he dared not sleep at home for fear of assassination and spent his nights in mountain caves.

It was at this time that he joined the Communist Party. 'Back in those days,' he said, 'I knew little about communism, but I did understand the need to drive the invaders from our country. And it was the Party that was leading the struggle against the Japanese. Besides, at that time, with death hanging over me I had the idea, "If I die as an ordinary person that's the end of me; but if I die as a Communist, I go on living in the Party." '

In 1943, in the the first democratic elections ever held in Ten Mile Inn he was chosen village head. In 1948 he was elected head of his township. With the co-ordination of trading co-operatives under the county government in 1949, he was transferred to work in trade. His first job was in Ten Mile Inn's consumer and marketing co-operative (which had suffered from mismanagement, first by a competent but private-profit motivated director, then by public-spirited but unbusiness-like leaders). Wang Xi-tang, combining competence with public spirit managed to set things right and was then put in charge of several village co-operatives. Under his leadership and with increased working capital these too were soon running well.

Wang Xi-tang continued to lead them during the transition from semi-socialist to socialist farming co-operatives. This was a crucial period ending in a decisive victory for socialism on the economic front. It was won not only in farming but also in trade (the main basis for which lay in the countryside) and included the transformation of rural capitalist trade and traders.

Yangyi Commune's Many-sidedness

Until 1955 a number of fair-sized privately-owned shops had been carrying on business in the Yangyi area, mostly in Yangyi townlet itself. These were capitalist enterprises not engaging in feudal types of exploitation. In 1956, in accordance with the policy of the 'peaceful socialist transformation of capitalist enterprises', these became 'joint state-private' undertakings. That is to say, the state bought a controlling interest of the shares. On the shares remaining in his hands, each 'capitalist' drew interest at the rate of 5 per cent per annum for a period of seven years (later extended to ten years) and received pay for his work. But he no longer ran the shop. This was done by a management committee which included, besides himself, employees and representatives of the county (later commune) trade department.

When the commune was set up, co-operatives and joint state-private stores were placed under its department of trade and industry. By the summer of 1960 this had 66 shops with a staff of 149. Only two interest-drawing capitalists now remained in Yangyi, purveying traditional funeral robes and Marxist pamphlets with equal enthusiasm. As the total value of privately-owned shares was just under 16,000 *yuan*, they drew rather less than 800 *yuan* a year in interest. This sum represented the dwindling remnant of direct exploitation in Yangyi commune.

SOME PROBLEMS OF COMMUNE COMMERCE

In public trade organizations the profit motive had given way to that of 'increasing production'; the principle of the 'sound business risk' had been supplanted by that of 'serving the people'. But there were still individual commune members engaged in trade for their private profit. Villages situated on the highway had long gone in for carting as a side-occupation. Some brigade members had business and carting experience going back to the pre-land reform trade-and-transport expeditions. Now, to individuals such as these, the brigade might turn over a cart and animal to use as he pleased, so long as he handed 90 *yuan* a month to the brigade. Technically this carting was a service trade which played an important part in commune economy by handling short-haul transport. It paid the carters well, some of them taking in 150 *yuan* or so a month. This gave them an income far higher than that of the ordinary field hand.

Some commune members, too, engaged in peddling. In 1959 (after the ownership of private allotments had been sanctioned by the April check-up), at the height of the fruit and vegetable season, as many as a hundred farmers might be seen peddling their home-grown produce in the streets of Yangyi townlet.

Peddling was not illegal, provided the pedlars abided by government regulations (covering what and where they might sell and the

148

Commune Commerce

prices they could charge). Supervision of this private trading fell to the commune trade department. Its investigations revealed that some peddling was going on which was clearly speculative. In Ten Mile Inn, for instance, there was a former middle peasant named Wang Shao-yu (who had been dismissed from his post as head of the united front anti-Japanese village government in 1944 for being involved in graft). Fifteen years later he was buying up commodities at above their fixed price and re-selling them still higher—until investigators from the commune trade section exposed him. 'There may be an average of one of these speculators in each of the commune's larger villages, that is those of 400 families or more,' said Party Secretary Jin.[4]

The commune leaders were not happy about even the legal types of private trade which they regarded as survivals from the bad old days. 'You can't exactly call it exploitation,' one of them said of the carting, 'but it's not a proper way of doing things.' As to the pedlars, whose labour was urgently needed in farm work, the full-time ones, who sold handicraft and small manufactured goods, were prevailed on to work for wages in the commune supply department (whose personnel went up from 122 to 149); the others, who sold produce from their own allotments, were urged not to allow peddling to interfere with their work in the fields. By the summer of 1960 peddling had all but disappeared.

The question of whether private trading should be permitted or not was being widely debated throughout the country. In 1956, the Central Committee had called for consolidation of the system of co-operation 'while continuing to combat the spontaneous development of capitalism in the countryside'.[5] At the same time 'every positive factor' for the building of socialism was to be 'mobilized'. The question was how to classify operations such as those of the Yangyi carters and pedlars? Were they 'a positive factor' or a 'spontaneous development of capitalism'?

The conclusion reached in the broad debate was that individual trading carried on in the context of a socialist market and carefully supervised by the state, would serve socialism, just as within a capitalist market, it served capitalism. A lively local market would encourage the commune members to grow on their private allotments a variety of crops, which had not been included in the state plan owing to the concentration on staples. It would also encourage household handicrafts. And while providing a greater variety of daily necessities it would raise household incomes.

Encouraging but supervising a market for private trade to serve and supplement the socialist market involved new problems. In the

[4] See Chapter XVII, p. 217.
[5] National Program for Agricultural Development, 1956–67, F.L.P., Peking, 1960, p.3.

149

past village fairs, held at frequent and regular intervals, had been an important part of rural economy. They had served to gather together the marketable surpluses of scattered private households in the form of a free market. With the collectivizing of farming these fairs had been discontinued with a consequent loss in cottage industry and private allotment production as well as in convenience to the customer. Now in various parts of the country, they were being revived and made to serve the socialist market.

The advantages of the fairs were summed up in an article in the *People's Daily*[6] under the following eight headings:

1. Under the leadership of local state trade departments they set free trade in motion and thus liven up rural economy.
2. They spur on communes, brigades and individual commune members to adjust their own supplies. This helps raise their standard of living.
3. They also spur on communes, brigades and individual commune members to go in for a variety of economic activities, such as raising barnyard animals and poultry, carrying on cottage industries, etc.
4. They are an excellent way of combining business and pleasure, affording an opportunity not only to buy and sell things but to eat out and see entertainments, to feel free and easy and have a real holiday.
5. They are not just a market but a place for publicizing policy and current affairs, for cultural activities such as singing and dancing and generally enriching the life of the people.
6. They increase the income of commune members and raise their standard of living.
7. They tighten the links between agriculture and trade and help state purchase and supply by solving the problem of short distance transport (through saving manpower and transport equipment) and shortening transport lines.
8. They provide material conditions for stabilizing the supply of small commodities.

In brief, private trading of this type, so long as it was carefully supervised by the state, helped strengthen the socialist economy. Thus, in the transition period between new democracy and socialism, the private profit motive could still play a useful part in stimulating short-distance transport and getting a variety of subsidiary products to the consumer.

Two of the main problems facing commune commerce, therefore, were controlled use of the private profit motive and vigorous application of the socialist principle of 'increasing production and serving the people'.

---

[6] Song Lin, 'Promote Trade Fairs and Liven Up Rural Economy', *People's Daily*, 18 January, 1961.

Chapter XIV

SOCIAL SERVICES

BY the summer of 1960 Yangyi Commune had a network of social services consisting of:

315 community dining-rooms (each work team having at least one);
37 sewing centres (each brigade having at least one);
136 nurseries attended by 1,600 babies or toddlers (78 per cent of this age group);
37 kindergartens attended by 1,300 children (81 per cent of this age group), each brigade having at least one;
4 old folks' homes with 91 residents;
7 maternity homes.

These services were estimated to have freed 5,000 of the commune's women from the greater part of their housework.[1] This opened up opportunities both for easing the commune's acute shortage of labour and for enabling women to become full-fledged citizens.[2]

COMMUNITY DINING-ROOMS

The key to the freeing of women from housework, to their taking part in productive employment and public life, was the community dining-room. In Bailin, for example, there were 1,445 households. Previously this had meant 1,445 cooks. These could put in at the most half a day's work in the fields. Now Bailin had 27 canteens—with a total of 81 cooks. The estimated saving in labour was 400,000 days in the course of one year alone.

Such importance was attached to running the dining-rooms well that they were ranked as second in importance to farming itself. Commune and brigade Party secretaries were made responsible for their success, by 'putting politics in command' and 'going into the kitchen'.

The commune had introduced community dining-rooms into the villages and the rectification had succeeded in re-establishing them in those brigades where they had been closed down. Now, in the summer of 1960, the Communist Party called for a great effort to

---

[1] In the commune's 24 brigades there were 6,723 women between sixteen and forty-five.
[2] For more on women's emancipation see Chapter XIX.

get them functioning smoothly so that their advantages would become clear to all. This called for efficient organization, skilful cooking and good leadership.

The staff of a community dining-room or canteen was elected by the work team running it, from among its own members.

In addition there was a canteen committee consisting of the head of the team, the head cook and one or two elected members. The task of the committee members was to obtain the team members' views about the food and the general running of the canteen. Finally there was the Brigade Welfare Committee, made up of the brigade Party Branch Secretary, the brigade head and elected members. This committee, though concerned with all aspects of welfare, made the success of the canteens its chief concern. It paid special attention to finding out which canteens were managed well and might have some experience worth passing on to others; and also which were in difficulties and needed help.

Ten Mile Inn's Work Team Three had two canteens. The first had been going scarcely a fortnight when two households withdrew. One consisted simply of Sun Xu-de, an old woman living on her own, who found it inconvenient to walk to the dining-room on her small bound feet. The other was a young couple with one small child. They thought that the canteen cooking was not up to their own home standards.

After losing two households in such short order the canteen staff talked things over. There was no old folks' home in Ten Mile Inn, as yet, and there were a number of old people in the team who, they concluded, must be feeling much the same way as Sun Xu-de, even though they had said nothing about withdrawing. So the canteen committee set up a meals delivery service for older people. The second withdrawal cast a reflection on the canteen's cooking. The cooks did in fact find it hard to cook for 78 people, especially just before the reaping of the winter wheat in late May or early June, when grain supplies were at their lowest and the choice of cereals limited. The mainstay was dried sweet potatoes. Day in and day out these had to be served as the main dish for at least one of the meals. But sweet potatoes were a crop fairly new to the area (they had been introduced only seven years before) and no one knew much about how to make the dried chips palatable. So every day the cooks just soaked and steamed them. People grumbled. And it was not long before the complaints reached the ears of the head cook, Wang Guei-ling.

(Wang Guei-ling, now twenty-nine, having been orphaned at an early age, had grown up self-reliant and willing to tackle anything. He was a member of the Communist Party and though he had been away working on the railway when the team decided to set up the canteen again, he had been elected head cook by acclaim.)

Now, faced with these complaints, Wang Guei-ling turned to a *Sweet Potato Cookery Book* which was being recommended to canteens. He found seven of its twelve recipes suited to local tastes. By milling the dried chips into flour, the book showed, several new dishes could be made. These included sweet potato cakes, sweet potato noodles (containing a fifth part of wheat flour), sweet potato dumplings. Then, together with the canteen committee, the cooks worked out a menu for a whole week, during which the same sweet potato dish never came up twice. This menu was posted on the dining-room wall beneath a large poster which announced:

> Seven new dishes
> All different
> All better
> Than steamed sweet potatoes!

This variety, together with the feeling of anticipation aroused by the weekly menu raised the diners' spirits.

Head cook Wang Guei-ling was not satisfied with this success. He even set about improving dishes over which there were no complaints. Corn cakes, for instance, were a traditional food and no one complained about having them every day, even though, cooked in the local fashion, they were heavy. Wang Guei-ling took to using soda, and made the lightest corn cakes ever tasted in Ten Mile Inn. Then he tried mixing a little sweet potato flour with the corn meal to make the cakes sweeter and softer. Soon the members of Work Team Three began to boast that their corn cakes were even better than steamed wheat bread—which was high praise indeed.

The skilful and varied cooking of staple cereals was one secret of the canteen's success; the variety of vegetables served was another. At the time of the commune check-up in April 1959, 5 per cent of the brigade's farmland had been given to the individual households for use as private allotments. But when the canteen was set up a number of the families had insisted on giving it their plots, saying: 'We'll be busy working for the team. Why should we waste time pottering about on little plots of our own? You take them over and run them as canteen kitchen gardens. Then you can give us back the vegetables cooked, together, with our cereal, in the canteen.' (Until this time staple cereals were cooked in the canteens and eaten with relishes or vegetable dishes brought from home.)

Wang Guei-ling and the rest of the canteen staff took this as a challenge. They decided that those who had given up their plots should not regret it; and that their vegetables should be so well cooked that the other team members would want to give up their plots too. The success of this scheme demanded good cooking and sound psychology. The vegetables, freshly picked in the canteen kitchen-garden, were never cooked until the diners were on hand.

Then, with fragrant herbs and seasoning they were tossed into a sizzling pan. This was calculated to fill the dining-room with an aroma which was hard to resist. Any doubts that remained were removed by the knowledge that the oil and seasoning were provided free by the canteen. One by one the allotments were given up, till all the team's plots were pooled. They were tended by a woman and two old men who by August 1960 had seven different kinds of vegetables ready for the canteen table.[3]

Not all the improvements were to do with cooking. Accounts were entered every day and posted up at the end of the month. This was a matter of the utmost concern to the work team members, each of whom had his individual monthly allocation of grain, part of which, following the April check-up was free.[4] A member consuming less than his share in the canteen took home the balance in cash or grain, as he wished. The prompt and clear statement of individual particulars regarding this and of such items as the cost of wages, fuel, oil, seasoning, etc., gave considerable satisfaction.

Following their success with the seven kinds of sweet potato dishes the canteen staff went on, in the summer of 1960, to offer two complete menus each day: a 'soft' one for the old folk and children and a 'solid' one for the rest. The 'soft' menu featured such food as wheat or maize flour dumplings, with finely minced filling, and soups of whatever vegetables were available in the canteen kitchen gardens. The 'solid' menu provided substantial food better suited to the more stalwart, such as wheat or maize buns and vegetable dishes. This dual menu inspired a work team rhymster to comment that after eating in the community dining-room:

> The youngsters feel they can aim sky high,
> And the old 'uns feel that they'll never die

A sign of success was a demand for the merging of the two canteens of Work Team Three, under Wang Guei-ling.

Not all the Ten Mile Inn canteen cooks were as enterprising as Wang Guei-ling. Wang Yau-he, head cook of Team Two's canteen, was a member of the Communist Youth League, but the diners were far from satisfied either with his cooking or with the general management of their canteen. The Brigade Welfare Committee had a talk with Wang Yau-he and suggested, among other things, that he should pay more attention to his accounts. 'Why? I've never taken so much as one penny from the canteen supplies,' the young man flared up. 'Every grain of millet and every speck of flour has been eaten by the team members.' When the Welfare Committee suggested the posting of a weekly menu, he countered: 'That would be a waste of time.

[3] This transfer of all private allotments was contrary to policy, for preserving a margin of household production was valuable.
[4] See Chapter III, 'Tempering the Winds of Communism'.

Social Services

I cook whatever we've got. If there's wheat we have wheat. And if there's maize we have maize. No matter how many menus you stick up, you can't change that.'

Since Wang Yau-he was a Youth League member the Brigade Welfare Committee asked the League to give him some 'socialist education'—in other words to help him see his job as a cook as one of importance to the whole team and directly affecting its output. All this was pointed out to Wang Yau-he at a special meeting of the Youth League Branch.[5] And it was followed by definite instructions: 'No more steamed sweet potatoes—starting from tomorrow.'

Next day the diners, to their surprise, were served sweet potato cakes; and the day after that sweet potato balls. These were followed by sweet potato dumplings and other novelties learned from the cooks of Work Team Three. This gave rise to the quip: 'Socialist education is a great thing. Without it we'd never have found out how many good dishes you can make from dried sweet potatoes!'

Helping the kitchen staff look on their duties with socialist eyes was one aspect of 'putting politics in command'.

In one of the work teams where two canteens had merged, one of the cooks had a soft spot for the members of his original canteen; so he gave them larger helpings. Those who had come from the other canteen complained to the committee. The matter was investigated and the offending cook was given a lecture on the evils of 'localism'.

In another team there were complaints that the cooks were spoiling good food. The dumplings, usually a popular dish, were too stodgy. 'The dough's heavy and the filling's tasteless' was the general opinion. The canteen committee failing to give the diners satisfaction, the complaints found their way up to the Welfare Committee, headed by Brigade Party Secretary, Wang Mi-shan. So Wang Mi-shan, putting politics in command, went into the kitchen and became one of the canteen cooks. After working for a while he came to the conclusion that what these cooks lacked was not skill but enthusiasm, because they looked down on their job. He talked things over with them. Why did Wang Guei-ling of Team Three do such a good job, he asked? Partly because he wasn't ashamed of being a cook; he was proud of it. Some people weren't, because in the old class society cooks and others in the service trades were despised. But those days were past. One had to see one's job as 'noble work in the service of the people',[6] and link it with building a communist society.

Perhaps more than this explanation, the fact that the most respected person in the village, the Party Secretary, was not above working in the kitchen, increased the cooks' enthusiasm.

In the spring of 1960, by which time 18 work team dining-rooms had been merged into 13, 4 (including Wang Guei-ling's) were con-

[5] See Chapter XX for the Youth League's handling of this case.
[6] 'Resolution on Some Questions Concerning Communes', Part V.

155

sidered first-rate, 4 satisfactory, and 5 (including Wang Yau-he's) poor. By the summer, as a result of the Brigade Welfare Committee's attention and of 'putting politics in command' and Party Secretaries 'going into the kitchen', the number of first-rate canteens had risen to 8 and the remaining 5 were considered satisfactory. There were no poor canteens left in Ten Mile Inn.

Some of the work teams had ambitious plans. Wang Guei-ling's Team Three intended to put up a new building as soon as the busy season was over. This was to serve in the first place as a dining-room but ultimately as a work team community centre with a bath-house, club and spare-time school. Meanwhile building materials were accumulating, some bought, some contributed by team members.

Although none of the Ten Mile Inn work dining-rooms were yet housed in special buildings, all of them already served as community centres to some extent.

'We do three things in the community dining-rooms now,' said Branch Secretary Wang Mi-shan, 'eat, meet and read. And there's generally a "praise corner", too, where notices about especially good work are posted up.' Meetings were of various kinds. Besides those concerning the canteen itself there were regular discussions of the team's work. Current affairs were also taken up, each dining-room having a loud speaker which might be tuned in to national, provincial or county networks. The evening meal was now and then followed by some informal entertainment, ranging from the latest songs the children had learnt at school to a newly-composed patter on current brigade affairs. Several evenings a week the dining-room became a classroom for adult education.

In Yangyi Commune as a whole there were variations from one brigade to another, but the general picture was: the canteens had been in existence for several months and this in itself was an advance in village housekeeping. The experience of Ten Mile Inn's Work Team Three showed that canteens could be successful provided they were reasonably run and conditions were not unfavourable. In this particular case, the village being a compact one and the team members all living together in one part of it, no one had to walk more than a few doors to get to the dining-room. Secondly, the cooking was good and the menu varied. Thirdly, the accounts were detailed, business-like and public. Fourthly, the prospect of a work team club—a community centre with a dining-room, bath-house, reading-room and other facilities—aroused the enthusiasm of the members.

*   *   *

Despite these successes a fundamental problem remained—though in the summer of 1960 it was not yet apparent. The work team as yet hardly had the resources to support such a social service. A community dining-room involved considerable expense which did not arise in household cooking. First there was the pay of the staff. To make a success of cooking for so many people a staff of able-bodied men had been chosen. The work was skilled and the hours were long. Some had to get up at three in the morning to light the fires and steam the maize cakes for breakfast. Such men could not be paid less than good field hands. Besides these, there were those who tended the canteen kitchen-garden and the old women who now and then put in a few hours' work cleaning the chopping vegetables and doing other odd jobs for the cooks. Apart from all this there were accounting and management. These were also skilled jobs, though when cooking was done at home people hardly gave them a thought; they were just the unpaid work of the housewife. Secondly there was the fuel. This too was an item that rarely entered a household budget, for after school the children scoured the hillsides for brushwood. The big canteen stoves, however, needed coal, and this had to be bought, and transported by work team carts and animals.

The cost of wages and fuel, which nobody in the village had had to face before, had now to be borne by the work team. This took a sizable slice out of the funds for distribution to work team members.

These two were the main problems, but there were others. In the Yangyi area, as in the whole of North China, household cooking was done on a little stove in the front of the *kang*; and the flue from this stove, passing under the brick bed, heated it and the whole house. Even if cooking was done at the community dining-room, in winter these stoves would still have to be lit for space-heating and brushwood would have to be gathered as before.

This was not all. For some families the canteen service was well worth their contribution (as work team members) to its running costs. These were the ones where the women released from cooking proved to be good field workers and earned work points. Those families in which the cooking had previously been done by an old woman or a young girl, however, earned little or no extra income to offset their share of the canteen's expenses.

Certain canteens were run in such a way as to keep these problems in check. In Bailin, for instance, some of them went in for sidelines, such as growing vegetables, raising pigs and poultry, making bean-curd and condiments. These not only met their own needs; sale of the surplus brought in cash which went towards covering running costs. But this meant developing an extra branch of work team economy for which only the best run teams could spare the labour.

Another serious matter was the transfer of some of the work teams' best hands from field to kitchen and to the transport of coal. Efforts were made to keep this down to a minimum by raising canteen labour efficiency. Cooks devised methods of bringing running water into the kitchen, for in many canteens water-carrying alone took the full-time work of one or more members of the staff; they invented vegetable-choppers powered by bicycle pedals and constructed noodle-making machines (which had long been in use in the cities). Thus a minor technical revolution was taking place in the canteens of the more advanced brigades. To speed it up the county government called for a number of 'innovations', from running water to mechanical milling. Even with these, mechanization was still too limited in scope and at too early a stage to offset the loss of labour from production.

The new use of coal by community dining-rooms presented a problem not only of transport but of the supply of coal itself, the local mines being suddenly faced with a demand from all the ten to twenty canteens in every brigade in the area. While rapidly increasing output to meet the growing demands of industry, they could hardly keep pace with this suddenly added demand for domestic use.

A problem of a different nature was setting canteen sights too high. Persuading all team members to eat in the community dining-room or to hand over their allotments to it were cases in point. The first drew in the families where the cooking had been done by women too old or girls too young to join the team's work force, and saddled them with a share of the canteen's cost without benefitting them or the team. The second prevented men too old for regular work in the fields from raising crops on allotments and thereby from adding to both the family income and the variety of produce on the market. In an era of such acute labour shortage, due to the still low level of mechanization, work teams could ill afford to dispense with the work of their older or younger members. This marginal labour force still had a contribution to make. Leaving it idle meant a loss to the economy, social and individual.

The ramifications of the revolution in household arrangements proved to be broad and complex. Valuable experience was gained in 1960, but the solution had still to be worked out.[7]

SEWING CENTRES

Another means of decreasing household duties by collectivizing (and mechanizing) them were the Sewing Centres.

The villages of Yangyi Commune, still hardly a decade from the era of homespun cloth, were only just entering the age of store-bought clothes. With the rise in purchasing power following the bumper yields of 1958 and the setting up of the commune, people started buying ready-made garments. This was when knitted vests and long fleecy pants and sweaters became popular. But most clothes, especially outer garments, were still made at home, as were cotton-

---

[7] In the winter of 1960–61 the canteens were closed once again. With the natural calamities of those years the revolution in housework had to mark time.

padded mattresses and quilts. Even shoes, with cloth uppers and thick, hemp-stitched soles were made at home. All this meant hours of handwork, the cost of sewing-machines being beyond private means. The liberation of housewives demanded that these tasks be put on a social basis.

Sewing centres were the easiest of all the services to set up, and every brigade in Yangyi had its centre. Bailin, the brigade most advanced in social services, had three employing altogether fifteen people and equipped with twelve sewing-machines. Set up at the same time as the commune, within six months they had turned out 1,896 suits of clothes and made 868 pairs of cloth shoes. By the summer of 1960 the Ten Mile Inn Sewing Centre, with its six machines, was making clothes for 65 per cent of the villagers. Though often described as a special boon to bachelors, the sewing-room was less conspicuous for the men's garments than for the green trousers, gay jackets and flowered blouses of the girls, who now that they worked in the fields had money of their own to spend on clothes.

THE TEN MILE INN KINDERGARTEN

Child and baby-minding was the third field in which social services were needed to relieve the housewife. Bailin and Yangyi both had model kindergartens. Ten Mile Inn's was more representative. It was set up in September 1959. A pleasant, sunny courtyard was allocated and two elderly women were persuaded to take charge. The only thing lacking was the children. This deficiency was not easy to make up, many mothers being beset by doubts.

The Party and Youth League branches called meetings of their members to discuss the importance of kindergartens in freeing women for productive employment and to urge them to set an example. So the Communists and Youth Leaguers were the first to agree to send their children. As an attraction a kindergarten canteen was to be set up which would provide the children with better food than that served in the work team canteens. At last enough children were enrolled. But the kindergarten was not a success. Its only goal (other than feeding the children well) was to keep them out of mischief and danger. The children found this boring and many ran away to play. The elderly matrons could not desert the children who remained, so they made no attempt to look for those who had run off. In any case, having bound feet, they had little chance of catching the truants. Those mothers who had parted with their children reluctantly had consoled themselves that at least they would know where the youngsters were. Actually, not even this could be counted on. Some parents took their children home again.

When it was clear that under these circumstances the kinder-

159

garten would collapse, the brigade leadership took matters in hand. First they checked on policy and found that kindergartens should aim not merely at collective care of children so that their mothers could be free to work, but at teaching useful and interesting things.[8] Then they went to see model kindergartens in Bailin.

Bailin had long experience in this field, Guo Heng-de having organized nurseries and kindergartens back in the co-operative stage. But these had been small and temporary, for rush seasons only. With the commune they were expanded and made permanent, while standards of hygiene and education were raised. Now in this one brigade alone there were 27 nurseries and kindergartens taking in 93 per cent of the village children of pre-school age. All the children wore gay pinafores and the toddlers 'never went around in wet pants'. The kindergarten children had learnt 30 written characters and the new romanized alphabet. They could sing songs from local operas, recite ballads to their own castanet accompaniment and dance.

Their visit to Bailin convinced the Ten Mile Inn brigade leaders that what was needed was a competent kindergarten teacher. So they sent off twenty-year-old Wang Chung-ai for a special course of training by the Women's Federation in Handan, the regional capital. There she learned something of hygiene and dietetics, obtained the city style pattern for boys' and girls' clothes and learnt a number of games, songs and dances. Then she returned to Ten Mile Inn to take charge of the kindergarten. She soon found that health, hygiene, diet, songs, dances and general education were more than she alone could cope with. And the two older women were incapable of helping her carry out a program of this type. So she asked for and was given two assistants of her own age.

Gradually, as the team of three young women got into its stride, things began to improve.

There was no equipment to speak of, but simply lining up, numbering off and marching out to the threshing-floor, all to blasts on a whistle, appealed to the children. Songs, dances and recitations were taught as well as handicraft with simple local material such as clay, straw and paper. What did most to win popularity for the kindergarten was the teaching of the new romanized alphabet. The gaily coloured clothes made of flowered prints, too, gave prestige to the kindergarten children and their parents. Gradually enrolment rose, though attendance fluctuated from day to day.

---

[8] 'Nurseries and kindergartens should be run well, so that every child in them has better living conditions and education than at home and so that the parents want to put them there and the children want to stay there. The parents may decide whether their children should board or not and may take them home at any time. In order to run nurseries and kindergartens well, the communes should train a large number of qualified child-care workers and teachers.' 'Resolution on Some Questions Concerning the People's Communes', December 1958.

Social Services

One of the main problems facing Ten Mile Inn's kindergarten was health and hygiene, for with such a concentration of children, infections could spread rapidly and a much higher standard of hygiene had to be maintained than in the village as a whole. But whatever the difficulties still facing the young staff, the key problems had been solved. The kindergarten had become recognized as a part of brigade life. Now, instead of reluctance there was a waiting list of sixty and the brigade cadres criticized themselves for inadequate planning and for 'underestimating the masses' demand for the new' once its advantages were made clear to them.

While the four- to six-year-olds were taken care of by the brigade kindergarten, arrangements for infants and toddlers were left in the hands of the work teams. This meant improving and adapting a system of mutual aid or labour-exchange in baby-sitting, introduced during the anti-Japanese production drives of the early forties.[9] The baby-sitters were now paid by the mothers, in work points, which the mothers earned in the fields.

SOCIAL SECURITY AND THE BAILIN OLD FOLKS' HOME

While canteens, sewing centres and kindergartens aimed at lightening women's household tasks and freeing them for productive employment, another social service was for the purpose of providing security. This was the old folks' home, officially called 'Home of Respect for the Aged'.

In the past, a peasant's only security in old age had rested with his family. But the old poor peasant, whose family had always been on the brink of beggary, could not count on support even there. Once bereft of children, and himself incapable of toil, he could only beg or starve to death. Rather than this, some old poor peasants put an end to their own lives.

With the setting up of democratic village government in the forties, some relief was given. For old folk whose sons were in the army or had died at the front, a rear service corps was organized in all Liberated Area villages, to plough, mill, cut brushwood and carry water. In the early forties, the care of widows, orphans and the destitute was gradually taken over by the farming co-operatives. As the co-operative movement developed and took in entire villages, the system known as the Five Guarantees arose.[10]

After the organization of the commune, some of the more prosperous and enterprising brigades set up old folks' homes. In Yangyi

---

[9] Kindergartens and nurseries in Yangyi Commune (except for one or two in Bailin) did not take boarders; but most of them had kitchens for serving the children specially prepared food. For this they received a bigger proportion of fine grain (wheat) than the ordinary work-team dining-rooms.
[10] See Chapter I, p. 13.

161

Commune there were four. One of these was a special home for support of the aged parents or orphaned children of those who had given their lives in the revolutionary struggles. This home, which was in Yangyi townlet, was only partly maintained by the commune, for it received a good share of its funds from the province. The three ordinary old folks' homes, however, were brigade ventures. One of these was in Bailin.

The Bailin Old Folks' Home was housed in low buildings surrounding a spacious courtyard and adjoining a good-sized kitchengarden. The rooms had *kangs*, and a little simple furniture.

The 27 old people living in the home in 1960, had spent most of their years in misery and squalor.

Guo Xiao-de, for instance, had spent a lifetime washing clothes and sewing for landlord families. She had had seven children of which not one had survived. Three died very young. Then she was left a widow and life was so hard that in time the remaining four children followed the first three to the grave. Even when the landlords had become only a bitter memory, hardships remained. 'In the old days I had grown-up sons and daughters for a time,' she said, 'but they couldn't even keep themselves alive, let alone me. In the new society I had food but it's hard to gather fuel when you have bound feet. And to carry water. It was just one long worry to me to keep myself alive. So when the brigade set up this home I was one of the first to move in. I didn't hesitate a moment.'

Another old woman had a similar story. She was seventy-two. In the old days she had been called 'Old Clipperty Clop', because her limbs were deformed through undernourishment and she walked with an awkward gait. Under the Kuomintang she had eked out a living by using her home as a gambling-den. It was squalid, but she managed to keep the *kang* warm and to have a kettle of boiling water on the hob, and when a winner took the pot he would toss her a copper or two. 'I was lonely before I moved in here,' she said. 'My old man died 25 or 30 years ago and then both my sons, two years ago. After that I was left all alone.' Her two sons had been in their fifties, but the widowed mother had been too poor to arrange marriages for them—until it was too late; so she had no grandchildren. 'I'd have died of a broken heart after that,' she went on, 'if I hadn't moved in here. This place is quite friendly. And all the young folk in the village are like our sons and daughters.'

Not all the old people, however, were free from doubt at the start. When the home was set up only seven chose to move in. Some hesitated because they had a notion to die in the homes they had lived in so long. Others feared that possessions they treasured and wished to hand down, would become the property of the home once they moved into it. It took the assurances of those who had moved

162

in first, and the appointment of a Party secretary to lead the management committee, to win their confidence.

One with fears for his property had been Xi Jen-jing. He had little to bequeath. But at last, after more than fifty years of privation, during the last fifteen years he had come into possession of something. He had different clothes for winter and summer now (in the old days, as the weather grew warmer, he just took the padding out of his winter suit); and he had enough bedding, so he no longer piled every garment he owned on top of a ragged quilt during the cold winter nights. He had good shoes instead of clogs, too, and a wash-basin made of enamel instead of coarse earthenware; and a torch and a thermos flask. Now one of the pleasures of possessing them was the thought of handing them on to his relatives. He did not want them taken over by the old folks' home.

The Party secretary explained that the home was only for the happiness and convenience of people like himself, who had been left without sons and daughters to take care of them; that his belongings were his own and would remain so in the home, to use during his lifetime and to bequeath as he thought fit. 'You just try it for a while,' concluded the secretary. 'And if you're not satisfied, you can move out again.' Xi Jen-jing tried it—and stayed.

Besides food, shelter and pocket-money, the old people were provided with clothing—including machine knit vests that were pulled on over the head, instead of doing up with cloth buttons as traditional Chinese garments do. These new vests created a sensation when they were first handed out. 'I'm seventy-three this year,' said one old man 'and this is the first time I've ever pulled a garment on over my head.'

By prevailing standards the old people were well provided for as far as material needs went. Other needs were being met as they became apparent.

The first to appear was work. In village picture-histories the old men were usually portrayed playing chess under the trees in a quiet courtyard, while the old women were shown either fanning themselves or puffing on long-stemmed pipes. These pastimes were in fact popular. But these old people had spent their lives working from dawn till dark. They could not get used to doing nothing.

The old men, after sitting around for some weeks, asked to be given work. First some ground was set aside by the home, for kitchen-gardens and pig-pens. When even this proved insufficient, it was arranged for the more hale and hearty to put in some time in the nearby fields. The women helped in the kitchen and, if their eyes were good enough (which in many cases they were not) did knitting or stitched soles for cloth shoes.

Whenever one of the county opera companies came on tour, the front row of seats was reserved for the old folk. Over the lunar new year, brigade members came with their children to pay their respects, as they would to their own parents. And the old folk, so that they could play their part as grandparents in traditional fashion, by giving the children little gifts of money, received an extra holiday allowance all in small change.

This touched on the biggest question after that of material needs: the fact that these old people had no families. In one of the brigades the old folks' home and the kindergarten were in connecting court-yards and there was mingling of young and old. In Bailin the home took in four little orphans to help provide family life.

MATERNITY HOMES AND MEDICAL SERVICES

Like old folks' homes, maternity homes were not yet numerous in Yangyi Commune. There were seven altogether. In this field, too, Bailin brigade had been a pioneer.

Bailin's maternity home consisted of three adjoining rooms with latticed windows opening onto a quiet courtyard with pomegranate and cassia trees, typical of the old landlord or rich peasant homes. It was supervised by the doctors of the village clinic, who had origin-ally been trained along traditional lines but had also been given short courses in modern medicine. The regular staff were old-style mid-wives, who had been given new training. (This was highly necessary for the old ways combined some sound experience with a certain amount of superstitition and a total lack of asepsis. Twenty years before, midwives had worked with large rings on their fingers, long finger-nails and unwashed hands. They often sharpened their scissors on the soles of their shoes before cutting the umbilical cord. The Communists, pending the training of new midwives, taught the old ones cleanliness, stressing the importance of cutting finger-nails, removing rings, washing the hands and dipping instruments in the potent local spirit distilled from sorghum. This sharply cut the rate of mother and infant mortality. Now to such training was added instruction in natural childbirth.)

The maternity home was opened in 1958, but it took the successful delivery of the first half-dozen babies to win public confidence. One woman, who had lost all her first three babies, decided to have her fourth in the home. When the news got round that mother and child were both doing well, the battle for confidence was largely won. By the summer of 1960 (that is, in just under two years) the maternity home had delivered 111 babies without a single death.

While maternity homes were a new venture, the brigade health services were the continuation of work started by the Communists over twenty years before. Their guiding principles[11] were:

[11] Laid down at the First National Health Conference, 1950. See *Culture, Education and Health in New China* (pamphlet), F.L.P., Peking, 1952.

Social Services

1. Serving the workers, peasants and soldiers;
2. Placing the main emphasis on preventive medicine;
3. Establishing close unity between traditional and modern medicine.

There was one hospital in the commune (in Yangyi); sixteen of the brigades had clinics, the rest first-aid posts and medical personnel. There were altogether 56 doctors and nurses. Everyone in the commune was regularly vaccinated and inoculated against typhoid, cholera and whooping cough and special attention was paid to the ancient art of acupuncture, in which one person from every twenty households was given elementary training. In line with the principle of unifying traditional and modern medicine, acupuncture needles, contrary to custom, were sterilized before use.

In Ten Mile Inn, the head doctor of the clinic, one of the brigade's six model workers, made 'medicine serve farming' by going regularly to the fields. There he would treat minor ailments and during breaks give talks on 'illnesses in season'. In between times he took a hand in field work and gave the canteen and kindergarten cooks talks on hygiene.

The result of this health service, according to Ten Mile Inn brigade statistics, was that there had been no infectious or contagious diseases in the village for two years and no infant mortality. Similar results were claimed by the other villages of the commune.

*   *   *

Yangyi was fortunate in having among its 24 brigades one which it could look to as a model for social services. This was Bailin, which had become a centre for on-the-spot conferences, where cadres not only from other brigades but from other communes and even counties came to learn how to launch social services and keep them up to the mark.

One of the secrets of Bailin's success had been that it did not put services first, but developed them on the basis of increased production in the fields. So at the very time that visitors to Bailin were studying its services, the brigade was achieving record yields. In 1958, on a one *mu* experimental plot, a group of women, under the leadership of Guo Heng-de, got a yield of 2,612 *jin* of millet. On a second field, 8 *mu* in size, they got a yield of 1,056 *jin* per *mu*. In 1959 they turned their attention to wheat and raised a crop of 1,108 *jin* per *mu* on a plot 1·4 *mu* in size and on fields covering 113 *mu* (just under 20 acres) they reaped an average of 300 *jin* per *mu*.

In leading Bailin to its position of a model brigade or pilot plot for social services, Guo Heng-de stuck to the principle that only through raising production could people afford to improve their living conditions.

So far as possible all the services provided in Yangyi Commune in the summer of 1960 were run along these lines. But in shouldering responsibility for the welfare of the mass of working people from the cradle to the grave, was a task never before attempted in China's long history. It involved an endless series of problems. In running social services the commune had taken on a job second only to production in its complexity.

Chapter XV

EDUCATION

NEARLY 15,000 children and adults were attending primary and secondary schools in Yangyi in 1960. Statistically the picture in the commune was:

Primary schools[1]	schools	pupils
to junior leaving (grades I to IV)	49	c. 4,000
to senior leaving (grades I to VI)	12	c. 1,340
Secondary schools[2]		
to junior leaving (grades VII to IX)	5	678
to senior leaving (grades VII to XII)	1	726
Total	67	c. 6,740

In addition, 8,230 adult members of the commune were studying in spare-time primary schools; and a sizable number of commune members had already reached secondary school level.

THE TEN MILE INN PRIMARY SCHOOL

Typical of village schools in Yangyi Commune was the Ten Mile Inn Primary School. In 1960, for the first time in the history of the village, every child of primary school age was going to school. The attendance figure of 330 was more than 10 per cent above the previous peak, reached in 1959, the year after the commune was set up. The girls, not one of whom went to school twenty years before, were now on an equal footing with the boys. There was no exclusion on the basis of class.

Before the land reform only 20 to 30 children attended the village school, nearly all of them from landlord, rich peasant and well-to-do middle peasant families. With the land reform schooling was officially made available to those previously deprived of it and enrolment roughly tripled. But with the small family farm and work

---

[1] Primary school (junior and senior combined) covers the first six years of education, starting at the age of seven.

[2] Secondary school (junior and senior combined) covers the years from primary to college.

force, which gave no guarantee of economic security, the labour of children was of value. Even a ten-year-old might be useful doing odd jobs in the fields and scouring the roads for manure, or at home fetching water and minding younger brothers and sisters. Besides, for farming of this traditional type education did not seem necessary. So though some families seized the chance of sending their children to school, others did not. With the rise in standard of living and with the need for book-keeping and records brought by the farming co-operatives, school enrolment again more than doubled. But it was the commune which cleared the ground for universal primary school education. Within a year of its founding enrolment rose from 178 to 298. By the following year all children of primary school age were at school.

Estimated Average Enrolment at Ten Mile Inn Primary School During Key Periods from 1940–60[3]

Before land reform	20 to 30
From land reform to farming co-operatives (1948–54)	70
Period of semi-socialist and socialist co-operatives (1954–58)	150 to 170
After consolidation of the commune (1960)	330 (all children of primary school age)

The school at Ten Mile Inn was housed in an old temple, with twisted trees and ancient inscriptions in the courtyards which now served as playgrounds. But the old walls were covered with new murals of irrigation works, tractors and trains.

The curriculum included reading, writing and arithmetic, drawing, singing, physical training and 'productive labour' throughout all grades; and in the higher grades, geography, history, politics and natural science.

One text on the subject of science used in the summer of 1959 was an adaptation of an editorial in the Peking *People's Daily* entitled: 'Toppling Idols and Smashing Superstititions.' The science

[3] The following figures for school enrolment as a whole were given by Premier Chou En-lai in his 'Report on the Work of the Government', delivered at the First Session of the National People's Congress, 18 April, 1959:

Primary school pupils

1952 over 51,000,000
1957 over 64,000,000 (an increase of 26 per cent)
1958 over 86,000,000 (an increase of 34 ,,)

Secondary school pupils

1952 over 3,000,000
1957 over 7,000,000 (an increase of over 100 per cent)
1958 12,000,000 (an increase of 70 ,,)

teacher introduced it with the words: 'Some people have an inferiority complex about science. What is an inferiority complex? It is looking down on yourself. Well, there's nothing to be afraid of about science. It's no mystery. Anyone who works can master it. . . .'

The biggest difficulty the school faced was finding enough teachers to handle the fast growing number of pupils, especially since enrolment had risen not only in Ten Mile Inn but in the entire area.

In landlord days the Ten Mile Inn school had one or two teachers. Soon after land reform it had three. At that time teachers of landlord and rich peasant class were replaced by others from poor and middle peasant families. These, though politically dependable, had little education, and some parents complained that they knew little more than the children. With the consolidation of the land reform a few teachers of landlord and rich peasant family background, who themselves had 'a clean political record', were drawn back into the school, where their literacy could be put to use. They not only taught pupils but helped the less educated teachers who came from poor and middle peasant families; but care was taken at all times to see that they did so under suitable political guidance.

In the following years growing numbers of young people of poor and middle peasant origin, having received primary school education, were able to take up teaching. In 1960 most of the Ten Mile Inn staff—now totalling ten, including two women teachers—were of poor or middle peasant origin. Their academic education was still limited, the principal himself being a graduate of senior (six grade) primary school. He had first worked as a village cadre. Then, after receiving three months' teachers' training, he was assigned to his post at the Ten Mile Inn school. Half of the younger teachers, however, had completed junior middle school (equivalent to 9th grade) and all ten teachers went on studying as they taught. During 1959, for instance, they all attended courses in geometry and algebra especially arranged for primary school teachers by the commune. In addition to such courses offered during the term, summer schools for teachers were organized by the county. In the summer of 1960 one of these, attended by 180 teachers, was conducted in Yangyi townlet. (These were the teachers who helped mend the breach in the Long Sea Dam.) Finally there was another system for upgrading teachers. This was releasing them for full-time training in the towns, while new normal school graduates took their places in the villages.

By the summer of 1960 not only were all children of primary school age (7-12) in school, but opportunities for further study had greatly increased. All 44 pupils of the top class left school for further study as follows:

Secondary school	22
Agricultural secondary school (i.e. part study, part work)	12
Training in public health	5
Training as mechanics	3
Training as technicians (in iron and steel)[4]	2
Total	44

The graduating of this class in 1960 brought the total number of graduates (from the time the school was organized during the war against Japan) up to 300. Of these, altogether 92 pupils were doing further study. When the Communists first came to the village, Ten Mile Inn had only two pupils at secondary school.

THE SHIDONG AGRICULTURAL SECONDARY SCHOOL

Adjoining the Ten Mile Inn Primary School was an Agricultural Secondary School. This had been set up in 1958, not by the state, but by the people of the Shidong District, to serve all eight of its villages—including Ten Mile Inn. It had only one class to begin with but was adding a class a year until the whole secondary school course was taught.

Like other schools of its kind, the Shidong Agricultural Secondary School was run on a 'half work, half study' basis. Thus, while in the primary school 'productive labour' was just one subject in the curriculum taking up from one hour a week in Grade I to three hours in Grade IV, in the Agricultural Secondary School it took up half the pupils' time. This arrangement permitted it to be entirely self-sufficient, with contributions from neither the state nor the pupils' parents. At the same time it brought education beyond primary school level within the reach of every child.

The basis for the school's economic self-sufficiency was seven acres of land allotted to it by the brigades concerned and planted mainly to wheat and cotton. The school time-table was flexibly co-ordinated with the working of the land (and other productive labour), sometimes part of the day being devoted to work, part to study, or at other times concentrated periods of a week or so being devoted to one or the other. During the 1960 cotton planting, for instance, classes were suspended for twelve days to let the pupils help fight the drought. Carrying water, sometimes for over two miles, to fill

[4] The commune was preparing to set up a small iron and steel works in the autumn of 1960 to handle the ore from its newly-opened mine. This would supply the growing commune Farm Tool Manufacture and Repair Works with its needs.

170

Education

every seed hole, inspired two Young Pioneers[5] to compose the couplet:

Swollen shoulders, aching feet.
We won't give up till the drought is beat.

Not all work was agricultural. Besides supplying itself and the primary school with desks and chairs, maintaining buildings and helping put up new ones, the secondary school had 'hook-ups' with nearby factories and mines (not necessarily in Yangyi Commune). In 1959, for instance, the pupils helped put up buildings in Wu An mining district, twenty-one miles to the east.

Such contact with industry not only helped the school economically. It was considered important for turning out technically-minded farmers or agricultural technicians such as commune farming required.

The Agricultural Secondary School was, in fact, geared to the needs of the commune. It provided education without cost to either family or state; and it kept badly needed labour within the commune while raising its proficiency.

THE YANGYI SECONDARY SCHOOL

The Yangyi Secondary School, which took pupils right up to senior leaving (12th grade), served the whole commune.

Set up in 1956 with 240 pupils in 4 classes it expanded to 6 classes in 1957. With the founding of the commune, enrolment rose to 653 pupils in 12 classes. By 1960 it was 726 pupils in 14 classes.

The school was on the outskirts of Yangyi townlet, next door to the machine shop and tractor station. Unlike most of the schools in the commune, which were in old temple buildings, with curved tiled roofs and wrought iron incense burners in the courtyards, the secondary school was housed in simple one-storey brick buildings put up largely by the teachers and students themselves. This applied not only to the classrooms, but to the lime and brick kilns, a small chemical fertilizer plant, a clothing factory and buildings belonging to the school farm (which in 1959 produced 275 tons of vegetables and also raised pigs, sheep and rabbits).

Besides studying such subjects as mathematics, chemistry, physics, botany, Chinese language and literature, Russian, politics, history and geography on five days of the week, the pupils did one day's industrial or agricultural work a week—eight hours for the seniors and six for the juniors. Staggering of work days for the different classes made it possible to keep the various enterprises fully staffed.

[5] An organization led by the Communist Youth League, for children from 9–15. Some three-quarters of the country's 40,750-odd children within these age-limits belonged.

171

The pupils also did some work for the commune. From the autumn of 1959 to the summer of 1960 they put in an average of 70 days each, mostly during the holidays. They took part in the fight against the drought, helping with the sowing, hoeing and harvesting, worked at reservoir and highway building and tree-planting. On the more technical and industrial side, 120 pupils learnt to drive tractors and a similar number to operate and repair generators. Thirty pupils with training as electricians, installed the electricity in newly-built classrooms and others did carpentry, iron moulding and so on. In the campaign of 1958 staff and pupils made seven tons of iron and low-grade steel in small furnaces which they built on the sportsground. In 1960 on Saturday afternoons a group of pupils, accompanied by the chemistry and physics teachers, went to work in the commune rocket factory.

During the five years of its existence (1956-60) the school had had an enrolment of 1,136 pupils, of whom 410 had completed junior leaving. The great majority of these (326) went on to further study, many continuing at the Yangyi Secondary School itself, others transferring to teachers' training or technical schools:

TABLE 8: *Numbers of Pupils at Yangyi Secondary School going on to further study and those taking up work*

I. *Those going on to further study:*

Secondary school (senior leaving)	130
Teachers' training school	33
Technical school (advanced)	25
Technical secondary school	138
Total	326

II. *Those taking up work:*

Education	52
Public enterprises	4
Cadres	10
Industry (mines or factories)	9
Agriculture	5
Military service (an additional 32 were called up before junior leaving)	4
Total	84
GRAND TOTAL	410

Tentative plans for the coming five years (1960-65) were for steady yearly expansion, bringing the numbers up from the present 726 pupils and 53 staff members to 1,115 and 86 respectively.

Education

In 1958 schools throughout the country were called on to implement the nation's new educational policy. This required education to 'serve working-class politics' and to be 'combined with productive labour'.[6] Its long-term aim was to bridge the gap between mental and manual labour, to produce a new generation of 'cultured, socialist-minded workers', and to prevent the creation of a stratum of intellectuals who would consider themselves entitled to a privileged position in society. This new concept was directly opposed to long-standing tradition, according to which scholars despised manual labour and peasants regarded book-learning with almost superstitious reverence.

This gap between mental and manual labour was related to that between town and country, the tradition being for young people who managed to obtain some education, to leave the country for jobs in town.

The transformation of agriculture, however, called for educated farmers; and education which fostered the idea of a privileged position and leaving the countryside had to be combated. The new educational policy was designed, among other things, to deal with this situation.

To put the policy into effect, the teachers—themselves intellectuals—had first to be convinced.

Yangyi Secondary School's teaching staff was mixed. Some teachers were 'rural intellectuals' not far removed from their landlord or rich peasant background. One of these openly favoured 'the capitalist road'. Over the years he had been politically active outside the field of teaching, opposing the Party's policy of planned purchase and supply and the development of co-operatives. Another opposed Party leadership in the field of education, trying to win adherents to the view that 'the Party should mind its own business—politics, and leave education to the educated'. In trying to form a faction among the teachers to oppose Party leadership, he attempted to undermine the prestige of the only communist teacher by belittling his academic qualifications.

Others on the staff had come to Yangyi from the towns, some enthusiastically, some not. One of them, at least, felt that working in the commune was beneath him and regarded his post in the Taihang Mountains rather as imperial officials had looked on banishment to the barbarian borders. Finally there were teachers who had

---

[6] The Central Committee of the Communist Party had raised the question of adding productive labour to the school curriculum in 1954; but finding that the majority of teachers had mixed feelings on the subject and that a certain number were strongly opposed, it postponed action.

For fuller treatment of this policy, see Lu Ting-yi, *Education Must Be Combined with Productive Labour* (pamphlet), F.L.P., Peking, 1958.

173

been educated locally. These tended to lack confidence in their academic qualifications.

While the number of teachers who firmly opposed communist leadership of education was small, so was the number who gave it wholehearted support from the start. The majority were in between these two extremes and had certain reservations. They were open to the influence of one minority or the other. Putting Party policy into practice depended on winning them over. This was bound to involve a struggle.

This struggle over educational policy reached a climax in two mass movements, one in 1958 the other in the following year. Both brought about big changes in the teaching and outlook of the staff.

The first of these movements was the anti-rightist campaign of 1957-58.[7] In the course of it the question of who benefited from planned purchase and supply was thrown open to discussion by the staff and students. The outcome was that the great majority of teachers gained a better understanding of the system and gave it stronger support. The view that 'the Communist Party can't lead education' was discussed in like manner. The conclusion drawn was that the Party, which 'had mastered military, political and economic affairs and given leadership to them throughout the revolution', could and must do the same in education.

In this discussion issues were clarified and linked to the choice between the two roads. Putting matters in this perspective helped to win over the centre group, which had to some extent been influenced by the view that the Party should leave education to 'experts'. Thus the few who persisted in opposing the new approach to education found themselves isolated. The two teachers who had taken action against the Party and Government (in trying to organize opposition to planned purchase and supply and to Party leadership of the school) were labelled 'rightists', but retained their positions and were not punished.

The field was now clear for the second mass movement—for 'Educational Reform'.

This began early in 1959. It started with systematic study of certain extracts from the works of Mao Tse-tung, of the Party's policy for education and of the achievements of outstanding schools elsewhere in China. After this there was a public airing of views at meetings, some of the whole school, some of groups of a dozen or so. Here criticisms and suggestions were made regarding the work of individual teachers as well as about current practices and arrangements—all in the light of the standards set forth in policy statements.

---

[7] This was a nation-wide movement against certain members of the bourgeoisie, who in 1957 had worked to bring about in China events similar to those in Hungary, under the slogan: 'Now it's our turn.' In the countryside it was connected with the Great Debate between the Two Roads. See Chapter I.

Education

The students also made 'presentations' to their teachers in the form of placards containing comments on their way of teaching. These were hung in classrooms, corridors and courtyards. The general tenor of these criticisms was that much of the teaching was divorced from productive labour, from reality and from politics. One mathematics teacher, for instance, had maintained that his subject could not be related to reality because that would interfere with the systematic presentation of the subject in the text-book. A teacher of political science insisted that courses in his field should be confined to the classroom, not connected with èvents going on in the world. Some of the older teachers stuck to their texts quite rigidly, one of them saying: 'The central or provincial authorities compile the text-books; and they can revise them. Our job is just to teach what's in the book and do it in the classroom, not go all over the place.' The rights and wrongs of such views and of the criticisms of them were thrashed out in more meetings and debates.

In the course of the movement the teachers examined their attitudes not only to the new policy but to teaching in general. Some acknowledged that they had not wanted to be teachers at all. Others, particularly older teachers, said they felt they would be unable to adapt themselves to the changes they saw in the offing and even feared they would no longer be able to teach at all. And while some of the younger teachers, who had only recently left secondary school, felt unsure of themselves, a number of their seniors feared that these same newcomers would overtake them and that they themselves would be cast aside.

Once these fears were brought into the open they could be, and were, discussed in the light of the commune's growing need for trained personnel and the general expansion of education. This placed a premium on teachers and guaranteed that all who made an effort to abide by the policy would be secure in their posts. The revealing of these worries and the realization that they were unfounded, brought a sense of relief which the teachers described as 'shedding burdens'.

With their minds at rest following these discussions, the teachers began to take initiative in relating their lessons to what was going on in the world. The mathematics teacher started using commune production figures in his problems. The science teacher, who had taught his subject in an abstract fashion, began making electrical equipment with his students. The geography teacher took the route of the historic Long March[8] as his subject matter and helped his students make a relief map of it. The botany teacher started an experimental plot on which he tried crossing potatoes and tomatoes, sunflowers

[8] The 8,000-mile fighting trek of the Red Army in 1934–35, starting from the old Soviet areas in south-east China, ending in the setting up of a new base in the north-west, with Yenan as its capital.

175

and ginger. The chemistry and physics teacher, with a group of students, began working at the commune rocket factory. Teachers of politics organized visits to the sites of events significant in revolutionary history, in which the Taihang Mountains are rich, and invited old revolutionaries as guest speakers on current affairs. The teacher of Chinese added to his course instruction in the writing of criticisms and suggestions!

The students too helped to make their courses more practical. They drew 850 maps, charts, diagrams and visual aids of one sort or another; made a combined microscope-projector for the study of bacteria; preserved specimens of frogs and other creatures and, in keeping with the principle of 'all-round development', turned out a wide range of equipment for physical training, from table tennis to weight-lifting.

When the new term started there was an upsurge of enthusiasm among the teachers.

By July 1960, in the regular appraisal for five good qualities: 'Selfless communist character, good work style, good attitude to manual labour, good ideology, concern for the masses' (held monthly or fortnightly in the school), the rating was:

Good on all five counts	25
Good on four counts	24
Good on three counts	2
	—
Total number of teachers	53[9]
	—

The headmaster associated this record showing with the firmer grasp of Party policy and strengthening of Party leadership which accompanied the movement. The number of Party members was, in fact, considerably increased, both by the appointing of new teachers who were already Communists and by the recruiting of new Party members among the staff and students, four of whom joined in 1960. This brought the total number of Communists in the school (students and teachers) to thirteen, in addition to 153 members of the Communist Youth League and 356 Young Pioneers.[10]

WIPING OUT ILLITERACY IN TEN MILE INN

In the portrait gallery of model members of the Ten Mile Inn Brigade was a picture of Party Branch Secretary Wang Mi-shan. The inscription under it read:

[9] The two unaccounted for were the rightists.
[10] Age qualifications were: for Young Pioneers, 9–15; for the Communist Youth League, 15–25; for the Communist Party, 18 and up.

176

Education

Wang You-lin (Mi-shan), age 40.

For generations no one in his family could read or write. He studied in the part-time school and the 'Red and Expert' school. Now he can read and write and take notes. Eighty per cent of the men of his age in our village are now literate.

324 adults of Ten Mile Inn had 'taken off their dunce's caps' by 1959. That is, they had learned 1,500 characters—enough to read simple books and write ordinary letters. These newly literate grown-ups, together with the 256 graduates of the Ten Mile Inn primary school, had changed the old picture of illiteracy that had prevailed in the village twenty years before.

One indication of new educational standards was the figure for subscriptions to daily newspapers, which now stood at 80.[11] Twenty years before, even after the land reform, individual subscriptions were unheard of among farmers.

The struggle against illiteracy started during the anti-Japanese war. Then, in the winter, during the lull in farm work, 'Resist Japan' schools were set up, for discussion of current affairs and Communist Party policy. Reading and writing were also taught. Conditions were hard, and obtaining even an elementary command of China's complicated script required concentration and constant effort. Nevertheless a drive to instruct cadres in the writing of road-passes and the filling in of forms was successful and a number of young men learnt to read the blackboard newspaper in the village street. Some could also cope with pamphlets and write letters and reports.

In 1945 there was a drive by the Women's Association to teach all women under thirty to read and write. This met with some success, but some of the gains were later lost through lack of consolidation. The 1,500 characters which constituted only an elementary level of literacy had to be constantly practised or they were forgotten—and the newly literate slipped back into illiteracy.

After the land reform literacy increased, but the number of adults who could read and write was still small. Learning characters was hard, especially for adults, and the old small-scale farming had not demanded literacy. But for mutual aid and still more so for co-operative farming, with their book-keeping and records, literacy was essential. Thus one of the big obstacles the co-operatives had to face at first was the lack of accountants and work-point registrars. Ex-landlords and rich farmers were literate but not trusted; poor peasants were trusted but—the adults, at least—were not literate. So in many of the early co-operatives the books were kept by fourteen- or fifteen-year-old lads, of poor peasant families, just out of

---

[11] The most popular papers were: the provincial *Hopei Daily*, the regional *Taihang Daily*, the county *Fuyang Daily* and the *Farmer's Daily*.

primary school. With the co-operatives' urgent need for literate members many older men attended courses; but they often found that after struggling through the textbooks prepared by the Provincial Government they still could not keep work-point records. This was not because keeping records called for many characters (two to three hundred might well be enough) but because those that were needed differed from one village to another, comprising as they did the names of particular people, fields and other geographical features. These were by no means the most common and generally useful characters in the Chinese language as a whole. It was therefore impossible to have a standard textbook for learning them. This problem persisted until the time of the socialist co-operatives. Then a solution was found and publicized throughout the countryside.[12] This was for each co-operative to work out its own initial list of two to three hundred characters, made up of the names of its members, fields and local places and of different types of farmwork, implements and crops. After mastering this list (for the purpose of record keeping) the students could go on to the ordinary provincial or national textbooks. Many farmers who had stopped studying when they found it did not help them with record keeping, now started studying again.

It was not only because of the need for accountants and record-keepers that progress was made in education after the setting up of socialist co-operatives. Technical advance demanded it. In this situation a new approach to literacy campaigns was adopted. Previously these campaigns had drawn in as many adults as possible, men and women, old and young. But in 1956 the national leadership of the Communist Youth League, recognizing that the majority of young people throughout the country were still illiterate, or only semi-literate, proposed that a special drive should be carried out to help them. This was to take into account that young people, being keener on study and less burdened by family responsibilities, could make faster progress if the course was especially geared to them, not to the adult population as a whole.

In Ten Mile Inn, in the first phase of this new campaign, the majority of young men and a number of young women became literate. Then in April 1958, as part of the Great Leap Forward, a major effort was made to complete the wiping out of illiteracy among young people (from 14 to 25), as well as among men from 25 to 40 and any women of that age group who might be drawn in.

This campaign went on for two months, with five classes and ten teachers. In the case of young women who had small children and found it hard to go out, arrangements were made for teachers to go into the home and hold classes on the *kang*. To help consolidate

[12] 'How a Youth League Branch Established a Course in Work-point Recording', *Socialist Upsurge in China's Countryside.*

what was taught in class, amateur teachers in each work group 'took learning to the fields'.

This movement was a turning-point in some lives. Among the illiterate young men swept into it was the elder brother of C.Y.L. District Secretary Li Wei-guo, the village's classic example of a young man who never made the grade. As a child he had not been sent to school because his father had considered him slow-witted. So at this time, though twenty-five, he could not even write his name. He had in fact always lagged behind. He had hidden to avoid the embarrassment of not volunteering for military service; he had stayed away from meetings and hated the idea of studying. But with the launching of this movement, after great effort on the part of Li Wei-guo and his friends, he was finally persuaded to attend classes. He had a hard time at first, but he was swept along by the tide and in the end he passed the course. Once he did so, to the surprise of his family and friends he began to adopt a more forward-looking view of life. Once literate he no longer lagged behind and throughout Ten Mile Inn he became the symbol of what education could achieve.

Among the young women a typical case was that of twenty-year-old Li Wen-yun. Like many of her age, influenced by the traditional idea that learning was no use to a woman, she had always been lukewarm about study. But she was an excellent worker in the fields and was elected a work team leader. As such she had to attend meetings and report on them to her team-mates, which meant she had to take notes. This was beyond her, and she soon began to feel that lack of education was hampering her leadership of the team. So she enrolled for study. Within a few months she was taking notes along with the other team leaders.

Few women over 25 could be persuaded to take part in the movement. Most of them felt not only that they were too busy to study but that reading and writing would be of little use to them. Others felt they were not up to it or 'too old for such complicated stuff'. But there were notable exceptions. Li Shua-de, forty-year-old wife of the Party Secretary said, 'Others can learn, why can't I?' She attended classes in the work team dining-room and got her thirteen-year-old son to help her with her homework so that she could keep up with the class. In time she learned enough characters to read the paper. Encouragement and help from husband and children were important for older women.

By 1959, with practically all the men under 40 and all the women under 25 able to read and write, the battle for literacy in Ten Mile Inn was considered won.[13] The target for adult education was now

---

[13] According to official estimates for the whole of China, two-thirds of the young and middle-aged men and women in the countryside (110 million people) were literate by 1959. See Tan Chen-lin, 'Report to the National People's Congress, April, 1960), *Peking Review*, No. 15, 12 April, 1960.

advanced from reading and writing to general courses, political study and agricultural technique. Meanwhile two lessons were drawn from these experiences of conducting literacy campaigns among adults. First, the sooner that study can prove *its* usefulness in daily life, the greater the enthusiasm and confidence of the students. This was borne out by the effectiveness of the 'local list' of characters for work-point recording. Second, illiterates should not all be lumped together. Differences in age and sex should be taken into account.

'RED AND EXPERT' SCHOOLS

With the battle for adult literacy won, not only in Ten Mile Inn but throughout the commune, with universal primary school education and with the attendance and quality of secondary education higher than ever before, there were now opportunities for further advances in technique. To make the most of these, however, it was necessary to raise the level of general adult education. This was the function of spare-time schools led directly by the Commune Party Committee and by the Branch Committees in the brigades. These were known as 'Red and Expert' schools, to indicate the importance they attached to linking political (red) with technical (expert) education and to combining theory with practice.

By the summer of 1960 a network of these schools had been established. Their existence could not be seen in the form of school buildings or libraries, but each brigade had at least one room which served as the centre of its study program. This was a combination reading-room, lecture-hall and exhibition centre housing the pictorial history of the village and the portraits of outstanding brigade members.

Furniture was sparse. A typical reading-room would have a long, narrow table against one wall, with sixty or eighty paperbacks and some stacks of magazines on it. Many of the volumes were of popular agricultural science and technique: on sweet potato growing, pig-raising, pest control and so on, as well as on the technical trans-formation of agriculture. Others were stories, often about popular heroes such as Huang Qi-guang or autobiographies such as those of Gao Yu-bao or Wu Yun-duo.[14] Besides these and stories of revolutionary struggles there were simplified pictorial versions of the popular classics such as *The Romance of the Three Kingdoms*, *Water Margin* and the *Western Pilgrimage*. Among the political writings

[14] Huang Qi-guang was a Chinese People's Volunteer who gave his life to destroy an enemy machine-gun nest in Korea; Gao Yu-bao is a P.L.A. man who has written of his poor peasant boyhood under the landlords and the Japanese invaders; Wu Yun-duo joined the Chinese Red Army in the early thirties and writes in his autobiography *Son of the Working-Class* about his work in guerrilla arsenals like that at Lianggou.

180

Education

were volumes of Mao Tse-tung's selected works and various pamphlets on current policy, such as the 'Report on the National Plan for Agricultural Development', delivered at the National People's Congress Session of April 1960 and the twelve year plan for the modernization of agriculture drawn-up in 1956.

General education courses covered both primary and secondary school curricula. These were given in the evening at the regular schools, by volunteers from among the teachers. In 1960, 8,230 adults were signed up for them. Political study, which included Marxist theory as well as current Party and Government policy, was carried on in work team dining-rooms.[15] As for technical study, each brigade was encouraged to arrange sessions on farming technique one evening a week. Commune industrial or trade units were expected to organize technical study in their own particular fields. This was done most energetically by the youth teams on the high yield tracts, usually in close connection with the running of experimental plots. On the Silver Sea Tract such courses were given by the graduate agronomist in charge of technical guidance of the tract.

The term 'Red and Expert' might have been applied to all education in the commune. Primary, secondary and spare-time schools for adults all fitted into an overall strategy. This was designed to close the gap between mental and manual work. Its object was to prevent the emergence of a new stratum of intellectuals divorced from manual labour and the labouring people; and to produce instead individuals of a new type, fit to take over and carry forward their revolutionary heritage. These would be at once both 'intellectuals' and 'labourers'.

Such were the main considerations underlying the emphasis on 'combining education with productive labour', making it 'serve working-class politics' and permeating it with a spirit of class struggle.

[15] See 'A Movement to Study Dialectical Materialism', Chapter XXI.

Chapter XVI

MILITARY MATTERS AND COMMUNE POWER

SECURITY AND THE EXERCISE OF STATE POWER

'THE people's commune . . . is the basic organization of socialist state power.'[1] But while other attributes of the commune—such as farming, industry, commerce, education and social services—were to be developed and perfected, state power, which included military forces, was to be maintained only during the period of transition to communism and of danger from abroad. After that, according to Marxist theory, it was to 'wither away'.

The State—'the executive committee of the ruling class'[2]—wielded its power in the first place to defend the commune from its enemies. In almost every village around Yangyi there were ex-landlords like Wang Dian-yuan of Ten Mile Inn (whose father had been executed as a traitor), who had served in the Kuomintang power structure as 'head of a thousand households' (*lianbao zhuren*) and his former rich peasant associate Wang Jia-wen. Such men had a long record of law-breaking and opposition to the communist-led reforms.[3] Men of this type were regarded as coming from the 'enemy classes' defeated in the New Democratic Revolution. Then and in the socialist revolution that followed, they were under surveillance by the rank-and-file—including their one-time tenants, debtors and hired hands, some of whom had once been jailed and beaten-up at their orders.

This surveillance was not only for the purpose of preventing sabotage or other crimes. It was to ensure that these former exploiters reformed themselves by engaging in productive labour. Regulations for this had been laid down during the land reform. At that time ex-landlords and rich peasants were given a share of land comparable to that of the mass of the peasants. This was intended to provide them with means of livelihood and prevent them becoming beggars tramps or thieves. In addition, the working of this land in the sweat of their brows alongside those they had once exploited, was meant to help them change their outlook on life. If they did so their social status was changed and they took their place among the working people, ex-landlords after working for five years, ex-rich peasants for

---

[1] 'Resolution on Some Questions Concerning the People's Communes.'
[2] See V. I. Lenin, 'The State and Revolution'.
[3] See Chapter VI, 'Rectification and Canteens in Ten Mile Inn'.

three. This led in time to former landlords and rich peasants becoming members of co-operatives and later of communes, provided the membership agreed that their outlook had changed.

While experience of landlord and rich peasants changing their outlook was still limited, the view of many peasants in the days following land reform was: 'Ex-landlords and rich peasants are easy to lead. They do as they're told.' And this idea was fostered by the former landlords and rich peasants themselves. As cases of sabotage and theft came to light, however, this view was changed into: 'Ex-landlords and rich peasants have sweet tongues but vicious hearts.' Accordingly an investigation was made in all co-operatives in 1955.[4] In one county in the Taihang region there were found to be 538 ex-landlords and rich peasants in 227 co-operatives. When their personal histories were examined, 260—nearly half of them—emerged with clean records. These retained co-operative membership. 241 did not have clean records. They had constantly complained, spread rumours and shirked, turning up late for work and leaving early, feigning sickness and breaking work regulations, damaged or stolen public property. These were allowed to remain in the co-operatives but without the title and full right of members. In local terminology they 'had their landlord and rich peasant caps put back on them.' 34—just over 6 per cent—had committed serious crimes, such as arson. These were expelled from the co-operatives and handed over to the judicial authorities to be dealt with according to the law.[5]

Explaining how one-time enemies were treated in Yangyi Commune, Party Secretary Jin said: 'If they work well and don't stir up any trouble, we take off their landlord and rich peasant 'caps'. That is, they're treated as ordinary citizens and commune members and have the same rights as everyone else. But we still keep an eye on them. And if they do start any tricks, we put their 'caps' back on them. If that happens, they're no longer commune members and lose their rights. They still have to work for their living of course.

'Take Meng Shang-yi in the Yangyi brigade,' Secretary Jin went on. 'After the land reform he worked quite hard without any prodding, so his rich peasant "cap" was taken off. After the commune was set up he went to work in a canteen and in time he was even elected head cook. Of course people did have a suspicion that he'd been working hard in the kitchen because he thought he could get himself a soft job as some sort of canteen manager instead of sweating over the stove or out in the fields. But they reasoned that whatever his motives, he was the best man for the job: he knew how to cook and he could keep accounts. So he was elected.'

[4] As part of a nation-wide movement for suppressing counter-revolutionaries See below, this chapter.

[5] *Socialist Upsurge in China's Countryside*, p. 351 ff.

(This election was contrary to Party and Government policy, which stressed the importance of electing 'politically reliable' members—preferably of poor peasant origin—to all such posts in the commune.)

'Well,' continued Secretary Jin, 'just before the lunar new year's festival the County Government called on all canteens to make the holiday a success. There was to be a thorough spring cleaning, the rooms were to be decorated and the windows re-papered. And of course the food was to be extra-special—a regular feast. It was the first new year's festival since the canteens got going and the idea was to give people the best holiday they'd ever had with a proper community 'do' in the work team dining-rooms.

'When the day came County Head Wang and I went up to the Silver Sea Tract and helped cook the meals so that the regular cooks could have some time off. Late in the afternoon we came back to Yangyi. It was dusk. A biting wind had sprung up and there were a few flakes of snow. As we entered the village we saw some people hurrying home in the wind and snow, carrying bowls of food. This doesn't look like much of a community festival, we thought. So we asked which canteen they came from. It turned out to be the one Meng Shang-yi was in charge of and we went to see what was going on there. When we arrived we found out that the place hadn't been fixed up at all. The food was all right, but nothing special—just about the same as on other days. After that we did the rounds of the other canteens—Yangyi's a big brigade and has over twenty altogether. All the others had made a great success of things and the people were in high spirits. It was only Meng Shang-yi who hadn't taken any trouble. Well, we looked into this and at the same time went into Meng's whole record. When we did so all sorts of little incidents and actions of his, which hadn't seemed important in themselves, began to form a pattern. It gradually became clear that Meng had worked his way into the position of head cook because it was a vantage point for stirring up dissatisfaction with the canteen and with the commune as a whole. So we removed him from his post and put his rich peasant "cap" back on him.

'Not all the former rich peasants are like Meng Shang-yi, though,' continued Secretary Jin. 'For instance, Guo Pei-jie, another ex-rich peasant in Yangyi brigade, worked quite well after the land reform, so during the co-operative stage he had his "cap" taken off. He's kept on working well ever since, so now he's a member of the commune. It's all up to the man himself how he's treated.'

This was borne out by an incident in a commune further north.

In a certain village there were two brothers named Gao, formerly rich peasants. After living by their own labour for some years, both had their 'caps' taken off. But while one put his heart into his work, the other, once he had been accepted as an ordinary citizen, began to take things easy. When some grain disappeared this Gao was suspected of stealing it. But nothing could be proved, so the matter hung fire. Actually he had been pilfering grain and burying it—and when a sudden downpour came, his cache was flooded and the grain soaked. The only way to save it was to spread it out in the sun to dry; but that meant risking detection. In the end, fear of loss proved greater than fear of being found out, and he quietly spread the grain on the flat roof of his house. But little escapes public scrutiny in a village, least of all the actions of a one-time enemy. The grain was spotted and Gao could not but admit he had stolen it. In addition to receiving due punishment for theft, he had his rich peasant 'cap' put on again. His brother, who was not implicated, remained an ordinary citizen and commune member.

In Yangyi, according to Secretary Jin's observations, a good two-thirds of the one-time landlords and rich peasants were considered to have genuinely changed their outlook while working in the fields during the twelve years since the land reform. But there were some who still set themselves against socialism and slid back into their old ways if they could.

Such reversion had its own laws. When things were going smoothly there was little of it. In times of sharp struggle between the capitalist and socialist roads, when difficulties arose in running some new venture or through bad weather, when some sweeping change was causing temporary dislocation—up it cropped. (In 1955, when the proportion of China's farming households belonging to co-operatives suddenly rose from 2 per cent to 63 per cent, there was a striking upswing of sabotage in the co-operatives, a semi-feudal swan-song. In one Taihang county, 49 cases occurred. This was nearly twice as many as in the previous year.)

And in 1959, when the Ten Mile Inn brigade was having its first difficulties in setting up the canteens, the ex-landlord Wang Dian-yuan and the former rich peasant Wang Jia-wen became extremely active. Both spread complaints and twisted facts about the canteens to rouse the maximum dissatisfaction with them.

If a one-time landlord or rich peasant did not seize the opportunity to stir up trouble even during difficult times, he was taken to be genuinely breaking with his past. Wang Dian-yuan's three brothers, for instance, were of this latter type and all were commune members in good standing.

But of all the peasants' former enemies, Li Feng of the Fort had gained most respect. Before the land reform he had been a rich peasant and a dealer in mountain products, his trade being highly profitable because he combined it with money-lending. In the spring, when the peasants were in need of money, he lent it to them; and in the autumn, when the walnut, wild pepper and jujube crops came in, they repaid him in kind at prices and rates of interest highly favourable to the lender. Li Feng had worked on his own land alongside his labourers and he was notorious as the meanest employer in the village. The story went round that he preferred to hire hands from neighbouring villages rather than from Ten Mile Inn—for local men might go home to answer calls of nature and thus deprive their employer of fertilizer! Li Feng himself was not afraid of work. In fact he could not bear idleness, on the part of himself or any other member of his family. In the land reform he lost his large holdings and with them went the need to hire labour; but he kept his capacity for work. So as time went on, ex-farmhands who had hated him as a miserly slave-driver found him a not unsatisfactory team-mate, who pulled his weight well enough.

Thus Li Feng was an example of a former rich peasant whose attitude to work helped him adapt to the new ways; Wang Dian-yuan and Wang Jia-wen, on the contrary, were diehards who held out at least in words, if not in deeds, as long as they could and dared. Not all of the former landlords and rich peasants, however, went to this extreme.

Public order, therefore, could be and was for the most part maintained by mass surveillance. But as experience during the up-surge of co-operatives had shown, it was still necessary in order to guard against sabotage, besides preventing other types of crime. Mass surveillance was therefore guided and supplemented by the work of the Commune Security Department.

This department, in the commune structure, was under the Commune Council. It was, however, under dual leadership, being directed on the one hand by the Commune Council and Party Committee, on the other by the County Public Security Bureau, which gave it a place in the national security structure. This was because local sabotage was carried out in a national or even inter-national context. When the Kuomintang collapsed and fled to Taiwan, it left behind on the mainland two million disbanded armed men, as well as 600,000 key members of reactionary parties and organizations and a similar number of secret agents of various kinds. These counter-revolutionaries engaged in considerable disruption when the People's Republic was first established, but large number of them were soon rounded up, after which counter-revolutionary activity subsided. At the time of the Korean war it again rose to a pitch of extreme violence, then subsided once more. Again in 1955, during the socialist transformation of capitalist industry and com-merce, agriculture and handicrafts, the counter-revolutionaries, though now reduced in number, increased their sabotage in town and country. And in 1957, as the political and ideological revolution swept China, the remaining counter-revolutionaries and anti-socialists revived their activities, this time in response to the attacks of the 'bourgeois rightists'.

Military Matters and Commune Power

Meanwhile, two nationwide campaigns for suppressing counter-revolutionaries were launched, the first in 1950-51, the second in 1955. Hundreds of millions of people took part in each, and it was this which largely accounted for the high degree of peace and order throughout the country, much of which had previously been prey to warlordism and banditry. The first movement had been to protect the democratic reforms from attacks by remaining Kuomintang forces; the second, to protect the co-operative movement. This was led locally by county Party committees working through township security organizations and local Party branches. The aims of the movement were made clear, as well, to the general membership of each co-operative, after which there was an investigation of the political background of members, especially those serving as cadres.

Until this time public security had been a function of the government, not of co-operatives, which were regarded as economic organizations. But as it became clear that disruption of the co-operative movement was the main line of the counter-revolution, co-operative councils were forced to take a hand in this branch of work. Convincing the inexperienced and already over-worked cadres of the newly-developing co-operatives of the need for this, was one outcome of the 1955 movement. Most co-operative councils, therefore, had one member in charge of security. (This was one of the many fields in which overlapping functions of socialist co-operatives and township government was done away with by the forming of the commune.)

In the course of its security work during this whole period, as well as during the previous twenty years in its own base areas, the Communist Party had evolved certain principles. These now served as a guide to the Security Department of Yangyi as of communes all over the country.

The first principle was to 'rely on the masses' and 'not to create an air of mystery'. If public order were to be upheld by ordinary people, security could not be surrounded by such an atmosphere. Any tendency to veil it in this way was regarded as a left-over of the old regime in which a small minority oppressed the vast majority, and so had to resort to such means. The task of the Commune Security Bureau (and of the member in charge of security in each brigade) was to keep a check on the activities of one-time enemies as well as on any suspicious activities or incidents. These were summarized by the Bureau which was required to report on them to the Commune People's Congress. The purpose of this was to maintain a constant state of vigilance on the part of the whole people; for if people were lulled into feeling that the enemy had given up the struggle, considerable loss might be suffered from sabotage, arson and poisoning; and following any such outbreak public sentiment might swing to the opposite extreme of general anxiety and sus-

187

picion, seeing counter-revolution behind any untoward occurrence and 'imagining that every tree or blade of grass concealed an enemy agent'.[6]

The second principle was that a clear distinction must be made between 'ideological questions' and 'political questions'. A person might have reactionary views or serious personal shortcomings; but these were not crimes. They were to be dealt with by criticism, persuasion and education. Legal action was to be taken only against those who engaged in illegal political activity.

These two principles guided security work in the commune.

THE LOCAL MILITIA AND ITS TRADITION

In addition to a Department of Public Security, the commune had a Department of Military Affairs. In Yangyi, military matters consisted mainly of providing recruits for the People's Liberation Army (PLA) and maintaining a militia.

The aims of the militia were:

To defend the country and safeguard world peace;
To serve as a partially trained reserve for the PLA;
To promote production;
To improve physique.

Each work team in the commune had its platoon, each brigade its company, each district its battalion—all these together forming the commune regiment. Though militia and production or administrative units existed on the same levels, it was a principle that they should not merge nor be under the same leaders. This was a necessary stipulation. The first Central Committee directive on communes had referred to farmers 'getting organized along military lines' and 'working as if fighting a battle'.[7] In some parts of the country this had been taken to mean that the militia form of organization should replace the work teams and that farming should be carried on under the command of militia leaders. Later it was made clear that 'getting organized along military lines' and 'working as if fighting a battle' meant simply that farmers should be as organized and disciplined as workers in a factory.[8] And to avoid confusion of the functions of work team or brigade leaders on the one hand with militia platoon or company commanders on the other, a rule was laid down that in principle one person could not hold the two posts. Ten Mile Inn's Work Team One, for instance, at first had as its leader an ex-PLA

[6] See Luo Rui-qing, 'The Struggle between Revolution and Counter-Revolution in the Past Ten Years', *Ten Glorious Years*, F.L.P., Peking, 1959.

[7] 'Resolution on the Establishment of People's Communes in the Rural Areas, August, 1958', F.L.P., Peking, 1958.

[8] 'Resolution on Some Questions Concerning the People's Communes, December, 1958', F.L.P., Peking, 1958.

man, who at the same time was commander of the brigade's militia and in charge of its public security work. This piling up of duties on the shoulders of one man (the result of shortage of experienced cadres) proved harmful to farm production and in accordance with the Central Committee principle he gave up his post of work team leader.

The 'basic' militia consisted of only the sixteen- to twenty-five-year-olds. All the able-bodied men and some of the women of the required age were enrolled (a fair proportion of them being pupils or teachers in the various schools). In addition there was a score of ex-soldiers, veterans of the PLA or its predecessor the 8th Route Army, with military and political experience, serving as company, battalion or regimental commanders or commissars.

Typical of these was Fu Tian-xun, political commissar of the Ten Mile Inn Company. Fu was a local man and at the age of thirteen he had gone to work for Fu Pei-yin, the rich peasant drug-trader, usurer and ward-head.[9] His father and uncle both worked for the same master and were driven so hard that they sought relief in drugs. They had previously reclaimed half an acre of stony, hillside land and as they fell into the clutches of their money-lending, drug-trafficking master, they offered this as security for heroin on credit. The hard-won patch of land was soon forfeit, but after foreclosing on it Fu Pei-yin became alarmed. He sensed that the two brothers were seething with hatred for him and he dared not keep them in his employment for fear that they might rob him or even slit his throat. So he drove them out, together with Fu Tien-xun, then a boy in his teens.

It was impossible for them to find work in the village, so they scattered, each to try and keep alive as best he could.

This was in the late thirties, shortly after the Japanese invasion, and the boy soon ran into a unit of the 8th Route Army. The guerilla fighters listened to the lad's story sympathetically and took him along with them as an orderly. In the army he received an education, joined the Communist Party and rose to the rank of battalion staff officer. In 1953, at the age of twenty-nine Fu Tien-xun was demobilized and returned to Ten Mile Inn, where he married and settled down. His fifteen years' experience in the army were immediately made use of in the village militia.

Militia activity in 1960 consisted mainly of drilling, shooting practice, stripping and assembling of weapons. It had not always been so limited; in fact, the militia had a record of twenty years of revolutionary activity in the area.

In most of the villages round Yangyi the militia had been formed in the early part of the war against Japan. In Ten Mile Inn it was set

[9] See Chapter XIII.

up in 1941, with six men and a total armament of three old rifles and one pistol. Its first responsibility was to lay plans for the evacuation of the village to hillside caves in the event of enemy mopping-up operations. Then, at a school run by the communist-led anti-Japanese County Government, the new militiamen learnt to use grenades and landmines. They also gained a broader understanding of the scope and nature of the war against Japan. On returning home they expanded their own forces and co-operated with those of nearby villages. These combined operations included harassing the rear of enemy columns (called 'cutting off the enemy's tail'), mining the country roads and tearing up the tracks of the Japanese-run narrow gauge railway a few miles down the valley. Another important task was maintaining an intelligence service for their own security and to provide the 8th Route Army with 'thousand league eyes and down-wind ears'. Even the children took part in this, shepherd boys signalling warnings of suspicious sights from the hill-tops, and young guards armed with red-tasselled spears, standing at the village gates to examine all travellers' road-passes. The old folk also did their bit. While the age-limit for the militia was 35, supporting it was a defence corps for men from 35 to 50 and an old men's corps for those of 50 and over. By 1944 the militia proper had grown from six to seventy-five strong. By then, together with other village forces, it was able to besiege and storm enemy block-houses, manned mainly by Chinese puppet troops.[10]

In the course of the war, according to commune researches, the Japanese killed 275 people in the Yangyi area (many of them cadres), raped or carried off to their brothels over 500 women, seized draught animals, destroyed housing and altogether did damage amounting to a million and a quarter *yuan*. Against this, over 1,000 local men joined the 8th Route Army and 11,500 the militia. The latter killed almost 2,000 of the enemy (including Chinese puppet troops) in twenty skirmishes, the largest being the 'Battle of Yangyi', a combined operation of 8th Route Army and local militia forces in which 1,300 Japanese were reported to have been put out of action.

In 1958, as the movement to set up communes swept across China, to an accompanying campaign of condemnation abroad, there was a mass surge into the militia. This was described as a step towards 'turning the whole people into soldiers in the event of imperialist aggression'.[11]

[10] In the Liberated Areas as a whole, which by the end of the Anti-Japanese War covered 950,000 square kilometres with a population of over 95 million, the militia totalled 2,200,000 strong; auxiliary defence organizations were over four times as big.

[11] 'Resolution on Some Questions Concerning the People's Communes', F.L.P., Peking, 1958, p. 43.

Military Matters and Commune Power

Recruits were provided for the PLA by means of an annual call-up of eighteen-year-olds. This was highly selective, only a small proportion of those eligible being needed in the army.

In Yangyi Commune, with standards of acceptance so high, there was keen competition for joining the PLA. In 1959, for example, eighteen boys from Ten Mile Inn reached call-up age. Registration was preceded by an educational campaign to point out the significance of serving in the army and to acquaint the young generation with its traditions. Meetings were held at the school, where village veterans spoke of their own experiences and of the exploits of national heroes; village poets wrote verses and the school-children sang songs for the occasion. At the end of the campaign all of the eighteen wrote pledges that they would volunteer on registration day. Meanwhile friends entered into compacts or issued each other challenges. Twin brothers Li Sheng-xi and Li Sheng-guei agreed to volunteer together and to win their parents' consent that both should join up. This they did, but when they reached the enlistment centre, one boy was turned down as under the required height. Another pair, who had been friends all through their schooldays, made a pledge to get 'excellent' in all their courses until call-up time and to gain their parents' consent to their joining up. They both succeeded on all counts, but again one boy failed to top the height requirement.

All in all, of the eighteen volunteering, only five were accepted. The age-old saying:

> You don't use good iron to make nails;
> You don't take good men to make soldiers

had now long been discarded. Ex-servicemen returning to their villages after regular or short-term service in the PLA were highly regarded and played a role out of proportion to their numbers. Of 547 demobilized soldiers in Yangyi Commune in 1960, 276 had been chosen Commune or Brigade Party Secretaries, or served as commune, brigade or work team leaders, or in the militia as commanders or commissars. They had been among the most public-spirited before volunteering for the army. During their service they had received general and political education in addition to military and technical training and experience. Some had fought the Japanese in North China; others had gone across the Yellow River and even south of the Yangtze in the war against the Kuomintang; still others had joined the Volunteers and fought in Korea. Younger national servicemen, though they had not seen active service, came back to the village with mechanical and technical training and experience as well as general and political education.

These ex-soldiers kept up the habits of systematic study they had

191

formed in the army. They organized 54 study groups in the commune and met once every ten days for classes or discussion. These groups were co-ordinated through six 'study stations', where books and periodicals were available and where members gathered once a month. This theoretical study combined with their practical experience and public spirit made the ex-soldiers an asset to the leadership at various levels in the commune. As rank-and-file members of work teams, too, they were looked to as pace-setters. In Little Yetao, for instance, the army veterans formed themselves into a shock team which they named the August 1st Team (after the founding day of the PLA). This team did much to set and maintain the high standards of that model brigade by fixing high targets and engaging in emulation.[12]

While ex-soldiers played a significant role in all branches of work in the commune, they were a powerful reserve for the army. As one of them remarked, 'Everyone of us is a soldier. If an enemy dares to invade our country, we'll put down our hoes and take up our guns.' In this they were at one with the militia, whose watchword was:

... there are still imperialist pirates abroad who are clamouring every day about wiping out this people's state. Therefore the whole of our people are determined to continue to arm themselves, and they declare: Be warned you pirates bent on plundering us. Do not dare to make a vain attempt to harm our people engaged in peaceful labour. We are fully prepared! Should the imperialists dare to unleash an aggressive war against our country, we will turn the whole nation into soldiers. The militia will co-operate with the People's Liberation Army and replenish it at any time to crush the aggressors.[13]

[12] See Chapter XX, 'Youth'.
[13] 'Resolution on Some Questions Concerning the People's Communes.'

PART THREE
*Politics of
Yangyi Commune*

INTRODUCTION

PARTY AND ADMINISTRATION

When 33 socialist co-operatives and 10 townships merged to form Yangyi Commune in September 1958, some people proposed that the Communist Party organizations in the area should also merge with the commune. This was overwhelmingly rejected on the grounds that it 'confused the highest form of organization of the working class' (the Party) 'with a non-Party revolutionary organization' (the Government).[1] The Party, it was pointed out, was responsible for political guidance and planning; it was not to take over administration.

Yangyi Commune had, in fact, parallel administrative and Party structures.[2] It had a Commune Council of 30-odd members and a Commune Party General Branch Committee (Commune Party Committee) of a similar size. These bodies consulted on day-to-day problems under the chairmanship of the Commune First Party Secretary, made decisions and assigned one of their number to see that they were carried out. This situation was duplicated at district and brigade levels.

At each level within the commune there was collective leadership and individual responsibility. This meant that decisions were made collectively but individuals were responsible for seeing that they were carried out. This was to avoid having 'everyone doing everything and no one responsible for anything' (the tendency which had once provoked the quip that 'the co-op's like a beehive', all buzz and bustle; and which in the early days of the commune accounted for brigade equipment being left out in the fields to spoil).

By the summer of 1960 every branch of work, every unit, every field and plot of land in the commune had someone responsible for it, seeing that decisions concerning it were carried out. In the case of a high yield tract it was a member of the Commune Council or District Committee, since tracts overlapped brigade boundaries; with a work team it was a member of the Brigade Party Committee and in a work group within the team it was a cadre or a Party or Youth League member. Every canteen had a Party or C.Y.L. guarantor whose name was posted up outside it.

---

[1] Liu Lan-tao, 'The Communist Party of China is the High Command of the Chinese People in Building Socialism', *Ten Glorious Years*, F.L.P., Peking, 1959.
[2] See Table 9.

TABLE 9: *Political and Administrative Structure of the Commune*
(Summer, 1960)

ADMINISTRATIVE AND STATE STRUCTURE	CORRESPONDING COMMUNIST PARTY STRUCTURE
Commune (Smallest unit of local government)	*General Branch*
Commune People's Congress (Elected every two years and meeting twice a year or oftener if need be)	*Commune Party Congress*
Commune Council (31 members, including 5 commune heads)	*Commune General Branch Committee* (28 members, of whom 11, including 7 Party secretaries, serve as the standing committee)
Departments (Staff of 20 full-time workers): Office Security Military Affairs Industry and Trade Education and Culture Technical Station	Departments (Staff of 15 full-time workers): Office Organization Propaganda Discipline Leadership of: Commune Communist Youth League Commune Women's Federation
District (six districts in all, with branch offices of the above departments and a staff of 25 full-time workers in the six districts)	*District Party Leadership* (Party secretaries in all the Districts are members of the Commune Party General Branch Committee and appointed to the job)
Brigade (Chief unit of ownership management and accounting)[4]	*Branch*[3]
Meeting of the Entire Brigade Membership: or Brigade Congress	
Brigade Council (Appointed by the Commune Council)	*Brigade Party Branch Committee*
Work Team	*Party Group*

[3] Brigade branches were not the only ones. Each of the seven industrial enterprises (the mine, farm tools works, printing shop, etc.), had a branch, as had schools. Of the commune's 40 high yield tracts, the larger ones, such as the Silver Sea also had their own branches. Thus while there were only 24 brigades there were altogether 61 branches.

[4] In 1960-61 the work team became the chief level of ownership, management and accounting.

Introduction

When the Commune Council of 31 members and the Commune Party Committee of 28 members met in joint session, there were well under 59 members, several of the Party Committee having been elected by the Commune Congress to the Council. Ren Qing-mei and Guo Heng-de, for example, were both vice-chairmen of the Council and members of the Party Committee. Like these two, many others of Yangyi's 1,100-odd Party members were among the commune's 2,000 cadres.

The overwhelming majority of the 2,000 were engaged in full-time production, only 60 to 100, at commune and district level, being full-time cadres and paid as such. All the others worked in the fields, workshops or social services, their duties as cadres being discharged as service to the community for which they received no pay except compensation for time lost from regular work. (Before 'leading on the job' was introduced in 1960[5] this compensation might amount to a good part of a cadre's earnings; after the new system was in operation it made up a very small one.)

At commune level there were altogether about 100 Party and administrative cadres, of whom 20 were full-time staff members in the departments under the Commune Council and 15 full-time staff members in the Party offices. In addition the commune had a full-time militia commander and political commissar as well as cadres in charge of the tractor station, farm tools manufacture and repair shop and other industrial enterprises. Leaders of the Communist Youth League and the Women's Democratic Federation of the whole commune were also full-time cadres.

At district level there were another 25 full-time staff members of the commune's administrative departments, supervising work in the brigades.

At brigade level there were about 500 cadres. These included brigade heads and vice-heads, chief accountants, militia company commanders and political commissars and one or two cadres in each brigade in charge of social services, the school and trade centre. There were also Party, Youth League and Women's Federation cadres (usually a secretary and two vice-secretaries each). This meant that each brigade had about twenty cadres, but none of them were full-time.[6]

At work team level there were 1,200 to 1,300 cadres, again none of them full-time. Each of the 35 or so work teams had a head and vice-head (a man and a woman), one or two cadres in charge of the canteen and a militia platoon commander.

All in all this accounted for close on 2,000 people out of 37,000 in the commune, who were entrusted with special responsibility.

[5] See Chapter XVIII.
[6] Ibid.

Cadres and Party members overlapped to a considerable extent and it was customary to speak of them together.

Nevertheless, maintaining a proper distinction and relationship between Party and administration was considered essential. The Communist Party was described not as a 'mass organization' but as a 'vanguard detachment of the masses'. Its leadership was elected by the Party membership (subject to ratification by the level above), whereas that of the administration was elected by the commune members. The Party's task was to explain and win support for its policies; that of the administration was to put into effect those policies the masses had endorsed.

<h2 style="text-align:center">YANGYI'S COMMUNISTS</h2>

Joining the Communist Party was not easy, requirements as to character, ideology and background being rigorous and subject to a process of recommendation, investigation and approval at different levels, which was followed by a probationary period. Duties involved placing the interests of the Party and the people before personal interests, being modest and unpretentious, studying and working hard, uniting with the mass of the people and overcoming all difficulties to make China a powerful, prosperous and advanced Socialist State.[7] They were summed up in the slogan: 'First to bear hardships, last to enjoy comforts.'

There were Party members assuming these responsibilities everywhere in the commune: in work teams, in the trade department and industrial enterprises, the militia, schools and social services and in the Communist Youth League and Women's Democratic Federation. They included a core of revolutionaries (all local men and women) with over twenty years' experience in the Party.

Before they joined the Party these old Communists had been illiterate poor peasants or hired hands.

At the end of the thirties, when the first communist armed work teams slipped into the villages around Yangyi at night, past the sentries of the local warlords or the Japanese, it was from among the 'poor and hired' that they sought 'activists' to serve as a bridge to the mass of the peasants. Once they got to know a likely individual, that is, one with the seeds of class consciousness as well as courage and energy, they began to explain Party policy. This was done in patient talks often lasting far into the night. Such was the case with 8th Route Army political instructor Wang Tie and the Little Yetao farmhand Ren Qing-mei, as well as with the communist woman cadre Guo Jing and the young poor peasant woman Guo Heng-de of Bailin. In time a number of these activists were secretly recruited into the then

---

[7] 'Constitution of the Communist Party of China', 8th National Congress of the C.P.C., *Documents*, Vol. I, F.L.P., Peking, 1956.

Introduction

underground Communist Party; they in turn recruited others. Ren Qing-mei joined the Party in 1938 and recruited a handful of other Little Yetao labourers and poor peasants. Thus the first Branch of the Yangyi area was formed. It was inaugurated in a cave outside the village, for discovery would have meant death. That first year, in the villages now forming Yangyi Commune, altogether 32 Party members were recruited by 8th Route Army teams working through local activists.

It was these early underground Party members who set up peasant associations in the villages and who, in accordance with the Party's General Line won fellow villagers for the broad united front struggle against the Japanese. And it was they who led the way in implementing the specific policies of Reduction of Rent and Interest, hiding grain from the enemy, growing cotton and organizing women to spin and weave, starting mutual aid. Again it was these local 'old Bolsheviks' who had spearheaded the fight against famine, dealt with pro-Japanese collaborators, built up the militia, joined and recruited for the 8th Route Army, organized rear service (stretcher-bearing and transport for the army and doing farmwork for soldiers' families).

After the victory over the Japanese, as soon as his forces had been moved up from the deep rear in American ships and planes, Chiang Kai-shek launched full-scale civil war to gain control of the vast areas which the Communists had freed from the invaders. The Communist Party, which had made proposals for avoiding civil war, finding them rejected put forward a new General Line: to form the broadest possible united front against the imperialists, the bureaucrat capitalists[8] and the feudal classes. The task of the Yangyi Communists now became to lead the mass of peasants and labourers in destroying the power of local landlords and rich peasants and taking the land for themselves; then to guide the newly-landed farmers to further economic advances by way of expanded mutual aid and marketing and credit co-operatives. Thus between 1946 and 1948, Yangyi's Communists were in the forefront of land reform struggles which set 90 per cent of the people in action. Land reform was linked with military operations—the forming of a militia to guard the newly-won land from the 'Homegoing Corps' of dispossessed landlords and rich peasants, and the providing of rear service and recruits to help the People's Liberation Army to defeat the landlord-backed Kuomintang.

Towards the end of this period the Yangyi Communists, till then underground, came out into the open. Those peasants and labourers who had been most resolute and active in the struggles were found

[8] Bureaucrat-capitalists were officials of Chiang Kai-shek's Kuomintang Government, who used their posts and public funds and property to run economic enterprises for their personal profit, or who simply put the profits from public enterprises into their own pockets.

199

to have been recruited into the Party. They formed the 'second generation' of Yangyi Communists.

Unlike these first two generations, both steeled in times of war, the 'third generation' of Party members were those recruited in the early struggles of the new socialist revolution. Following the brief period needed for restoring the war-torn economy and completing land reform in the newly-liberated areas, a new General Line was put forward: 'To carry out step by step socialist industrialisation and the socialist transformation of private industry, agriculture, handicrafts and trade.' Around Yangyi this meant strengthening mutual aid, then moving on to co-operative farming, first semi-socialist, later fully socialist. This set tests of a new nature—of the choice between two roads of development: the capitalist road of private ownership and personal profit and the socialist road of collectivized farming for the general welfare. This period, from 1951 to 1958, called for a clear-cut choice, for Communists and others, between going it alone and working collectively.

1958, the year of the founding of the commune and of the Great Leap Forward, marked the beginning of another stage in which newly-recruited Party members were put to the test of a new General Line of: 'going all out to make China a great socialist country with modern industry, agriculture, science, culture and national defence in the shortest possible time.'

During each of these periods new Party members were recruited from among those (mainly hired hands and poor and lower middle peasants) who fought in the campaigns with the greatest courage and understanding. But each successive stage along the socialist road set higher and higher demands on the Communists. So while fresh forces came in, a few who could not take the next step fell behind or even dropped out. Some who had joined the Party in response to the call to drive out the invaders, held back in the struggle against landlords and rich peasants. Others who fought hard to win land for the tillers could not bring themselves to lead the way in organizing co-operatives.

Those who dropped out did so as a rule in the course of rectification movements. The main aim of these was not simply to rid the Party of 'impure elements'; it was to refine the quality of the whole membership, to raise it to the level of the ever rising demands upon it. Dropping the few who failed to make the grade was a minor aspect. The major one was upgrading the many who stayed in.

In 1960 Yangyi Commune had altogether 1,140 men and women Party members in 61 branches and 286 groups.[9] (The branch was the basic organizational unit; groups consisted of the Party members who happened to be working in the same work team or small

[9] Figures for the whole country in 1959 were: 13,960,000 members in 1,060,000 branches. Liu Lan-tao, op. cit.

enterprise.) The branches were led by the Commune General Branch Committee which had a Standing Committee of eleven. Nine members of the General Branch Committee were engaged in full-time production in their own brigades, some of them also serving as Brigade Party Secretaries.

Under the Commune General Branch Committee were a number of departments (for organization, propaganda, discipline) and an office. These had a full-time staff of fifteen. Each of the commune's six districts had its Party Secretary (concurrently a member of the General Branch Committee) who supervised Party work in all the brigades in his district. Finally each brigade had one or more Party branches with their own Branch Committees, each led by a First Party Secretary and one or two Assistant Secretaries. These were responsible for Party work in the brigades, including the leading of Party groups.

CURRENT TASKS OF THE YANGYI COMMUNE GENERAL BRANCH COMMITTEE

In the summer of 1960, the General Branch Committee was responsible for the success of five key tasks in the commune. These were on five different fronts: the first was in political and ideological work, the second had to do with upgrading cadres, the third with modernizing agriculture, the fourth with developing social services and the fifth with work among women and youth.

Work on each of these fronts had its focal points.

The first, summed up in the slogan 'Politics in Command', was to tackle the political and ideological work which was necessary for the commune to move forward and not to be bogged down in administrative detail. This meant paying special attention to the 286 Party groups, sharpening their members' awareness of the class struggle going on and showing how current tasks fitted into the long-term goal; then, through the Party members, spreading this understanding among ordinary commune members. The Commune Party Committee estimated that this work was going well and as evidence cited the speed with which a mass movement could be developed. After the wheat harvest, for instance, when the county leadership issued instructions for making the regular deliveries of grain to the state, a mass movement was executed in a single day, as opposed to the three or four days required in the past. On this one day alone Yangyi delivered over a million *jin* of wheat to the county administration. This was achieved by 'putting politics in command'.[10]

The second key task called for changing cadres' 'work style'—that is, their grasp of the actual conditions in their field of work and their relations with the people, or 'mass line'. At this time the chief

[10] See Chapter XVII.

201

measure for improving 'work style' was the 'two: five system', which left full-time cadres in their offices (holding meetings, writing reports, filling in forms, studying directives) for only two days out of seven, and for the remaining five enabled them to be out on the production front.[11]

The third task called for implementing the policy that agriculture was the base of the economy, and striving for a bumper harvest by taking the high yield tracts as the 'battlefield', and promoting irrigation, mechanization, electrification, and 'chemicalization' (use of chemical fertilizers, insecticides, etc.).

The fourth was the organizing of social services to improve the living conditions of all commune members—especially of the women released for productive employment.

The fifth point was work among women and youth. This meant drawing women into the most important current tasks of the commune, particularly farming and social services. From this stemmed two other tasks: one was helping women to become technically proficient, the other developing their capacity for leadership. On the principle that the best way to train cadres was on the job, a new system was being put into effect: every brigade and work team had to have a woman as vice-head and efforts were being made to have woman assistant Party secretaries in every brigade branch.[12] Work among young people meant urging them to lead the way in carrying out the Party's policy. This called for strengthening the Communist Youth League, politically and ideologically.[13]

These five points were current tactics fitting into an overall strategy. The members of the Commune Party Committee, as 'scientific socialists', took it for granted that there were laws governing the development of society which could be discovered and made use of, just as there were in other fields. Commune Secretary Jin Han-cheng, for instance, explained the emergence of the commune and its growth in the following Marxist terms:

First the forces of production were fettered by the relations of production embodied in the socialist farming co-operatives. These were too small and too limited in scope to solve the farmers' problems: the need for larger scale soil and water conservation, mechanization, electrification and 'chemicalization' of agriculture. The six months period from the setting up of the commune to the check-up of April 1959, brought the relations into line with the forces of production.[14] This had the effect of releasing these forces, so that there was an advance in agricultural technique (shown in the widespread use of the Eight Point Charter); in agricultural capital construction

[11] See Chapter XVIII.
[12] See Chapter XIX.
[13] See Chapter XX.
[14] See next page.

Introduction

(to be seen in the digging of the North Zhang Channel, as well as smaller channels and some reservoirs, etc.); and in the development of local industry. With these changes in the economic base of society, measures had to be taken to bring about corresponding changes in the thinking and habits of the people. In other words, in order to achieve a fresh advance in the forces of production it was necessary to bring about changes in the ideological superstructure. This was done by the rectification and socialist education campaign in the winter of 1959-60.

As a result of the changes in the superstructure brought about by this campaign, a new upsurge of the forces of production was taking place, as seen in the widespread development of high yield tracts and technical innovations. It was the duty of the Party to grasp the main task of the moment and throw its whole weight behind it, to roll forward the wheel of history.

This cycle of advances in the forces and relations of production and ideological superstructure was not new in Yangyi. It was precisely what had taken place in the winter of 1955-56 with the setting up of socialist co-operatives. This had been followed by the burst of speed in production of 1956, then by the rectification and Great Debate of 1957 and finally by the Great Leap Forward of 1958.[15]

[15] The various problems of management in the brigades and work teams, aggravated by natural disasters, showed that the relations of production were still in need of adjustment. This was made only in the winter of 1960–61. It was not until the holding of the 10th Plenary Session of the 8th Central Committee, in 1962, that the Chinese Communist Party officially stated that these relations had been adjusted throughout the country and that the Party's attention could be focused on changing the forces of production. (See 'Communique of the 10th Plenary Session of the 8th Central Committee of the C.P.C., September, 1962'; *Peking Review*, No. 39, 1962.)

203

Chapter XVII

CLASSES AND THE CLASS LINE

CLASS ORIGIN AND POLITICAL STAND

IN 1960 four years had already passed since the socialist co-operatives with their collective ownership of land, had undermined the economic basis of capitalism. And it was a good twelve years since the land reform had 'eliminated the landlords and rich peasants as a class'. Yet in analysing commune problems the Yangyi cadres still spoke of landlords, rich, poor and middle peasants, even of upper middle and lower middle peasants. They still stressed the need to 'look at things from a class standpoint' and to do all revolutionary work according to 'the class line'.

In talking of classes, the cadres were referring not to existing economic relations but to ideology and behaviour which stemmed from social origin—on the principle that a person's social character is determined primarily by his class.[1] The former landlords and rich peasants they referred to were those who had been so classified at the time of the land reform. Upper-middle, lower-middle and poor peasants, were those who were of this class before joining the farming co-operatives.

Definitions of class were based not on standard of living but on ownership of the means of production and the social relations arising from it.

The classes or strata singled out as most politically significant in

[1] This Marxist theory of human nature was summed up by Liu Shao-chi in his essay, 'The Class Character of Man', in which he states:

'. . . if a given group of people have for a long time held the status of a given class, that is, a given position in social production; and have for a long time produced, lived and struggled in a given manner, they will create their particular mode of life and their particular interests, demands, psychology, ideas, customs, viewpoints, manners, and relations with other groups of people and things etc. All these are different from or contrary to those created by other groups of people. In this manner the particular characteristics of men, their particular class character, are formed.

'As people in different classes of society have different interests, demands, ideas and customs, so they have different ways of looking at, and different policies in dealing with, everything in society and history—such as politics, economics, culture, etc. . . .'

—in *How to be a Good Communist*, F.L.P., Peking, 1951. Appendix: 'The Class Character of Man.'

204

1960 were: ex-landlords and ex-rich peasants; upper-middle peasants; lower-middle and poor peasants. In Yangyi Commune the first group was extremely small; the second was estimated to make up about 10 per cent; while the third consisted of close on 90 per cent of the rural population.[2] Each of these three main classes or strata was regarded as having a characteristic outlook on life and its own attitude to developments in the countryside.

In the village of South Yangyi (south of Yangyi townlet), for example, in 1957 there were 849 households. Thirteen (1·5 per cent) of these were ex-landlord or ex-rich peasant families, who before the land reform had owned 1,795 *mu*. Eighty-two (9·8 per cent) were upper-middle peasants.[3] Before the land reform they had owned 4,264 *mu* of land and at the time of setting up farming co-operatives were among the best-off in the village. The remaining 744 households (88·7 per cent) were poor or lower-middle peasants. Before land reform they had owned 4,213 *mu*—less than the upper middle peasants. Many members of the poorest households had hired themselves out to the landlords, rich and upper middle peasants—288 as long-term hired hands, 144 on a short-term basis.

As part of the rectification and socialist education movement in the winter of 1957, the cadres made a study of the stand each South Yangyi household had taken during the long struggle to form and consolidate the co-operative. Three categories were defined: those who had supported socialism all along; those who had wavered back and forth; those who had actively opposed socialism and supported capitalism. 713 households (85 per cent) were found to belong to the first category; 113 (13·5 per cent) to the second and 13 (1·5 per cent) to the third. Analysis revealed certain features of each group.

Of the 744 lower-middle and poor peasant households, 659 (88·6 per cent) had consistently supported socialism; and though the other 85 (11·4 per cent) had vacillated, none had actually opposed collectivizing or supported individual farming.

Thus despite the waverers among them, the lower-middle and poor peasants were essentially united in their stand. This was in

[2] This did not coincide with nation-wide figures according to which poor and lower-middle peasants amounted to 70 per cent of the rural population.
[3] The upper-middle peasants had varying backgrounds. There were, for instance, 'the old' and 'the new'. The old upper-middle peasants (those who had been prosperous even before land reform) were harder to win over than the new. The latter, though their former poverty was fading from their memory could still be brought to recall it, and to see it as a product of exploitation. Many of them, too, had fought against the Japanese and later against the landlords and rich peasants. Thus their political insight was deeper than that of the old middle peasants. The South Yangyi figures included only old middle peasants as upper-middle peasants, and excluded new middle peasants. This accounts for the discrepancy with national figures, in which new upper-middle were grouped with old middle peasants rather than with lower-middle and poor peasants.

marked contrast to the scattering found among the other two classes. This investigation convinced the cadres and the mass of rank-and-file members of the South Yangyi Socialist Co-operative that classes were still significant. Without it, quite different ideas might have arisen: for instance, that wavering was typical of poor and lower-middle peasants (75·2 per cent of the waverers being of this class) and rare among ex-landlords and rich peasants (only 3·5 per

TABLE 10: *Class Composition of South Yangyi Village (1957)*

Class	Number of House-holds	Per-centage	Land held before Land Reform	Per-centage
Poor and lower middle peasants	744	88·7	4,213 *mu*	41·014
Upper middle peasants	82	9·8	4,264 *mu*	41·512
Ex-landlords and rich peasants	13	1·5	1,795 *mu*	17·474
Total	839	100·	10,272 *mu*	100·

TABLE 11: *Political Stand taken by Households of Different Classes of South Yangyi Village (1957)*

	Class			
Political stand	Poor and lower-middle peasants	Upper-middle peasants	Ex-landlords and rich peasants	Total
	744	82	13	839 (100%)
Those who supported the socialist road (active) (passive)	659 (88·6%)	48 (58·5%) (21)(25·6%) (27)(32·9%)	6 (46%)	718 (85%)
Those who wavered	85 (11·4%)	24 (29·3%)	4 (31%)	113 (13·5%)
Those who opposed the socialist road and supported the capitalist	—	10 (12·1%)	3 (23%)	13 (1·5%)

cent of the waverers being of these classes). The proportion of waverers, however, was almost three times as high among the latter as among the former. (Had the category of poor and lower-middle peasants taken in only 70 per cent instead of close on 90 per cent, many of these waverers might have been excluded.[4])

The political stand taken by the households of South Yangyi, as shown in the table, represented no natural tendency to support socialism. It was a result of almost twenty years of work in the area by the Communist Party. This was based on the following Marxist premises: The peasantry is a part of the petty-bourgeoisie, and while throughout history it has shown that it has its revolutionary side, its ideology is essentially individualist, not collectivist. The community of small producers which arose from the land reform, therefore, would if left to itself create a capitalist system in the countryside. The division, in the course of the transition to collectivism, into upper-middle peasants on the one hand and lower-middle and poor peasants on the other, accorded with the susceptibility of these classes to collectivism. The poor peasant small producer was a labouring man—but he was also a seller of commodities, who would tend to retain his individualistic, small producer's outlook even after the basis for it had gone—that is, after co-operatives had replaced individual holdings. But while naturally an individualist, the poor peasant was open to collectivist ideas—because of his vulnerability and insecurity under both the feudal and capitalist systems of farming.

It was by acting on these assumptions that the South Yangyi Party Branch was able to convert 88·6 per cent of this class into firm supporters of collectivism; to partially convince the remaining 11·4 per cent and to leave not a single household with the full-blown individualist outlook of the small producer.

The upper-middle peasants were not so easily weaned from individualism. Yet over half of them had been won over to at least passive acceptance of collectivism and only 12 per cent remained opposed.

Much depended on how satisfied each upper-middle peasant household was with its income and with the running of the co-operative or brigade it belonged to.

Within these families, too, different members might have different attitudes, the young folk on the whole being more collectively-minded than their elders. This was the case with the Meng family, the old man at first staying out of the co-operative but agreeing to join it when he saw it would bring him more money; his daughter-in-

---

[4] In South Yangyi, only the old upper-middle peasants were classed as upper-middle peasants. Those who became upper-middle peasants following the land reform were not counted. Had both sections been taken together (as was usual in classification) the figure would have come to between 20 and 30 per cent, according to findings for other areas. See *Socialist Upsurge in China's Countryside*.

law, whom he had rated lower than his mule, wishing to join as soon as the co-operative was set-up.

With the former landlords and rich peasants, too, various factors were involved in overcoming opposition to the co-operatives. One was the way in which the cadres carried out the policy. Another was time. Twenty years had brought a new generation reared in a social environment where property was not worshipped nor labour despised. During the last ten years almost all—even of the older generation—had given up hope that Chiang Kai-shek and his Kuomintang armies might come back and restore their property. They felt, however reluctantly, it was more practical to move along the socialist road together with the rest of the villagers than to stay back with a cause that was lost. Another factor was the progress of the economy, clearly seen in tractors, electric lights, reservoirs, local mines and steel mills, schooling for all children—including their own. These things among others made it possible for six out of thirteen ex-enemy households to support the co-operative, for four to waver back and forth rather than to oppose it, and for only three out of thirteen households to maintain a hostile stand, hoping for a restoration of the old regime and saying and doing what they could and dared to oppose the new, by rumour-mongering and sabotage.

ROUSING CLASS CONSCIOUSNESS

Class analysis had not come naturally to the peasants. It was cultivated by the Communist Party. When the 8th Route Army work teams first came to Yangyi they constantly urged the poor peasants and hired labourers to draw a line between themselves and the landlord and rich peasant classes, to recognize the latter's exploiting nature.

This had long been obscured by social customs and institutions. Family ties, so distant that in industrial society their existence would hardly have been realized, had been kept alive in an intricate system of relationship terms and by given names indicating a particular generation. Before land reform, ancestral halls and tablets and ceremonies such as sweeping ancestral graves, as well as the appointment of clan elders, upkeep of clan lands and other institutions were all kept alive and controlled by landlords and rich peasants to maintain their authority. In this social atmosphere clan rivalry (such as that between the Fu's, Li's and Wangs in Ten Mile Inn) and village rivalry (such as that between Bailin and Yangyi over water) had flourished. All this had served to obscure the fundamental relationship of class society: that of exploiter and exploited.

When the landlords and rich peasants ruled, theirs were the ruling ideas. Outstanding among these was the belief that the poor peasants and farm labourers were dependent on the landlords and rich peasants and should be grateful to them, for leasing land (at exorbitant rents), for lending money (at usurious rates) and for giving employment (at long hours and low wages), and that without all this the poor would starve. Thus the landlords and rich peasants were seen as benefactors, not as exploiters. The Communists maintained that it was not the landlords and rich peasants who supported their tenants and hired hands, but the other way round. If the poor peasants and farm labourers withdrew their labour, they asked, what would the land bring the landlord fanning himself in his courtyard? It was labour that created all wealth and the labourer who was heir to it.

Revealing the nature and relationship of classes was a powerful weapon in the Communists' armoury. They used it in big campaigns in the Yangyi area, both before and after land reform, to establish a class outlook among the hired labourers and poor peasants, to show them that they were victims of exploitation. One method employed was the 'Pouring Out Bitterness Meeting'. Here long pent-up feelings and facts were released through the telling of personal histories: of ruthless seizure of land for payment of rent or debt, especially in time of famine; of families driven to beggary, child-selling, starvation and suicide. The Communists helped speakers and listeners to 'get to the root of the bitterness', to trace it to its source and analyse its nature—exploitation. In this way the image of the landlords and rich peasants as benefactors was shattered. They were portrayed as parasites and murderers. At the same time the once despised and downtrodden labourers and poor peasants were offered a new image of themselves—as people worthy of respect and entitled to the fruits of their toil. Above all, by hearing from the mouths of others, stories of sufferings like their own, individuals began to grasp that their misery was due not to fate but to class; and that while the individual was helpless in the face of exploitation, the class as a whole could end it.

The concept of class and class solidarity, the use of such terms as exploiter and exploited, the establishing of the view that labour is admirable and idleness odious, were vital forces in the fight against feudalism, just as rejection or concealment of them had been bulwarks of feudal rule.

With the victory over the Kuomintang armies and the carrying out of the land reform, the class struggle became more complex. It was still directed against the defeated landlords and rich peasants to prevent them from undermining the revolution and to make them change their ideas. This was a struggle between 'the people' and their enemies.[5] But the main class struggle now was between those taking

---

[5] The people at this stage comprised the working class, the peasantry, the urban petty-bourgeoisie and the national bourgeoisie. See Mao Tse-tung, 'On the People's Democratic Dictatorship', *Selected Works*, Vol. IV, F.L.P., Peking, 1961, pp. 417–18.

the socialist road and those seeking to take the capitalist one. This was mainly a struggle 'within the ranks of the people', that could be handled peacefully. It was more difficult than that against the former landlords and rich peasants, for the upper middle peasants could not be kept in order with a 'cap'. They were secure in their position as full-fledged citizens, so long as they did not break the law.[6]

In 1960, therefore, the Communist Party had different approaches to the different classes in the countryside, based on their characteristic attitude to exploitation and to labour. These were: 'rely on the poor and lower-middle peasants; steady the upper-middle peasants; remould the former landlords and rich peasants.'

Re-moulding the defeated enemy classes was a major objective of the exercise of state power by the commune.[7] Steadying the upper middle peasants was the guiding principle for waging the main class struggle in the commune—between followers of the two roads. Relying on the poor and lower middle peasants was the guide to choosing cadres and training them to arouse and organize the rest of their class to transform agriculture, society and themselves.[8]

STEADYING THE WAVERING OF THE UPPER-MIDDLE PEASANTS

It was only after land reform that the upper-middle peasants became a significant social force. For only after the destruction of the feudal land-owning system could capitalist tendencies advance in the countryside and these peasants become budding capitalist farmers, a newly arising rural exploiting class.

In Yung An village, for example, there was a farmer called Wang Jing, who owned 15 *mu* of good land. As he was the only working hand in the family he hired help, in 1949 paying 120 *yuan* for 150 work days. The returns from the land cultivated by hired hands, after deducting the cost of seed and fertilizer, came to 220 *yuan*. 'So he got a hundred *yuan* from exploitation,' said a local cadre, 'and the following year he bought three more *mu* of land.'

At this time (around 1949-50) some 20 per cent of China's farmers, like Wang Jing, were going up in the world (these were the upper-middle peasants); most of the remainder were merely holding their own or were on the downgrade.

Towards the thriving 20 per cent the Party line was: encourage them to prosper through increasing their output, but curb their

[6] The concept of two types of class contradictions, those 'between the people and their enemies', and those 'within the ranks of the people', as well as the handling of this latter type of contradiction, were developments of Marxist theory by Mao Tse-tung. Though the concept had been applied for some time, it was first publicly presented in 1957 in his *On the Correct Handling of Contradictions among the People*.

[7] See Chapter XVI, Military Matters and Commune Power.

[8] See Chapter XVIII, Mass Line Leaders and Leadership.

opportunities for doing so by exploitation (hiring of labour, profiteering and usury). To achieve this, Government and co-operative loans were issued, relief was given to the needy and mutual aid was organized. These measures could not meet the needs of all the many peasants short of capital, but they did help check the hiring of labour and the rate of interest which well-off lenders could charge.

Steps were also taken to curb profiteering. After land reform, farm production had gone up; but with the growth of the industrial population and the fast-rising need for industrial crops created by the first five-year plan (1952-56), demand had risen still faster. Well-to-do peasants strove to take advantage of this. So in 1953 a new measure was introduced to prevent surpluses from falling into the hands of profiteers. This was the Planned Purchase and Supply, at fixed prices, of grain, oil-bearing crops, cotton and certain other farm products. The upper-middle peasants tried to rally opposition to this policy by portraying it as an encroachment on the peasants' freedom. Communist Party branches throughout the Yangyi area, in a movement launched to explain it, described the policy thus: 'If you have a big surplus of grain the state will buy a lot from you; if you have a small one, it will buy a little; if you have no surplus, you won't be asked to sell; if you are short of grain, the government will help you out.' Broken down into these terms the policy's class nature became clear and it won the support of the poor and lower-middle peasants. The upper-middle peasants opposed it because they had a surplus to dispose of and wanted no price ceiling.

These curbs on exploitation and profiteering were important. But a more fundamental means of preventing the emergence of a new exploiting class in the countryside was the organizing of a collective economy based on farming co-operatives.

When co-operatives were first being introduced in the early fifties, middle peasants in general and upper-middle peasants in particular, did not look on them with favour. Some of them merely did not choose to join; others were hostile. Both attitudes had their logic. At first few peasants could believe that simply through cultivating the fields collectively, without mechanization, substantial increases of output could be achieved. To those unwilling to join it seemed clear that if a group of poor farmers jointly tilled their poor land, without enough draught animals, manure or capital, they might have nothing to lose—but they could expect to do little better than when working on their own. It seemed, too, that if a better-off peasant were to join their co-operative, he could only lift them up—while he himself was dragged down.

Some of the upper-middle peasants looked further ahead, and did not like what they saw. With the poor organized in co-operatives, they foresaw, there would be less labour for hire and less land for sale.

So they did not merely stand aloof; they ridiculed and disparaged the infant co-operatives.

To do this was not difficult, for joint management of several individual farms, allocation of their man and animal power and keeping their accounts, posed problems more complex than any individual farmer had ever faced. 'The co-op's just like a bee-hive' was a common quip—with the accent on buzz and bustle not on achievement. For with inexperienced leaders who had not yet learnt how to plan work and assign jobs, the co-operative members seemed to be just buzzing about.

But before long the co-operatives' relatively large-scale soil and water conservation, their mass drives to accumulate fertilizer and their ability to concentrate a large labour force at rush periods, began to show results. So many middle peasants began to feel that they must set themselves the goal of beating the co-operatives. Even some of the mockers began to wonder whether they could stay the pace. Thus relations between middle peasant individual farmers and co-operative farmers entered a new stage.

For this the co-operatives, under Communist Party leadership, had a dual policy, to match the dual nature of the upper-middle peasants. On the one hand they strove to show their superiority to individual farming by obtaining higher and higher yields; on the other they lent a hand to neighbouring individual farmers who found themselves in difficulties, helping them get their crops in before a storm or when a member of the family fell ill. Such practices could not but convince these individual farmers that even though they might be locked in struggle with the co-operatives, they were still not regarded as enemies. This was in keeping with the co-operatives' aim: to win over the individual farmers, not ruin them through competition.

When the experimental co-operatives of the 1952–4 period at last proved that co-operation brought higher yields and incomes, middle peasants, even better-off ones, were 'converted' to the new organization. Some of them set up their own 'co-operatives', restricting membership to prosperous farmers. Such co-operatives were characterized by 'the strong seeking out the strong and elbowing aside the weak; squabbling for capable cadres; poaching of members and resultant disunity'.[9] Others applied for membership in already existing co-operatives and were admitted—Meng Qing-yen of mule versus daughter-in-law fame among them. But those who joined often did so with mixed feelings, for unlike the poor and lower-middle peasants who saw co-operation as their only way forward, the newcomers still felt there were two possible roads. While they had now chosen co-operation, they did not wish to burn their bridges behind them. If the co-operatives failed (and this was

* Mao Tse-tung: *The Question of Agricultural Co-operation*, F.L.P., Peking, 1956, p. 34.

212

not to be ruled out, for they still faced problems of organization, management and leadership) these middle peasant members wanted to be able to return to individual farming.

This desire to keep the old road open made them push for policies which would have cancelled out the very factors that gave the co-operatives their higher yields.

During this period of semi-socialist co-operatives, for example, the land though collectively tilled was individually owned, and boundary-stones marking-off different owners' plots were still in place. Their removal and the levelling and joining of several small plots into bigger ones, made ploughing, harrowing and sowing more efficient and cut labour costs. But a member who had in the back of his mind the possibility of withdrawing from the co-operative after the next harvest, would want his markers left in place. Again, many of the fields put into the co-operative by the poor peasants were less fertile than those put in by the better-off, because their owners had not been able to afford much fertilizer. If more fertilizer could now be put on these poorer fields, the co-operative as a whole would raise its output. But the better-off co-operative members were anxious to have their fields get the biggest share of fertilizer. Another way for the co-operative to raise output was to increase the ratio of double-cropping. For this the natural choice was the more fertile land of the well-to-do; but many of them would not permit it, fearing it might impoverish their soil.

The better-off members had other interests, too, which led them to advocate policies which would benefit them at the expense of the former poor peasants. They pressed for a considerable differential between the rate for jobs such as ploughing and that for less skilled types of labour. As the poor peasants had had little chance in the past of handling draught animals, and were consequently less adept at it, the upper-middle peasants had little difficulty in getting these jobs assigned to themselves at high rates of pay, leaving the less skilled and more poorly paid work to the poor. Similarly, when the price was being fixed for barnyard manure sold to the co-operative, they pressed for artificially high rates, for they owned most of the animals, not the poor peasant members.

During this period, too, when dividends were paid partly on land invested, partly on work done, a few well-to-do farmers who were accustomed to carrying on trade as a secondary occupation, put land in the co-operative but did not work in it, since trade brought them a higher income.

All these practices and policies, by which the better-off peasants hoped to have the best of both worlds, could only undermine the foundation of the co-operatives' success: the more rational use of labour, land and other means of production; and the enthusiasm of all the members.

213

In this situation Party policy called for: 'mutual benefit for poor and middle peasants.'[10] This could be achieved only if production rose, so co-operative leaders had to oppose any practices that would lower it. This meant waging class struggle inside the co-operatives. For if the policies urged by the better-off members were carried out, the cadres foresaw, production would fall and these very members would withdraw from the co-operatives. If the Party's policies were practised, output would rise and though they might complain they would probably stay in.

Such were the complex class relations within the semi-socialist co-operatives, involving struggle between classes but 'within the ranks of the people'.

With the change from semi-socialist to fully socialist co-operatives (in which the land was jointly owned and dividends were paid on labour alone), some of the earlier problems were solved. The road of individual farming was closed. The former upper-middle peasants instead of being full individual owners of fields collectively cultivated, were now part-owners of village-wide co-operative farms. They had burnt their bridges after all. Some did so because they finally found that co-operation was better than individual farming; others because they saw poor prospects for their individual farms in a village where the rest had merged. What this group yearned for was their own

[10] This policy was not one of 'equal benefit', for while raising the income of the upper-middle peasants, it rapidly closed the gap between them and the poor peasants. In a Taihang township where the co-operatives carried out the policy in exemplary fashion, the following figures were worked out:

INCOME FOR HOUSEHOLDS OF DIFFERENT CLASSES IN 1954
AS COMPARED WITH THEIR PRE-CO-OPERATIVE INCOME

Class of Household	Year's income for 1954 (in terms of grain)	Percentage increase (over income before joining the co-operative)
	jin	
Poor peasant	831	38
New lower-middle peasant	928	31
Old lower-middle peasant	816	28
New upper-middle peasant	1,090	5·6
Old upper-middle peasant	982	5

N.B.—Figures for this model township are all well above those for the whole county, where the average income in 1954 for all households was 650 *jin*.

(See Li Lin, 'The Comprehensive Plan for Pingshun County', *Socialist Upsurge in China's Countryside*, pp. 342 ff.)

individual farms amidst other individual farms. But they could not stop their fellow-villagers from collectivizing, so they found themselves voting for 'the lesser of two evils'—membership in the socialist co-operative.

With the Great Leap Forward and the setting up of the commune in 1958, things changed fast. And with this fluidity, the class struggle again sharpened. Once more upper-middle peasants spearheaded the attack on collectivism. When the 'winds of communism blew too hard', they were able to rally followers from other strata.[11] These included peasants dissatisfied because of the mistake of 'levelling' and 'transferring': and those who felt that free food was unfair, because those families with 'many hands and few mouths' were subsidizing the ones with few hands and many children and old folk. 'Levelling and transferring' and free food had tended to isolate the firmest supports of socialism. The correction of these mistakes in the April (1959) check-up removed the source of dissatisfaction of many poor and lower-middle peasant commune members. But the check-up aimed at correcting mistakes made and acknowledged by the leadership; and some upper-middle peasants, secure in their position as part of 'the people', were not afraid to make the most of this situation. They spread rumours about the cadres, at the same time distorting Party policy and pouring scorn on new ventures, complaining about the tempo of work, going slow, ignoring instructions, breaking regulations and generally doing slipshod work.

It was at this time that Fei Xi-suo, an upper-middle peasant of South Cunjing, went about the village streets openly complaining: 'This Great Leap is exhausting.' 'Eating at home is far better than eating at the canteen.' 'There's no freedom.' Fei had been one of the most prosperous peasants in the village. Before he had joined the co-operative, he and his wife had 18 *mu* of land, just for the two of them, besides a donkey and 30 walnut trees which brought in a good cash income. The village average just after the land reform was roughly 3 *mu* per person, but Fei had tripled his holding during the new democratic period. He had clearly moved fast along the capitalist road since the land had gone to the tiller. So had Zhang Feng-he, an upper-middle peasant of South Yangyi, who also complained. 'It's no use working hard,' he said. 'The policy in this commune is not "the more you work, the more you get"; it's "the more you work, the more you have to give away!" ' He was referring to rationing and Planned Purchase and Supply—a popular target for attack with his class.

When this system had first been introduced in 1953, it was the upper-middle peasants with a surplus who had opposed it. With the change-over to co-operative farming, it was no longer upper-middle peasant individual farmers who had surpluses for sale, but co-operative farms. The struggle had changed from one between the individual and the collective, to one between the small collective (the co-operative farm, later the commune brigade) and the large collective (the State). So village Party branches now took up the task of persuading the broad mass of commune members to support Planned Purchase and Supply. This could be achieved by the regular presentation of balance sheets showing what the members sold the state and what the state sold them in the way of tractors, pumps, fertilizer and so on as well as consumer goods. In other words by making clear that both sides benefitted from the system. Where this was not done systematically upper-middle peasants (always among the chief proponents of narrow sectional interests) could still stir up some dissatisfaction.

The rectification and socialist education campaign in the winter of 1959–60 was a political movement 'to expose and criticize incorrect views and actions before the village masses, so that the rank-and-file could judge who was right and who was wrong'. This way of dealing with those upper-middle peasants who still favoured the capitalist road—in words or deeds—helped unify brigade members' views. It also helped the brigade and work team cadres to apply the principle of unity-and-struggle to this well-to-do part of the population. As one brigade cadre of poor peasant origin put it:

'When I used to hear some of these upper-middle peasants running down our Party, twisting its policies and spreading downright lies, I used to get into quite a state. There seemed to be nothing I could do about it. They hadn't broken the law. And they weren't old money-bags' (former landlords and rich peasants); 'you could soon put them in their place. These upper-middle peasants were part of the people. So all I could do was scowl. But what did they care if I scowled? Now it's different. If I hear them spreading lies and slanders I feel much calmer. I say to them: "Is that what you really think? All right. Let's have a public debate on it. You give your views and I'll give mine and we'll see what everyone thinks." '

With the door to individual farming closed, upper-middle peasants who still sought 'the capitalist road', felt that one avenue was still open: trade—either private or brigade. They jumped at any chance of taking charge of brigade-run trade-and-transport enterprises, where they found considerable scope for profit-making. This was due to the common practice of assigning a cart and animal to a brigade member to use as he pleased, so long as he turned over 90 *yuan* a month to brigade funds.

Apart from these open and above-board trading activities, there were clandestine ones. Wen Tian-sun, for instance, an upper-middle peasant of Bailin, known as an experienced stockman (since he had had animals of his own in the past) was put in charge of some of the brigade's draught animals. His main interest, however, was not in using them for brigade work in the fields. He bought himself a cart, hitched up two of the brigade's mules and went in for private trade. Another upper-middle peasant, Du Jing-ming of Baicaoping village, also turned to trade of this sort. Long experienced in marketing mountain products, he discreetly offered 5 *mao* a *jin* for walnuts, though the fixed price was only 3 *mao*. The supplies he bought up at this inflated price he sold in Wu An town at one *yuan* a *jin*.[12]

The serious shortages of consumer goods created by the widespread and rapid rise of peasant incomes, as well as some mistakes in planning, favoured such speculators. Summing up this situation in the summer of 1960, Commune Party Secretary Jin said: 'Last autumn some of these upper-middle peasants were really throwing their weight around. So during the Rectification and Socialist Education campaign in the following winter we attacked the harmful ideas they were spreading. We used the methods of reasoning, of comparing the past with the present, of setting out the facts in each village. But they're still not satisfied. They still haven't given up their illusions about the capitalist road, where, so they say, a man could run his farm as he liked. What they mean is, where he was free to buy and sell, lend and hire and do down the other man in any way he pleased. And the other man, of course, was a poor peasant. Besides that they just can't get used to the system of "to each according to his work". The fact is, they don't like hard work. They prefer buying and selling to working on the land. So the struggle between the two roads goes on.'

But though the scene of struggle now was clearly in the field of trade, it was constantly shifting. The essential thing was to recognize it. This was one reason why the first item on the Commune Party Committee's work plan was: 'Put politics in command; give ideological and political training to the vanguard' (meaning Party members, cadres and Youth Leaguers) 'and strengthen the socialist education of the masses'. This alone could enable commune members to maintain the vigilance needed for seeing through the disguised forms of class struggle adopted by the bourgeoisie (represented primarily by the upper-middle peasants) and for forestalling them.

RELYING ON THE POOR AND LOWER-MIDDLE PEASANTS

In Yangyi relying on the poor and lower-middle peasants meant principally doing two things: consulting them and winning them for the Party's policies; and putting them into positions of leadership throughout the commune.

In choosing cadres for any branch of work, the first qualification

[12] 10 *mao* = 1 *yuan*.

was class, not 'capability'. In 1960, the list of qualifications was:

1. 'good class origin'—that is, poor or lower-middle peasants, preferably the former;
2. 'clean record'—that is, never to have fought on the wrong side in the class struggles over the years (this did not apply to having held wrong or confused views);
3. industriousness;
4. uprightness in personal matters;
5. high prestige among the people.

Election procedure was, first for the electors to hold discussions on the significance of these qualifications and why they were essential; then on possible candidates, who were sized up on each of the five points. Only after this was the voting to take place.

The cost of placing trust in 'capable' hands had to be learned in Yangyi not once, but many times right down to 1960. Back in the forties when the former landlord-businessman Fu Xin was relieved of his post as manager of the Ten Mile Inn marketing and credit co-operative (for not making the co-operative serve the people, but simply piling up profits for the better-off stock-holders), the Party Branch had pointed out that class was the decisive factor in selecting cadres. Later, when farming co-operatives were set up, the Communist Party proclaimed it a principle throughout the countryside that leadership and control must be firmly in poor and lower-middle peasant hands.

Where the Party's work among the rank-and-file was efficient, this principle was adhered to. Where it fell short, the most technically competent person was elected, even when it was suspected that he might not have the public interest at heart. This was the case in the election of the rich peasant Meng Shang-yi to his canteen post in Yangyi townlet.

One reason for the tendency to elect those who were 'competent' rather than those of poor peasant origin, was that the latter were often reluctant to take office. This was because they lacked confidence in their own ability. So when a poor peasant was elected, the first requirement was to convince him that he could and must develop the ability to lead; that management, accounting or any other field of work need not remain a mystery to him, but could be mastered. One poor peasant assigned to a task which he thought beyond him, complained: 'What you need is a horse, but I'm only a donkey.' 'But we haven't got enough horses,' came the answer, 'so you'll just have to be a horse.'

While many 'donkeys' did become 'horses', the shortage of 'horses' persisted because new demands were constantly arising. It was out of the question, however, to wait until there were enough qualified cadres of reliable class origin and outlook, and meanwhile to fall back on the 'capable' and 'educated'. Mao Tse-tung put forward a solution to the problem in 1955 when the advancing co-operative movement was grappling with the cadre shortage. 'Both cadres and peasants will change of themselves,' he wrote, 'as they learn from their own experience in the struggle. Get them into action themselves; they will learn while doing, become more capable, and large numbers of excellent people will come forward. This "fearing the dragon in front and the tiger behind" attitude will not produce cadres.'[13]

It was considered necessary, however, not only to elect cadres from a reliable class; but also to prevent them from becoming a new bureaucracy or privileged stratum (which could ally itself with the upper-middle peasants and strike out along the capitalist road). For this reason commune cadres were paid roughly the same as ordinary brigade members. Brigade and work team cadres took part in manual labour, for which they received work points like everyone else; and when they had to leave such work to attend to public affairs they were credited with a corresponding number of work days.

To ward off corruption various precautions were taken. Steps to prevent embezzlement included a system by which funds were not handled by any one cadre. Decisions involving finances were made by the collective leadership of the unit concerned; accounts were kept by other cadres; and the funds themselves were in the hands of still others. Bribery, especially in subtly-disguised forms, was harder to prevent. But cadres were alerted to the dangers of 'sugar-coated bullets' in the course of political study and rectification movements. Their conduct was also examined during check-ups, and by the local people's congress.

Under such circumstances, office held no great economic attraction for careerists. In fact being a cadre called for sacrifice of personal interest. It involved much hard work and heavy responsibility.

[13] Mao Tse-tung, *The Question of Agricultural Co-operation*, F.L.P., Peking, 1956, p. 2.

Chapter XVIII

MASS-LINE LEADERS AND LEADERSHIP

'GOOD class origin' was required of cadres because poor and lower-middle peasants, having most to gain from the socialist transformation of agriculture could be counted on to support it most staunchly. But to get farming out of the rut where it had lain at the mercy of the weather and a prey to pest, scraping along with poor seed, narrow range of crops and puny draught animals, called for comprehensive long-term planning and effective short-term measures. This strategy and tactics was worked out by the Communist Party. Without the study of Party policy, therefore, even poor peasant cadres would be 'blind, half-baked, muddle-headed revolutionaries', as Mao Tse-tung described those who forgot the Party's General Line and specific policies.

Furthermore the various policies had to be interpreted in the light of local conditions and applied in a flexible fashion. But to know what was flexibility and what was departure from principle called for grasping overall strategy. Thus cadres could not be satisfied with studying particular directives; they had to study the General Line, politics as a whole and even dialectical materialism.

In the spring of 1960, for example, according to policy the running of canteens was to be taken as the focal point for improving commune members' living conditions and freeing women for work in the fields. But in some brigades the cadres favoured persuading everyone to eat in the community dining-room and to contribute their private allotments to it. This, however, deprived old people of employment. It was therefore not in keeping with the spirit of the General Line, which called for the 'mobilizing of every positive element' for the 'rapid building of socialism.'[1]

Cadres found that without systematic study of both general and specific policies they could not reach sound decisions or put forward correct proposals. One brigade cadre remarked, 'I used to have the idea that I must be stupid, because I couldn't sort out which was the right thing to do and which the wrong. I couldn't reach prompt decisions and I was always making mistakes. Now I see it's not a question of being either stupid or clever, but of studying politics and grasping policy. Since I did that I seem to have grown a lot cleverer'.

[1] See Chapter XIII, 'Social Services'.

Mass-Line Leaders and Leadership

'PUTTING POLITICS IN COMMAND'

Even after a cadre did understand policy and support it, he still faced another and bigger task: getting the masses to do the same. This called for 'good work style'. Relying on administrative measures was seen as a hangover from an exploiting society, where those in authority were bureaucrats. Cadres in the commune were called on to 'follow the mass line' and 'put politics in command'.

Described as a fundamental political and organizational line of the Party, the mass line is based on the belief that 'the people are the real makers of history' and that they have 'boundless creative power'.[2] Therefore, while Communists should serve and keep close to the people, they cannot take the place of the people or take over from them. 'Merely through the efforts of the vanguard and without the genuine consciousness and mobilization of the people themselves,' says Liu Shao-chi, 'emancipation of the people is impossible, history will not move forward and nothing can be accomplished.' Thus the Communists cannot 'bestow emancipation' upon the people; they can only lead the people in struggle to emancipate themselves. And they can lead neither by ordering people about ('commandism') or by trailing behind them ('tailism'); but only by learning from them, systematizing and refining their knowledge and experience, returning it to them as their own policy and then leading them into action for it. The mass line thus 'comes from the masses' and 'goes back to the masses', though what comes from them is raw material, what goes back is processed. It arises from and expresses the unity between masses and leaders, just as its opposite, bureaucracy, arises from and expresses contradiction between them. To the extent that the mass line is practised, bureaucracy and the emergence of a privileged class of leaders is ruled out.

'Putting politics in command' meant explaining the long-term significance of an undertaking, showing its effect on the building of socialism, winning support for it by reason and persuasion, not by compulsion. It also meant urging people to put the interests of the group before those of the individual, those of the large collective such as the state or commune ahead of those of the small one such as the brigade or work team. It did not rule out material incentive, but it placed long-term before short-term and collective before individual material interests.

The Ten Mile Inn cadres, for instance, were anxious to afforest the hills beside their village, which meant covering them with thousands of fish-scale pits. While this was expected to bring ample reward in years to come, it could yield no immediate return. This meant that current income would have to be divided to cover not

[2] Liu Shao-chi, 'The Mass Line of the Party', *On the Party*, F.L.P., Peking, 1950.

221

only immediately profitable production but the long-term pit-digging project as well; in other words, more work but not more pay. At first there was opposition to the idea, so the cadres called a public discussion to win support for it. First they worked out how much could be gained from growing wild pepper, which produced a crop in three or four years and sold at a good price. Then they spoke of how afforestation would check erosion, reminding their listeners of the topsoil washed into the river and the stony soil washed down from the hillsides onto the fields during the heavy rains of past years, of the silting up of the river and the floods it had caused. Afforestation would help stop all this, they argued, and in the long run it would even change the weather. Despite some scepticism on this last point, villagers found the cadres' arguments convincing. They agreed to dig the pits. Politics had taken command.

It was the same when the Little Yetao brigade leadership set out to train some of its primary school graduates as technicians for the breeding station and poultry farm. The job called for living in. 'That old temple's only fit for monks and nuns,' the poultry girl's mother had at first protested. As to those working at the breeding station: 'No decent girl ought even to see such things,' was a common attitude in the community. But Ren Qing-mei called the Communist Youth League members together and explained the importance of the work to them. He contrasted their youth with his own and spoke of the Communist Youth League's special responsibility in building a socialist society. The whole nation set great store by them, he said; they should not be shy or timid or afraid of difficulties. Fortified in this way the young people went ahead. Politics took command.

When the commune leadership gave Little Yetao a small quantity of special seed for some extra large turnips, in recognition of the brigade's outstanding achievements, some brigade members took it for granted that they would be raising a crop for their own consumption. But after discussion initiated by the Party branch, the majority favoured letting the crop go to seed. The turnips grew 'two feet long and as big around as a rice-bowl'. When they did go to seed the members who had first favoured eating them suggested that the seeds should be sold, saying they would fetch a fine price. But once more after the matter had been discussed the majority favoured a different course. The interests of the larger collective should come first, the cadres and Party members pointed out. This view prevailed and the seeds were turned over to the commune, free, for distribution amongst the 24 brigades.

When workers on the newly set up Silver Sea Tract, despite hard work and cold, damp living quarters, put aside thoughts of going home; when Youth League members hankering for home cooking came to the conclusion that community dining-rooms accorded with their aim of fighting for communism and that the old way of eating belonged to the past, it was all a result of subordinating short term to long term interests, of putting the interests of the collective before those of the individual, of judging all words and deeds by their effect upon the building of socialism and communism.

An essential part of the process of putting politics in command was for the cadres to make clear to the people the whys and wherefores of proposals put forward and what must be done to implement them; and for the cadres to know what ordinary members thought about current developments and about Party and Government measures for dealing with them. The former called for a 'mobilization' meeting; the latter for 'airing of views'.

'Mobilization' aimed at arousing mass enthusiasm for a new policy or undertaking, and determination to see it through. The usual pattern was for the matter first to be put to the Party members and cadres, who in turn would take it up with the 'activists'. All of these might informally sound out public opinion in personal chats, so that when the meeting was held not only were the audience mentally prepared but the leadership had some idea how they felt about the matter on hand. First a mobilization speech would be made. This would generally be followed by discussion, which would centre first on the policy or project itself, to bring out its significance, then on how to implement it. Finally pledges would be made to carry it out.

A new means of airing views came into being with the wiping out of illiteracy. This was the writing of *dazibao* or 'large character posters'. Introduced in the late fifties this had soon become nation-wide practice and was widely used in the commune. Whenever some important task or controversy arose, commune members were called on to put their views in writing and display them. Writing *dazibao* had the advantage not only of providing a record which anyone could consult. It meant, too, that ideas were put pithily. This made it easier for the leadership to sort out and sum up the ideas of the rank-and-file. Writing *dazibao* was one of the methods used on the Silver Sea Tract when tract workers were called on to decide whether to push on with contouring or wait till the weather grew warmer. On that occasion 1,500 posters were put up, an average of almost seven for each of the 220 workers.

Putting politics in command called for long-term perspective, for seeing the future rising on the basis of present achievement and against the background of the past. It was a means of moving from the socialist distribution system of 'to each according to his work', to the communist one of 'to each according to his needs'. This perspective served as an incentive. But perspective alone was not enough for rank-and-file commune members in the early stages of the process. It had to be bolstered by immediate material incentives. Hence the communes' slogan: 'The more you work, the more you get.' Material incentive, however, might be either useful or dangerous; it might lead to either socialism or capitalism, depending on how it was guided and controlled. Its course was set by political education.

Broadly speaking material incentive grew less important as 'political consciousness'—public spirit and social conscience—rose. This needed to be accurately estimated at each stage of social development. Under-estimation of political consciousness and over reliance on material incentive was termed a 'rightist' mistake, leading to capitalism; over-estimation of it was a 'leftist' mistake in which the leaders struck out towards socialism but left the rank-and-file behind them. When the commune was taking shape, for instance, its cadres supported 'levelling and transferring' (equalizing the value of work points in the various brigades regardless of differences in output, and transferring means of production from brigade to commune or from one brigade to another). The result was what commune leaders first described as a contradiction between rich and poor brigades and a lowering of morale and production in both.[3] The Commune Party Committee tried at the outset to deal with this by putting politics in command. They pointed out to the rich brigades that though they were contributing something to the poor ones, they themselves were getting richer each year, not solely through their own efforts but as a result of belonging to the commune. At the same time they urged the poorer brigades to cultivate a spirit of self-reliance and become more prosperous by exploiting the special resources of their hilly land. This, while helpful, did not solve the problem. It assumed a degree of 'political consciousness' which had been reached only by the most advanced, not by the vast majority of commune members. What was needed at this stage was a change in set-up which would give fuller play to material incentive. This was provided in the check-up of April 1959.[4]

'LEADING ON THE JOB'

Following the mass line and putting politics in command were not enough. A cadre needed another aspect of good work style: a practical approach to a host of technical problems such as growing grain, planting trees, raising livestock, building dams, terraces or houses, running canteens, setting up new industries and keeping accounts.

[3] See Chapter IV, 'Tempering the Winds of Communism'.

[4] The danger of over-estimating the people's development had long before been pointed out by Mao Tse-tung. 'When we lift a bucket of water, for instance,' he said, 'aren't we lifting up something that stands on the ground and doesn't float in mid-air?' (See 'Talks at the Yenan Forum on Art and Literature', *Selected Works*, Vol. IV, Lawrence & Wishart, London, 1956, p. 75.) An accurate estimate of people's political and ideological level—of just where the bucket was to be lifted from—was the starting point for putting politics in command.

The Ten Mile Inn cadres, for example, by putting politics in command, succeeded in persuading the villagers to cover their hillsides with fishscale pits. But the wild pepper they planted did not flourish; it died. Why? Were the pits not well dug? Was the upkeep not careful enough? Could wild pepper not flourish on a northern slope? Whatever the reason, the promising pepper project was abandoned. Politics in command without adequate technique to back it up proved fruitless.

The importance of technical competence to leadership was one reason why cadres were urged to cultivate experimental plots. In 1960 Yangyi Party Committee called on all Party secretaries in the commune to 'go in for experimental plots in a big way'. The 'plots' were not limited to agriculture; they might consist of pilot projects in social services, animal husbandry or forestry. Their purpose was to improve leadership and increase production, by finding out what could be done and how to do it.

In addition to technical problems there were complex questions of management to be solved.

Early in November 1959, for example, the team leaders of the Ten Mile Inn brigade reported that their teams had finished the sweet potato harvesting and were moving on to their next tasks. A little later complaints reached the Brigade Party Committee that time limits set for the harvesting had been too short, the job had been rushed and many tubers had been left in the ground. The Committee investigated and found that this was so. Then it called a meeting of the brigade members and put the facts before them. First the Party Secretary dwelt on the work put into growing the sweet potatoes (a crop requiring much care) and the waste that had been brought to light. Then he showed how the Party's policy of 'increasing production and avoiding waste' was vital for the building of socialism. Finally he called on the teams to go over the fields again, this time with a plough to save labour. This was agreed, and so many tubers were turned up in the first ploughing that some teams ran over their fields twice. The additional sweet potatoes thus harvested in all nine teams came to over eleven and a half tons though over a ton of them were spoilt.

This loss of both crop and time was due rather to management than technique, and indicated the need for improvement in methods of leadership. This need existed throughout the commune, in fact throughout the country as a whole.

Measures were taken to strengthen management following the rectification in the winter of 1959–60, in the form of a newly-introduced system which brought brigade leaders into closer and quicker contact with the teams. It was known as 'leading on the job'.

In some brigades the new system was not adopted without misgivings,

'We brigade leaders are now supposed to lead and to take part in production at the same time,' said Wang Mi-shan, Party Branch Secretary of Ten Mile Inn. 'At first I had my doubts about it. I just didn't see how I'd be able to keep it up and lead the brigade as well.'

All the same, when in the spring of 1960 the call for 'leading on the job' came through to Ten Mile Inn, the brigade leaders did not hold back. When the wheat was being harvested they were out in the fields from dawn till dusk. And when the work team leaders said, 'Well, that job's done,' the brigade leaders disagreed. They saw ears of wheat among the stubble. They took a sample *mu* of land already harvested and went over it with eagle eyes, gleaning as they went. They got 2·4 *jin* from that *mu*. Then they took an abacus. There were 1,800 *mu* sown to wheat in the brigade and on the basis of 2·4 *jin* to a *mu* they would be able to glean over 4,500 *jin* (two and a half tons). 'That could just about keep a hundred men going for forty days,' said Wang Mi-shan. A brigade meeting was called and the situation explained. A mass 'gleaning movement' was launched, and 4,550 *jin* was brought in.

After the wheat was reaped the maize was hoed. As they worked, the brigade cadres saw some sickly, yellowish sprouts. They got together, compared notes and estimated the total area of such sprouts throughout all the teams they were in. It came to 125 acres.

Again a mass meeting was called. The outcome this time was a brigade-wide movement to collect fertilizer.

> Let's pile up muck both night and day,
> To drive those yellow shoots away.

With this couplet as a slogan, barnyards were scraped; cesspools were emptied; streets were swept, especially round the donkey-driven mill-wheels; chicken-coops and pig-sties were given a thorough cleaning. The occasion was seized, too, to knock down crumbling earthen walls. This helped make good compost. At the same time it helped to clean up the village, so that collecting fertilizer was combined with sanitation. Within less than the scheduled five days and nights over 400 tons of fertilizer was collected.

'After a few experiences like that,' concluded Wang Mi-shan, 'I realized that there was no contradiction between leading the brigade and working in the fields. As a matter of fact, the only way you can lead properly is to work in the fields. You can't do it from the brigade office. It's only if you're on the spot that you can find out right away if anything's wrong; or how to do things better and faster. If we'd been on the job with the sweet potatoes the way we were with the wheat, we'd never have lost that 2,000 *jin*.'

His conclusion was that 'leading on the job' not only speeded up the spotting of problems and shortcomings; it helped cement relations between the brigade and its teams and improved the general quality of work. Previous experience had shown that when work team leaders saw the brigade leader and Party branch secretary leading from an office instead of from the fields, they tended to do the same. And since these lower level leaders were among the best field workers, their divorce from production had meant a loss to the teams. Leading through taking part had the opposite effect. 'The rank and file put their hearts into it more when they see us cadres working beside them in the fields and shouldering our other responsibilities as well,' said Wang Mi-shan.

Thus leading through taking part not only improved the quality of the work. It also increased its quantity. While in 1959 the average number of work days put in by brigade cadres throughout Yangyi Commune was 165, in 1960 the average was already 150 by the end of May.[5] The cadres 'at the basic level' had become full-time members of their teams.

UPPER LEVELS OF LEADERSHIP AND THE TWO: FIVE SYSTEM

'Leading on the job' and running experimental plots were two of the chief systems devised for helping cadres at the basic level to keep in close touch with production and with the rank-and-file. The need and the difficulty of doing this was all the greater at the higher levels of leadership.

In 1960 there were five levels of administration from central government down to commune—the basic unit of the State. These were: central, provincial, regional, county and commune. Within the commune there were three levels of supervision or management: district, brigade and work team (the last two being considered basic levels of production).[6] Thus there were cadres at eight levels altogether, those at each level being responsible for implementing policy laid down above, and for investigating and reporting on the situation below, on which policy was based. This called for upholding the spirit of a policy while adapting it to the particular conditions existing in a given area. It demanded understanding of policy on the one hand and of the local situation on the other.

In combining the general lines and policies with the situation in their own areas, cadres were called on to 'learn from Chairman Mao' whose thinking 'combines the general truths of Marxism-Leninism with the specific reality of the Chinese revolution'.

This integration of the general and the specific was the practice all along the line. For example the 'Resolution on Some Questions

[5] 10 points counted as a work day. Experienced, able-bodied farmers could earn 12 work points in a day.
[6] At this time the brigade was the basic level of ownership, management and accounting. In the winter of 1960–61, the basic level in some brigades went down to the work team. In such cases the brigade became a supervisory level.

Concerning the People's Communes' was passed by the Central Committee of the Communist Party in December 1958 after a series of conferences reviewing the state of communes throughout the country. Soon after this the Hopei leadership convened a conference at which six points were selected as applying most directly to the communes of their province. This was followed by conferences called at county level but attended by cadres of the region, county, commune, district and brigade. It was by this detailed, step by step procedure that the Central Committee's resolution of December 1958 was implemented in Yangyi Commune through the check-up of April 1959.

In connection with leadership, Mao Tse-tung had warned: '... No leading worker can possibly give general guidance to all the units under his direction if he does not get actual experience in working on specific tasks with the individual workers in particular units. ...'[7] Various measures were taken over the years to enable leading cadres to get such experience. Outstanding among them was the two : five system. This meant that out of every week, five days should be spent 'on the production front' helping the cadres 'at the basic levels' to become good leaders; the other two days were to be spent at headquarters at meetings, studying policy documents, consulting, summarizing and analysing the situation in the district, commune, county, region or province, as the case might be.[8]

The two : five system was first evolved in Hopei Province in 1959. It was tried out in various localities, including Shexian, and after initial successes was taken up throughout the province. In 1960 all cadres from the district and up were being urged to use it. Some cadres, however, had slipped into a routine of office work and meetings; others knew no other way of working. Many cadres really wished to get away from their offices; but they had so many meetings to attend, so many reports to write or to study and so many forms to fill in that they did not see how they could spare the time. A few felt they were not the type to function well in the field. To overcome doubts much publicity was done to show how the system worked.

One case publicized was that of a bank manager in a county town not far north of Shexian. Emerging from his piles of printed forms and stacks of ledgers, this banker went to work in a commune brigade. It was at the height of the battle against the 1960 drought and every available person was carrying water from reservoirs and rivers, ponds and tanks, in buckets on shoulder-poles and basins in hands. The bank manager joined this army of water-carriers. At the edge of a field he noticed two steam-powered pumps lying idle. Why were they not working? he asked. No funds to buy coal, came the

[7] Mao Tse-tung, 'On Methods of Leadership', *Selected Works*, Vol. IV, Lawrence & Wishart, London, 1956.
[8] Sunday was not normally a day of rest. See p. 96.

answer. The banker put down his bucket, went to the brigade head-quarters, phoned his office, authorized a loan, and soon the pumps were working. According to established office routine the granting of the loan should have gone through four steps: application, investigation, authorization and issuance. By being on the spot the manager had been able to telescope the first three steps into one. He at once gave instructions that the office should get in touch immediately with each commune in the county to find out how many pumps were idle through lack of fuel and to issue the necessary loans.

A cadre's duty during his five days in the field was more than taking part in production. He was to give three types of help: in making plans, in arranging work, in solving problems. His relations with those he led were to be governed by 'the five togethers': he was to work, consult, eat, live and study together with them. Besides this there were 'the six types of work' that he was required to be proficient at: the work of a commander, as well as of a rank-and-file labourer, of a technician and a herdsman, of a cook and a propagandist. He was to carry with him 'three notebooks and one tool'. The tool might be a hoe, sickle or trowel; the books were for recording work points, for study and for work matters.

Despite its advantages the system was not easy to establish. The main problem was the amount of time taken up by committee meetings. The solution put forward was: if in doubt about holding a meeting or not, don't hold it; if in doubt about holding a short meeting or a long one, hold a short one; if in doubt about having many attend or only a few, have only a few. The same line was laid down for reports and form filling. Upper levels were not to ask lower levels for reports or to fill in forms if they could get on without them. These measures were an acknowledgement that for the two : five system to work there must be not only the will but the way, in the form of appropriate arrangements.

On the other hand the two : five method of leadership itself made many meetings and much paperwork superfluous. A leader on the spot had little need for oral or written reports. He could learn how work was going on by using his eyes, having talks with those on the job, by his own participation.

Co-ordination of the different levels of administration, however, from central government to work team needed direct links not only with the basic level, but with the intervening ones. One way of achieving this was for upper level cadres to engage in projects at the basic level together with cadres of intervening units. In Guzheng Commune, for instance, adjoining Yangyi, Party secretaries of five levels had a joint project in the form of a high yield tract, made by damming a big gully at intervals so as to form a series of steps, each with a reservoir and terraced fields. This experiment in land reclamation and flood and drought control was of significance for a large area. The five levels of Party secretaries involved were Handan Region, Shexian County, Guzheng Commune, the local district and the brigade on whose land the gully was situated. Yangyi Commune itself contained no projects involving any level higher than the county; but it had cadres at three levels (county, commune and brigade) working together on experimental plots or projects. The Long Sea Dam had been one of these; the Silver Sea High Yield Tract was another.

With cadres of various levels working together in this way, discussing problems on the spot, all levels were kept in the picture while a mass of written reports, conferences and meetings were dispensed with. At the same time valuable experience could be rapidly passed on.

COUNTY CADRES

Shexian County had ten rural communes and one urban one (in the county town). Responsibility for the rural communes was shared by the First Party Secretary, Duan Peng-xiang, and the County Head, Wang De-hen, Duan taking those in the western half of the county and Wang those in the eastern half (where Yangyi was situated). Both were local men.

County First Party Secretary, Duan Peng-xiang, born in 1910 in what is now one of Yangyi's neighbouring communes, had long been a hired hand.

'When I recall those years,' he said, 'no tears come to my eyes, but my heart weeps.

'We had little land of our own. Just on six *mu* for the six of us, my parents, my wife, myself and two children. Poor land it was, too, on a steep hillside. We cleared it and terraced it. But it wouldn't feed six mouths and my father and I both worked for landlords at the busy seasons. We tended our own land when things were slack.'

Duan's parents, worn out by toil and hunger, died in their forties. To provide them with a fitting funeral (by feudal standards of filial piety) Duan sold four of the six *mu* of land. He returned from the burial of his mother to a home bare of a single grain of sorghum (wheat was an undreamt of luxury) and to quiet the sobbing of his hungry children he went to borrow from the landlord who had bought his four *mu*. But no loan, not even a measure of grain, was forthcoming without security; so he mortgaged his last two *mu* of land. It was not long in following the first four. Thus Duan, in his early twenties, sank from the low level of a poor peasant and occasional farm hand to the lower one of a full-time labourer.

'We lived in a tiny broken-down rented room,' he said. 'And though the *kang* practically filled the place, it was too short for me and my feet dangled over the edge; so I had to prop them up on a pile of stones. When it rained outside it drizzled inside. One night

230

during a storm my wife was afraid the whole place would collapse and said we'd better move to the temple with the beggars. But I wouldn't go. I thought, "Let it fall and bury us, kids and all. So much the better". '

This was his state of mind when, in 1939, an 8th Route Army unit came to organize his village to resist the Japanese. Before long he became head of the militia and later of the peasant union, which struggled successfully for the reduction of rent and interest. In 1942 he joined the Communist Party. 'I knew from my whole life,' he said, 'that they told the truth when they said that the landlords had everything without working and that we poor peasants had nothing though we worked ourselves to death.

'Soon after I became a cadre there was a flood and some of the people were ready to give up. They didn't care whether they were saved or not. But I rounded up others to drag them from the flood waters and save them in spite of themselves. I knew what was going on in their minds. I remembered how I, too, once had no hope.'

When Duan was leading the rising struggle for reduction of rent and interest, the very landlord who had taken over his land came offering him a loan, hoping to blunt the point of the struggle. (This was before land reform and during the anti-Japanese united front.) 'How much were you thinking of lending?' asked Duan. The landlord hesitated. 'What about five bushels?' he said at last. 'That won't do,' said the peasant union chairman. 'You'll have to make it at least fifty. Mine's not the only poor family in the village. There are plenty of others.' He refused to let the issue become a private one between himself and the landlord who had foreclosed on his last two *mu*. He kept it a struggle of class against class.

Duan Peng-xiang was promoted step by step. By the early fifties he was in charge of trade for the region. Although now a middle-ranking cadre living in the city of Handan, his way of life remained frugal. In 1956 when experienced cadres were needed to strengthen the leadership in the countryside during the high-tide of the co-operative movement, Duan volunteered to go there.[9] It was then that he became a county cadre. In 1960 he was appointed first secretary of the Shexian Party Committee.

The administrative head of the county, Wang De-hen, was born in a village in the Taihang foothills a few miles to the east of Yangyi. Both his father and mother had worked for landlords (the latter as a weaver) and he himself had started to do so, herding sheep, at the

---

[9] With the setting up of the People's Republic in 1949 had come a trend towards centralization. This was largely a result of the shifting of the base of the revolution from the countryside to the cities. Strengthening centralized leadership speeded up unification of the country, stabilization of the currency, economic recovery in general. In 1956 it was found possible to simplify the central administration and there was a considerable reduction of personnel at higher levels.

age of thirteen. By then both his parents were dead (poor peasants died young in those days) and young Wang went on working for little more than his keep for another eight or nine years. Then his sister married and with the wedding gift from her husband's family was able to buy a small plot of land. This she gave to her brother to work. Thus the hired hand Wang De-hen became a poor peasant.

This was in the early forties when the 8th Route Army were waging guerrilla warfare in the area. Even before the Communists could operate openly in the village young Wang had secretly contacted them and begun to do underground work. They were impressed by his spirit, energy and intelligence. 'If you work and study hard,' they told him 'some day you'll be a village leader.' Recalling this, the County Head commented, 'I wasn't interested in becoming a leader. All I wanted was my own bit of land'.

He had it, and held it, but only through constant struggle. When he first started working on his own he borrowed from his former landlord-employer enough to buy himself a home, offering land as security. He saved all he could to keep up the exorbitant interest payments, but it was a losing battle. At last he was resigned to surrendering his security. By this time, however, the Communists had gained ground and had instituted a steeply progressive tax on land. The landlord was already cursing this. To have acquired more land by foreclosure would have put him in a still higher tax bracket.[10] He refused to take the land (the tax system had been specifically devised for just such an end) and demanded his money, threatening to have his toughs beat up young Wang if it were not paid. But the ex-hired hand now belonged to the communist-led village peasant union. The peasants rallied round him, no beating was even attempted and the debt was finally paid off—at the new, reduced rates with the usurious interest already paid being reckoned towards repayment of the loan itself.

This was one of many incidents which convinced Wang De-hen that the policy of the Communist Party was the policy for him and his whole class. In 1946 he joined the Party and in time became secretary of the village branch as well as head of the peasant union which had once saved him from a beating. From then on he won steady and rapid promotion, as well as a year and half of study at the Revolutionary University in Peking in 1949 and 1950. On completing the course there he was first given a regional post in Handan. Then with the decentralization which started in 1956, he became a county cadre, in 1960 becoming head of Shexian.

Shexian county leaders were among the first to take up the

---

[10] The whole of a village's tax fell on the richest 30 per cent of the families; among these the bigger their holding the higher was the tax-rate. For fuller treatment of the Communists' use of taxation as a weapon against feudalism, see *Revolution in a Chinese Village*.

two : five system. County Head Wang De-hen worked on experimental plots at several places in the five communes he led and whenever he could took part in the key task on hand, making the production of wheat and cotton his focal points. In 1959, he cultivated an experimental plot of cotton on the outskirts of Ten Mile Inn and attained a yield of 1,161 *jin* per *mu*. He drew into the experiment party secretaries from both Yangyi Commune and the Ten Mile Inn Brigade, the three working on the plot together, discussing problems and solving them as they went along. In 1960, when the breach in the Long Sea Dam was being filled, the County Head shovelled dirt and trundled a wheelbarrow, and from his vantage point on the job was able to streamline and speed-up the work. At crucial periods (during sowing, pest prevention and hoeing) he stayed at the Silver Sea Tract, where he had an experimental plot. When the Lunar New Year came round he went into the tract cook-house to make dumplings so that the cooks might have extra time off. Once while sowing cotton alongside tract members, he proposed that an ordinary seeder be used. This had never been done in this part of the country before and the suggestion provoked heated debate, some saying, 'You can't plant cotton with a seeder any more than a mother-in-law can give birth to her own daughter-in-law'. But the County Head offered to show that you could, and with one of the oldest farmers on the tract leading the donkeys he sowed cotton far faster than could be done with the old-style hand drill. His team-mate was impressed not merely by the efficiency of the seeder but also by the fact that the County Head was handling it. 'You never saw county heads like that when I was a boy,' he said. 'They used to go lolling around in sedan chairs carried by eight men, while we were sweating in the fields.' He felt that the new experiment demonstrated new social relations quite as strikingly as it did new technique.

Many cadres no longer tied to the office and bogged down in paper-work spoke of themselves as 'liberated'. Yangyi commune members put it differently. They said, 'The 8th Route Army has come down from the mountains again'.

'GRASPING EACH END TO PULL FORWARD THE MIDDLE'

Spending time in the field was one thing; deciding which particular unit to spend it with was another. The county cadres did not pick at random. They went by the principle: 'Grasp each end to pull forward the middle.' This meant on the one hand spending time with units which had achieved conspicuous successes, mastering their methods and helping them advance still faster; and on the other hand working with units where failures had occurred, giving them guidance and help. After the experience of both the backward and advanced had been summed-up, lessons were drawn and publicized for the benefit

233

of the mass of average units—'the middle'—so that similar mistakes might be avoided and successes achieved on the broadest possible front.

County Party Secretary Duan Peng-xiang, for instance, went to work in Mabu Brigade in Xishui Commune, which had the lowest production record in Shexian. After a preliminary sizing up of the situation he called a meeting of brigade members and had county and commune cadres attend. The farmers themselves made clear at the meeting that their main problem was the lack of water, both surface (rivers or ponds) and underground (wells or springs). They depended wholly on rain. Yet even after it did rain there was little water for their land; it drained so rapidly to the valley. How could this problem be solved? Duan asked. Some brigade members suggested that rain storage tanks might be the answer. After discussion this was agreed and taken as the focal point of the brigade's work, on which the maximum labour force should be concentrated.

The Mabu farmers knew every fold of their land, every path and outcropping where a rivulet formed after a downpour. At these points, carefully sited to trap the rain-water, they hollowed out and lined vat-shaped tanks ten to fifteen feet deep, leaving only a small opening so as to reduce evaporation. Six thousand of these tanks were dug in Mabu's rolling uplands. When the rain came it flowed into them and almost every field had its own supply of water close at hand. This made it possible to irrigate all the land once, some of it twice during the growing season. The next harvest showed that Mabu had moved up from being the most backward brigade in the county to one of the advanced. Following this it became the scene of county and even provincial 'on-the-spot conferences'[11] for the study of 'clusters of rain-storage tanks'. Soon brigades all around were following Mabu's example.

Secretary Duan achieved similar success with another backward unit—North Ridge Brigade in Henandian Commune just outside the county town. This time the problem was not lack of water but lack of drive. The brigade and team leaders worked hard but they could not get the rank-and-file to follow suit.

After working in the brigade some days Duan began to suspect that the leaders' weakness lay in welfare work. So he told them what he had learned in the Dragon and Tiger Brigade of neighbouring Xishui Commune, which was noted for its high morale. Just recently, he said, a number of the brigade members happened to fall ill. This made it hard to finish the field work on time and placed an extra heavy load on the brigade leader. Nevertheless he took the time to visit every one of the sick, discussed their needs with the doctor and helped in every way he could. This concern, especially at such a

[11] See below, this chapter.

difficult time, was appreciated by the sick people's families and by the patients themselves, who tried to show their gratitude by getting up to work. The brigade leader restrained them until they were fit; but when they were well enough to work they went at it with a will— and the whole brigade followed suit.

The North Ridge cadres were impressed by the story.

'Yes, that's the way to lead,' said the brigade leader. 'We haven't paid enough attention to welfare work. We should take a leaf from their book.'

'What about the members of your brigade?' asked Secretary Duan. 'Are they all in good health?'

'Pretty good. Just two or three of them aren't too well at the moment.'

'Have you visited them?'

'Not yet.'

'Could you find time to go and see them?'

'Yes, we ought to be able to manage it as soon as we finish this weeding. It's a rush job, you know.'

'Couldn't you find time before then? Even while the weeding's going on?'

The visits were paid right away.

The first result was that the brigade members started to talk. They commented that their leaders seemed to have become more human. At the same time, complaints which had not been openly expressed before, came out: that the cadres had been concerned only about work, targets, plans—but not people. The second effect was a speeding up of the weeding. Within a week 500 acres were completed—a record for this brigade.

The lesson the brigade cadres drew from this experience was: 'The more attention the cadres pay to the welfare of the masses, the more enthusiastically they work.' Secretary Duan reminded them also that: 'The more enthusiastically the masses work, the more attention the Party should pay to their well-being.'[12]

STANDARDS AND STANDARD BEARERS

While 'grasping the backward' meant giving them help to catch up, 'grasping the advanced' meant having frequent checks and competitions to discover who was advanced in each aspect of work. It also meant cultivating model units or individuals and publicizing their experiences. In the summer of 1960, for instance, Shexian County organized a competition and election of 'standard-bearers'— those who had achieved outstanding results in increasing production. Six were finally chosen from the whole county. Each had contributed

[12] 'Resolution on Some Questions Concerning the People's Communes.'

something different. The head of the Dragon and Tiger Brigade of Xishui Commune was singled out for his 'strong mass line', shown in his concern for the sick, which had heightened his brigade members' enthusiasm. Ren Qing-mei was chosen for the measures he had taken to prevent loss in output despite the damage done by the hail. A third 'standard-bearer' had raised output by using every possible patch of land in the brigade, his method being termed 'the sow more line'. A fourth paid special attention to planting high yield crops such as sweet potatoes and maize. This was called 'the high yield crop line'. Another had gone in for high yield tracts wherever possible. This was the 'better field management line'. The sixth was the 'Five Plum Blossoms' cotton-growing team of the Silver Sea Tract, led by Zhu Xu-mei, who had achieved outstanding results by using advanced technique. The achievements of all these 'standard-bearers' were summarized by the county leadership and their six different measures were publicized throughout Shexian.

Checks and competitions were carried out not only on a county scale, but at each level and in every branch of work. During 1959, for instance, Yangyi Commune won one red flag for production and another for trade from the Handan Region administration. From Shexian County Government it received red flags for tax collection, finance, military affairs and transport as well as for farm work—primarily for excellent wheatfield management and manure collection. At the end of the year the county graded Yangyi as one of its three red flag communes. (The Commune Party Committee, too, received a red flag from the County Party Committee for its Party work.)

While the selection of 'standard-bearers' and awarding of red flags was for specific achievements and limited periods of time, a more general and permanent award was the title of Labour Hero or Heroine. During the anti-Japanese war, when Shexian was first liberated, there had been a constant need to promote personnel to the higher levels. This unavoidably meant a loss to the villages of some of their most experienced and able cadres. Labour heroes and heroines were a notable exception to this trend, for whether in the local, provincial or national category they stayed at their posts in the village. Guo Heng-de, a provincial labour heroine, from time to time attended conferences in the provincial capital, but most of her time was spent in Bailin; Ren Qing-mei, a national labour hero, attended conferences in Peking and elsewhere, but his regular post was Little Yetao. Thus the choosing of labour heroes and heroines was a form of recognition which did not divorce the producer from the primary level of production. It meant that each area was able to honour its best people without losing them.

Labour heroes and the units they led provided examples for the less experienced or less able. In fact it was a standing joke
236

that their thresholds were worn down by advice-seekers. It was not only local people who drew on their fund of practical experience. The People's Government and the Communist Party called labour heroes and heroines to conferences at county, regional, provincial or national level as a means of keeping in touch with the people, preventing bureaucracy and guaranteeing a down-to-earth approach to problems in the villages.

Many methods were used for publicizing and popularizing achievements of advanced units and individuals. Summaries were written, duplicated and circulated. Reports were given at conferences and over the radio. Rolls of honour and accounts of special deeds and experiences were posted on bulletin boards together with photographs and biographical notes on those concerned.

One method considered especially effective was the 'on-the-spot conference'. This meant inviting the cadres engaged in a particular type of work to a conference at the spot where some success had been achieved. In this way they could see it in operation and talk things over, not only with the cadres in charge, but also with the rank-and-file participants. In the first few months of its existence the Silver Sea Tract was the scene of ten on-the-spot conferences and fifteen checks arranged by cadres at three levels—Handan Region, Shexian County and Yangyi Commune. Over 1,000 visitors went to see for themselves what the tract had achieved and how it had done it.

Competition and emulation were another important method of leadership. Here the current slogan was 'Learn from, catch up with and overtake the advanced'. (This was subsequently broadened to: 'Compare yourself with and learn from others, catch up with those ahead and help forward those behind.') This was the opposite to merging backward units with advanced ones. The idea that differences between the advanced and the backward should be concealed rather than exposed had arisen perhaps from the feeling that emulation was socialist, competition capitalist. After discussion this view was rejected. As the Silver Sea philosophy tutors observed in their study of dialectical materialism, 'There are contradictions in everything under the sun. They exist between the advanced and the backward. These contradictions are the motive force of society. So we should not be afraid of them, but bring them to light and solve them.' Merging meant glossing over problems. Comparison and competition were a way of revealing contradictions between the advanced and the backward; emulation was a way of solving them. Competitions, checks and emulation drives were therefore popularized as a method of leadership.

The two : five system, leading on the job, competition and emulation, the election of labour heroes, on-the-spot conferences, 'grasping both ends', all created conditions for fostering unity between leaders and led, for combining centralized leadership with 'the boundless creative power of the masses'. They were specific measures for practising the mass line and avoiding bureaucracy.

Another important means for helping a cadre improve his work style were rectification movements. These started inside the Party with a study of current policy, which was followed by a check on its implementation by the branch leadership, by the branch as a whole and by individual members. After this a rectification movement might be taken to a new, public phase in which non-Party cadres and even rank-and-file commune members were drawn in on a voluntary basis. In the course of both inner-Party and public phases, the class stand of Party members, cadres and others was checked in the light of their actions during the period under consideration, especially during certain critical moments. Rectification for example, took place on the eve of the check-up on Yangyi Commune in April 1959, as preparation for the clearing up of mistakes of 'levelling' and 'transferring'.[13] This gave people who had clearly strayed from the socialist road a chance to consider their conduct and if they chose— like Yuan Tian-fu of Liuqu to—return to it; or if they chose not— like Guo You-lin of Baicaoping—to be expelled from the Party. At the same time the work style of Party and non-Party cadres was examined in order to root out bureaucracy, subjectivism and departmentalism, or sectarianism.

[13] See Chapter VI, 'Rectification'.

Chapter XIX

WOMEN

WOMEN made up half the population. Potentially, therefore, they were a tremendous force. So even the first communist armed work teams that slipped into the villages of the Yangyi area during the war against Japan, paid attention to arousing women as well as men to resist the invaders. These work teams themselves had women members. One of them was Guo Ying, who in 1938 went to Bailin and drew the young poor peasant woman Guo Heng-de[1] into revolutionary activity.

By 1960 Yangyi Commune had a core of outstanding women, Guo Heng-de, the first woman Communist in the area, being the veteran among them. Besides being a provincial labour heroine she was a vice-chairman of the commune and of its Women's Federation, as well as a member of the Provincial Women's Federation Executive, and of the Bailin District and the Commune Party committees. Though now well on in her forties she still worked 'at shock task tempo' and year after year broke farm yield records.

Ye San-ni, another former poor peasant, though only in her thirties was also a veteran organizer. Soon after joining the Youth League in 1950, she became secretary of its General Branch Committee for Yangyi townlet. As such she was responsible for guiding work in all the townlet's branches. Next she was an organizer of the movement to set up co-operatives and herself became vice-head first of a semi-socialist then of a socialist co-operative. In 1956 she was given the job of organizing women in Yangyi township; and when the commune was set up in 1958 she headed its branch of the Women's Democratic Federation (W.D.F.).[2]

Zhu Xu-mei of the Silver Sea Tract, also of a poor peasant family, was another of the commune's outstanding women. She was no veteran, but a sturdy, red-cheeked girl of the generation born at the time the 8th Route Army arrived in Yangyi. She had known hunger and cold as a child and had grown-up in a period of fierce but victorious struggles. She had seen the defeat of the Japanese, the overthrow of the landlords and the first steps towards mutual aid and co-operative farming. On the tract she studied as she worked,

[1] See p. 16 ff.
[2] The full name was 'The All-China Women's Democratic Federation'.

239

taking spare-time secondary school courses while mastering cotton-growing technique. Zhu Xu-mei could be counted on to volunteer for tasks that others might shy away from. She was good at applying what she learnt from books to life and explaining it in terms that others could grasp. By 1960, at the age of twenty-two, she was already an effective organizer of women workers, a skilled cotton-grower and leader of one of the tract's record-breaking teams. That summer she joined the Communist Party and was appointed a vice-head of the tract.

Other women had come to the fore in mastering technique. Two of the commune's three tractor drivers were young local women trained in Handan. In Little Yetao's livestock breeding station and in its chicken hatchery the majority of the newly-trained technicians were girls. During the iron and steel-making campaign of 1958 large numbers of young women worked shoulder to shoulder with the men and earned proficiency certificates. Educated young women, the first generation of graduates from the new local schools, held jobs as brigade accountants and as clerks in commune trade enterprises. And in the field of social services, kindergartens throughout the commune were run by literate young women who had received short-term professional training in Handan.

Women were coming into their own in field work, too. Almost every brigade had its 'March 8 Team'[3] of women farmers who ran experimental plots to improve their technique and achieve record yields. Every high yield tract had women on it.

'WOMEN'S WORK'

The popular term for the carrying on of revolutionary propaganda and organization among women was 'women's work'. This began in the Yangyi area with the arrival of the first 8th Route Army work teams which came to organize resistance to the Japanese.

Before this time women were subject not only to the same oppression as the men of their own class. They suffered this and more. In poor peasant families, when there was not enough food to go round, it was the girl children who were sold first, as child brides (to save the expense of supporting them during the years when they could not work for their keep). And it was the girl babies who were killed at birth, for boys would support their parents in their old age, while girls married into other families.

Women's main work was in the home, grinding the grain by turning heavy chaser mills, gathering firewood and herbs, cooking, drawing and carrying water, sewing, twisting hemp to make string for use in stitching cloth shoe-soles and, of course, minding the children.

[3] The date of International Working Women's Day.

240

Women

This work and tradition tied them to their homes and courtyards. Footbinding, which had only gradually been discontinued during the previous years,[4] meant that when the 8th Route Army arrived in the late thirties, all the women and some of the girls suffered a physical handicap which made it hard for them to travel any distance from home. Within the home their status was low. According to the Confucian code woman was born to obey—first her father, then her husband and finally, if widowed, her son. Widows were not supposed to remarry, though a man might marry as many wives (or concubines) as he could afford. It was considered the natural right of a husband to beat his wife. Symbolic of the status of women was the reply given to male visitors when the man of the house chanced to be out. The customary answer to the question: 'Is anybody at home?' was, 'No, there's nobody in'—given by the housewife herself.

To educate and organize women for struggle against their double oppression, the Communists first helped them to set up Women's Associations.[5] These associations aimed at safeguarding women from oppression and drawing them into both revolutionary activity and production. On the one hand they took up cases of maltreatment of wives; on the other they organized women for spinning and weaving, making quilts, uniforms and cloth shoes for the 8th Route Army and for working in the fields. The women responded, often in the face of opposition from conservative husbands and fathers (as well as mothers-in-law). They span and wove, cut and stitched and some even sowed and reaped. This meant that they earned money, though it was not paid into their own hands (except in the rare cases of widows who were heads of families). As contributors to the family income they commanded more respect than when they toiled only at unpaid housework. So their contributions to the struggle against the Japanese invaders both strengthened the economy and raised their own status.

It was not easy to maintain the correct relationship between women's struggle for emancipation and their revolutionary tasks. In Ten Mile Inn, for example, in 1948, women were called on to take an active part in the current land reform campaign, and to throw off all remaining oppression. For this purpose they were urged to reveal their sufferings. As they did this, in some cases the target of their attack became their own menfolk, even in poor peasant families. But it was poor peasant men who were bearing the brunt of the land reform struggle. So the land reform work team stepped in and persuaded these poor peasant women to treat their offending menfolk as erring comrades to be reasoned with, and to direct their

[4] After the revolution of 1911 a law was passed prohibiting footbinding; but its enforcement was slow and uneven, occurring first in the biggest cities, last in remote rural areas.
[5] Later federated into the All-China Women's Democratic Federation.

241

Politics of Yangyi Commune

attack against their joint oppressors. The work team's approach accorded with a Central Committee resolution on women's work passed in the same year. This stated that the freeing of women could not be isolated from the revolution as a whole and that two wrong tendencies were to be guarded against: one was to think that all would be well with women so long as general revolutionary aims were fulfilled and that there was therefore no need to pay special attention to women's problems or to have separate women's organizations; the other was to think that women's emancipation was a cause in itself, not part of the revolution. Actually, the resolution declared, one of the first lessons of women's work was that the two causes—the freeing of women and the revolution as a whole—had to be combined.[6]

An important part in raising the status of women was played by legislation.

In the late forties, as part of the land reform, land deeds were for the first time issued in the name of individual members of each family. This included women and children. (Previously they had been in the name of the head of the family only.) Then in 1950, the Marriage Law of the People's Republic of China abolished 'the arbitrary and compulsory feudal marriage system, which is based on the superiority of man over woman . . .' This law prohibited concubinage, betrothal of children, interference with the re-marriage of widows and the exaction of dowries. It made the free choice of partners and equal rights for men and women the basis of marriage.

In 1954 the Constitution of the People's Republic of China was adopted. This decreed that 'women enjoy the same rights as men in all spheres of political, economic, cultural, social and domestic life'.

The women of Yangyi, like tens of millions of others in the Liberated Areas, had for years been legally entitled to much the same rights as those guaranteed by the Marriage Law and the Constitution. But the law alone could not change habits, traditions and ways of thinking. For instance, although with the land reform land deeds were issued in the name of individuals, they were generally in the keeping of the head of the family, who also controlled family finances. While he had to obtain his wife's consent if he wished to dispose of her land, it was up to her to exercise this right. This meant casting aside tradition and called for strength of character and even physical courage on the part of the woman. It was the same with the Marriage Law. Rights of divorce, re-marriage of widows or deserted wives, free choice of partners could be exercised only by women refusing to be dominated by tradition.

[6] 'On the Present Women's Work in the Rural Districts of the Liberated Areas,' Decision of the Central Committee of the C.C.P., 20 December, 1948; in *Documents of the Women's Movement of China* (pamphlet), New China Women's Press, Peking, 1949.

For this reason mass movements were conducted for both the drawing up and carrying out of these laws not only among the women but throughout the community. These movements made clear that the law was a powerful weapon, but it must be used with courage and skill. Unless a woman was prepared to stand up for her rights, her life would go on as before. Emancipation could not simply be bestowed by law.

The Women's Associations played a major part in these movements, organizing the women and securing general recognition for their legal rights and status.

In the early and middle fifties the chief task of the revolution in the countryside was organizing co-operatives. These opened up new opportunities for women to take part in production. Back in the days of the Anti-Japanese War women had already been called on to break with tradition and work in the fields, for with men in the army and militia extra labour was needed, especially at sowing and harvest time. Following the land reform, women were again called on to 'take their place with men on the main production front'—farming, which would enable them to exert their influence on the life of the community. This, however, could then be done to only a limited extent, for one of the main problems of small scale agriculture was under-employment. Not even the men were fully employed for most of the year. The co-operatives changed this situation. As they began to undertake sizable soil and water conservation projects, to organize big movements for collecting fertilizer and to accumulate capital for secondary occupations, the demand for labour rose. This not only took up some of the slack of men's labour but gave women greater opportunities of employment outside the home. The upsurge of socialist co-operatives in 1955-6 and the increase in farm production, gave women greater opportunities still.

One result of this was that some people came to the conclusion that women no longer needed special organizations any more than men did; and that they should simply exert their influence through the ordinary machinery of co-operative councils and township congresses. This view was rejected, however. At the Eighth National Congress of the Communist Party in 1956, Teng Ying-chao, a member of the Party's Central Committee as well as of the National Executive Committee of the W.D.F., declared that though much had been achieved much remained to be done before women's emancipation was complete. There was still a high percentage of illiteracy among women, she pointed out; those who had been drawn into jobs were not yet well qualified technically or professionally; in some places there was a prejudice against giving women jobs, while in others they were given work but without consideration for their health or home responsibilities; thus there still existed a contradiction between going out to work and coping with household duties and caring for the children. Women's special problems still existed in society.[7]

Meanwhile the Communist Party called on women to play a still bigger part in socialist construction and re-affirmed its long-standing principle that they should take part in production and thus help raise the general living standard and their own status at the same time. Concrete proposals included: implementation of the Party's policy of equal pay for equal work, expansion of social services to lighten the burden of housework and child care, gradual elimination of illiteracy. The whole Party was called on to take action along these lines. At the same time, local women's organizations, so far from being dissolved were to be strengthened.

Following this, new action was taken in the Yangyi area. The Youth League organized literacy drives to make all women (and men) from 16 to 25 literate, and in some of the socialist co-operatives rush season nurseries and kindergartens were set up.

For the women of Yangyi, 1958, the first year of the Great Leap Forward, was a notable period. In the spring there was a new drive for literacy among both women and men; by the end of the year practically all the women from 16 to 25 and a number of the older ones had learned to read and write. Then, with the Great Leap in agriculture and the nationwide campaign for making iron and steel, immense opportunities opened for women. In making iron and steel and driving tractors, they were doing work which even most men had not attempted a couple of years before. Another innovation was the commune's issuing of pay directly into the hands of those who earned it (regardless of age or sex) instead of to the head of the family. This helped tilt the balance towards paid work in the fields and away from unpaid work in the home. It brought more women than ever into the labour force. At the same time it struck a blow at the remains of the patriarchal system.

By 1960 there were a thousand women working in the commune's social services, a number of them professionally trained, and all the 'March 8' experimental plots in the different brigades were under unified leadership to form a 'dispersed high yield tract' for upgrading women farmers throughout the commune. Thus not only had the number of gainfully employed women increased. There was a marked trend among them from unskilled to skilled work.

THE DRIVE FOR SOCIAL SERVICES

In spite of all these advances women were not yet on an equal footing with men. Housework, a branch of the economy entrusted

[7] See 8th National Congress of the C.C.P., *Documents*, Vol. II, F.L.P., Peking, 1956, p.227

exclusively to women, remained on the old narrow family basis and still held them back.

In 1959, when the Ten Mile Inn Brigade Party Secretary Wang Mi-shan was asked why there was only one woman Communist in his village after 20 years of revolutionary work, he replied: 'Women have a lot of work to do in the home and a Communist has a lot of work to do for the Party. He has to attend meetings, too. If you don't, you can't understand Party policy and do your job as Party members should. This makes it hard for a woman to be a Party member. Still, it's partly our own fault. Other villages have more women Party members and cadres than we do. The reason is that their men cadres have paid more attention to drawing women into things than we have.' The question of Party membership was, of course, a special one, directly involving only a small number of villagers (perhaps 2 or 3 per cent). But for women in general the contradiction between putting in full time in the work teams and doing hours of work in the home was becoming increasingly sharp.

Some women were given help to avoid it. In Ten Mile Inn young Wang Yun-de was able to excel in farmwork because her husband's mother and grandmother encouraged her and took over the household chores, though normally, after slaving in the household for a couple of decades, a mother-in-law felt entitled to place most of the housework on the shoulders of her daughter-in-law. But this was a 'Red Star' or model family. The father was a model cook in a restaurant, the son was a model student, the grandmother was a model for her age in doing field-work. Wang Yun-de herself was a model field-worker and a probationary member of the Communist Party.

In most households, however, the younger women still had to do most of the housework. This put a heavy strain on them. Young Li Chai-de, for instance, eager to become a full-fledged member of her work team, could not help taking off one whole day a week to grind the grain for the family's meals. On top of that she was expected to do the cooking. And if meals were late or there were other hitches in the housework, her mother-in-law would scold her. Once the older woman got so worked up that she started smashing bowls. Li Chai-de's husband, a filial son, sided with his mother. He approved of his wife's working in the fields, but thought she should put 'first things first'. And in his mind the first duty of a woman was to run the home.

Things were much the same in the family of young Party member Wang Sheng-you. Though this was considered a rather democratic, modern household in which mother-in-law and daughter-in-law were equals, the two were always bickering. 'You ought to do the milling,' the mother-in-law would say. 'You're younger than I am.' 'I don't know anything about these household matters,' the daughter-in-law would answer. 'They're your job. I work in the fields all day.'

Sometimes both went to work in the fields and both came back equally tired. Then neither of them wished to start cooking. Even in a family without a mother-in-law there could be friction. Wang Lin-rong, the young militant who had spoken out in the Great Debate against the former rich peasant Wang Jia-wen,[8] had been an orphan since early childhood. So after he married there were just his wife, himself and eventually two children in the family. His wife was keen on working in the fields and it often happened that the young husband came home to find that the meal was not ready. Wang Lin-rong was an active C.Y.Ler with many duties to attend to and such delays upset his tight schedule. The result was frequent family flare-ups.

Advances in household economy were clearly desirable and the Communist Party had called for them in 1956. At that time, as experience was limited and the resources of the co-operatives were still small, the first step was to conduct experiments in a few places such as Bailin, where the cadres were exceptionally competent and had some experience with kindergartens.

By the time the commune was formed both the need and the possibility for social services had increased and canteens, nurseries and kindergartens were set up in almost every village. But in the first few months the leadership were faced with so many new tasks that they could not manage to put social services on a sound footing except in model brigades like Bailin. Many of the new social services, therefore, were soon closed down.

During the check on the work of the commune in the winter of 1959–60, however, the question of community dining-rooms came to the fore. It was clear that agriculture could now provide full employment for women as well as men if only the problem of household and family arrangements could be solved. A technical solution, however, based on household gadgets, was out of the question (China's industry not yet being sufficiently developed), but socialization was feasible.

It was in these circumstances that canteens, kindergartens, and sewing centres were developed to the point of freeing 5,000 of the commune's women for productive work alongside the men.

In Ten Mile Inn 180 women now turned out regularly for field work, out of a total turn-out of 470. Twenty to thirty of these women were described as 'old'; that is, they were over 45. The rest were 'young and middle-aged'; that is, between 16 and 45. This meant that roughly two-thirds of the women in this last age-group were now regular workers. Not only were many more women working in the fields; a number were becoming highly competent farmers. Eight women cadres of the village W.D.F. branch had started a 'March 8' five *mu* experimental cotton plot, with a target of 500 *jin* of (unginned)

[8] See p. 25.

cotton per *mu*. Another eight women were members of the Ten Mile Inn team on the Long March high yield tract.

Not all the women between 16 and 45 who had been tied down by household duties were eager for a place in the 'front line' of rural life.

One of these was Guo Xi-fu of Ten Mile Inn

Guo Xi-fu was a housewife in her early forties. She had a son of five and a daughter who had just married and left home. All her life she had done housework and accepted it as the normal occupation for a woman. When the work team her husband belonged to set up its canteen, she ate in it with him and the little boy. (The husband was a strong supporter of the canteen.) When the kindergarten started, her husband urged her to send the boy. She was not eager to do so— but thought it wrong to oppose her husband. So she did as he wished. No longer having to cook or look after her son during the day, she found herself with little to do. But working in the fields seemed quite out of the question. 'I can't tell wheat from barley,' she said when the work team leader asked her to help with the weeding. At this time the work team was so short of labour that its fields were thick with weeds. At last, because it was an emergency and because her husband thought she ought to, she agreed to try and put in a few days at the job. When the wheat harvest came round the team was again short of labour and this time she turned up every day for reaping. After this work Guo Xi-fu received the first pay she had ever earned. By the autumn she was turning out quite often.

The case of Guo Xi-fu showed that some women were satisfied with their circumscribed existence and inferior position in public life, or at least were reluctant to make the effort needed to change it. But it also showed that even they could gradually be drawn into community work.

The proportion of women taking a passive attitude differed from brigade to brigade. In Bailin, for instance, in the summer of 1960, 796 out of 823 able-bodied women were doing farmwork fairly regularly. This was proportionately almost 50 per cent more than in Ten Mile Inn and took in practically all the women physically capable of working.

One conclusion to be drawn from this disparity was: an important condition for women taking part in public life was the carrying out of ideological work to arouse their enthusiasm for socialism and increase their desire to take part in revolutionary activity and achieve equality with men. Such work was the task of the local branch of the Women's Democratic Federation and indirectly of the Communist Party. In some brigades these branches worked more effectively than in others; the results could be seen in the number of women taking part in farm work and public life. If a well-meaning hard-working Brigade Party Branch, made up of men, decided that freedom from house-work and equality in building socialism should be bestowed on women, the results would not be the same as if the women demanded it themselves. Here lay the difference between Bailin and Ten Mile Inn. In Bailin the education and organization of the mass of the women had gone on energetically and systematically for years.

In Ten Mile Inn, on the other hand, according to Party Secretary Wang Mi-shan: 'We didn't pay enough attention to women's work in our village in the past. We didn't train a core of women cadres.'

Steps were being taken to change this state of affairs. 'Since the rectification last winter ' said Wang Mi-shan, 'we've been trying to improve things. First the Branch Committee decided to recruit some women into the Party, had talks with them and assigned them tasks to carry out under the Party Committee's guidance. So by this spring we had three women Party members: Zhi Di-de, head of the W.D.F. branch in our village; Wang Yun-de, a very able young woman, and Wang You-fen, who was outstanding in the steel campaign. But we've only two members now, because Wang You-fen married a man from Shidong village and went to live there. At the moment we're cultivating another five candidates; three of them may be admitted quite soon.

'Secondly, whenever the Branch Committee is considering an important piece of work, it discusses how to draw the women in. Thirdly, we're now appointing some women cadres. In the past we didn't train women to be cadres because we didn't have enough confidence in them. Now we've even made Wang Yun-de vice-head of the brigade. She's very capable and we sent her to attend an advanced workers' conference in Handan. And we've re-organized the leadership of the work teams so that now each team has two leaders—one man and one woman. We've still got a long way to go in women's work, but it's being done twice as well this year as last.'

WOMEN CADRES

Women cadres and Party members played a big part in the success of women's work and a new generation of them was growing up in Ten Mile Inn. This was indicated in the 1960 membership figures of the Ten Mile Inn branch of the Communist Youth League. Seventeen of the thirty-nine members were girls.

During the previous twenty years Ten Mile Inn had not been without women leaders. The first was Wang Chui-de, who became head of the village Women's Association in the early forties. Some twenty years before, together with her husband she had been driven out of a prosperous middle peasant family by her husband's step-mother, who wanted the whole family inheritance to go to her own children. The couple eventually got work in a nearby town, the wife as a weaver, the husband as a cook. They made their living as wage-

248

workers for several years before returning to Ten Mile Inn to farm. By the time she became head of the Ten Mile Inn Women's Association at the age of fifty-five Wang Chui-de had long ceased to be a typical village housewife. Having the makings of a militant leader she was sent on a training course. She came back to the village filled with new ideas and with bobbed hair and unbound feet. She proved an able and energetic organizer and soon had most housewives spinning and weaving. In fact under her lead they won the county record in spinning and weaving and Ten Mile Inn became outstanding for its women's work during the last critical years of the war against Japan. But the movement rested largely on the shoulders of Wang Chui-de. This prevented women's work from taking deep roots.

After the war was over, during the land reform struggles, Wang Chui-de's husband's once prosperous family were disenfranchised; and Wang Chui-de herself, was therefore no longer eligible to lead women's work in the village.[9] A poor peasant woman named Wang Xiang, now came to the fore in Ten Mile Inn. Wang Xiang had been a child-bride brought up in a decaying middle peasant home, which was finally bankrupted by her husband's profligate habits (he was notorious for having all 'the four big vices'—opium smoking, gambling, gluttony and promiscuity). He died leaving Wang Xiang all but destitute and with a young son to bring up. Only by cultivating poor hillside land did she manage to keep herself and the child alive.

In struggling against oppression and poverty Wang Xiang had cultivated a spirit of independence together with a ready and bitter tongue. It was largely for this reason that during the land reform struggles the women of Ten Mile Inn, most of whom dared not speak in public, elected Wang Xiang their spokesman. Some of the men, however, particularly the middle peasants, had a low opinion of her, for as a fan of the local opera she invited the (all-male) village music club to use her home as its headquarters. By traditional standards this was unseemly behaviour for a woman—particularly a widow. In fact at this time many men, convinced that woman's place was in the home, even opposed having their wives and daughters attend women's meetings and threatened to drive them out if they attended 'those gatherings of prostitutes'. This attitude existed even among the men on the village Party committee who complained that it was almost impossible to cultivate women Party members or cadres since 'militant women aren't virtuous and virtuous women aren't militant'.

The adjustment campaign of 1948 brought a swing towards 'virtuous' and away from militant women, with the election of Zhi Di-de to the chairmanship of the Ten Mile Inn Women's Association. Zhi Di-de was known as the finest spinner in the village and as a model daughter-in-law—traditional style. Since the traditional style

[9] This was not in accordance with policy, as they were middle peasants, not rich ones. For details of this 'deviation' see *Revolution in a Chinese Village*.

daughter-in-law could not presume to hold forth in the presence of her mother-in-law, when Association committee meetings were held in her home, Zhi Di-de stayed silent. In the years that followed she continued as head of the women's organization. She was respected as intelligent and hardworking and proved to be such a good field-worker that she was able to support her family with her work points. In 1959 she was accepted into the Communist Party, becoming the one and only woman member of the Ten Mile Inn branch at the time. During the wheat harvest of 1960 she was voted a model worker, the caption under her water-colour portrait in the village exhibition stating: 'She led a team of ten women who each worked at top speed during the harvest, reaping 3 to 5 *mu* each a day (30 per cent more than the average for men) and gleaned 5 *jin* of wheat.'

But though Zhi Di-de set the women a good example as a worker, organizing and doing propaganda were not her strong points. She still would not speak at meetings, no matter where they were held.

An outstanding example of a successful woman cadre was Guo Heng-de. Like Zhi Di-de she was a competent worker. But she also knew how to organize. One of her characteristics was single-minded-ness. Once a decision had been made by the Party Committee to carry through some plan, Guo Heng-de would go at it and keep working at top speed until it was done. When, under her lead, Bailin was tackling its water shortage by digging hundreds of rain storage tanks in the fields, Guo Heng-de was here, there and everywhere, despite her bound feet. Fellow villagers claimed that no one had ever heard her say she felt tired. When the old folks home was being set up in Bailin she worked night and day. Some of the men cadres became concerned about her health when they saw how red her eyes were from lack of sleep; but try as they would they could not persuade her to rest.

Some years earlier she had organized one of the first kindergartens in the area in the same fashion. Her own youngest child was then a baby, so to give her undivided attention to her work she had found friends to take care of it. Then in a whirlwind campaign she got the kindergarten going. In setting Bailin's first community dining-room on its feet, Guo Heng-de took her bedding and settled down in a little room adjoining the kitchen, so as to be on the spot to help the staff. Whenever any canteen in the brigade found itself facing prob-lems, she did the same, moving in with her bedding and staying night and day until things were going smoothly.

Guo Heng-de never rested on her laurels. She used each success as the starting-point for a fresh advance. The pioneer kindergarten she had launched in 1952 with 20 children, by 1956 had 113—though in the intervening years her chief work had been in the co-operatives. Her all-round ability as a cadre contributed much to educating and organizing women throughout the area.

Women

YANGYI WOMEN'S CONGRESS, 1960

In 1960 the national leadership of the W.D.F. called on its local organizations to sum-up and consolidate their work, so that fresh advances might be made. For this purpose a Commune Women's Congress was convened in Yangyi.

First came the election of delegates. It was decided that for every 35 women one representative should be elected. This made a total of 256 delegates for the whole commune. Of these, 251 were from brigades, 3 from schools, one each from commune industrial and trade enterprises. The election itself was an important part of the strengthening of women's work. First the W.D.F. Committee proposed a list of qualifications which, after being discussed in small groups throughout the commune were accepted as necessary if the delegates were to do their job well. The candidates were to be: of good class origin (i.e. former hired hands, poor or lower-middle peasants or their children), industrious, enthusiastic in farm work; respected and supported by the people, models in publicizing the Party's policies and in carrying them out. With these qualifications in mind, candidates were discussed and elections held.

Following the elections the congress was convened. Its first task was to sum up the achievements and problems in work among women since 1958. This covered the whole period of the commune's existence.

Under achievements, the unanimous view was that women did now stand shoulder to shoulder with men. They were mastering technique. The high yields of the 'March 8' teams, the work of women on high yield tracts, where the most advanced technique in the commune was used, the women's handling of machines, especially tractors, and their mastery of iron and steel production, all bore this out. Advances in technique were giving women ever more favourable conditions for equality with men in farming. This was a new factor favouring women's emancipation.

Three problems were singled out for immediate attention. First, women's organizations in the brigades and villages needed to be revitalized. Accordingly a decision was taken to carry out a check-up and consolidation of each, so that women could be aroused to the opportunities before them and take a new step in their emancipation.

The second problem was the safeguarding of women's health. Some of the young women refused to pay attention to this. When, as during the anti-drought or steel-making campaigns the task had the urgency of a battle, they could hardly be restrained. Besides this, when women first started to turn out regularly for farmwork, most teams had an all-male leadership. Not being accustomed to allocating work to women, the men sometimes gave them jobs which were unsuitable or quotas which were too high for them. The Central

251

Committee of the Communist Party had already issued its directive on women's work in the communes, which was summed up as the 'three musts and three must nots' (See page 126.) The women's congress decided that stricter measures were needed to ensure the carrying out of this directive.

The third problem had to do with current farmwork, for women's work was not divorced from that of the community as a whole. The main farm task at this period was field management for the late crops, cotton and sweet potatoes; so the congress decided to launch a campaign among the women to improve this work.

On the basis of these decisions and of the general discussion the congress elected a new committee. Nine of its twenty-five members ranked as chairmen of the W.D.F. of Yangyi Commune. Ye San-ni was first chairman, Guo Heng-de one of the vice-chairman. A standing committee was put in charge of day-to-day work. The general feeling among delegates at the conclusion of the congress was of a fresh surge forward in the emancipation of women.

The struggle for this emancipation had been going on in Yangyi without cease for twenty years. Much progress had been made. With the Great Leap Forward and the establishment of the commune it had clearly entered a new stage. Women for the first time had become a major force in agricultural production, the basis of the whole economy. But their emancipation was not yet complete. There was still work for the Women's Democratic Federation.

Chapter XX

YOUTH

THERE were 3,900 young people (from fifteen to twenty-five years of age) in the Yangyi area in 1960—and they were much in evidence in commune affairs. Far more so than their counterparts in the period of land reform. For since then the conclusion had been drawn that young people should not be lumped together with everyone else if their full powers were to be brought into play.

Youth had special qualities. Two in particular were of significance to the commune. One was physical energy. With farming still unmechanized and the vast bulk of farmwork being done by man or animal power, the vigour of youth was of immense importance to the work force. The other was flexibility and freshness of approach, which made the young folk eager to try new techniques and methods of management. Most of the older farmers had to see with their own eyes that an innovation really worked, before they would give up their tried and trusted ways. So when labour heroes or Party Committees advanced new proposals and sought to prove them in practice, it was the young people who acted as their mainstay and served, under their guidance, as trail-blazers. They did so in the drive to spread Eight Point Charter farming methods, in running high yield tracts, in building the Republic Channel and the Long Sea Dam, in afforesting the hills, running canteens and kindergartens and in the steel campaign.

To tap the potentialities of youth the right methods of work had to be used. Emulation, competition, titles, praise and awards for outstanding individuals and teams, forming Youth Shock Teams, assigning shock tasks, waging 'battles'—all these gave scope for 'heroism' and so had a special appeal for youth.

The steel campaign, for instance, was felt by almost all the young people to be a high point in their lives.

'We lived in mat-sheds all the time,' said one Yangyi lad. 'The roofs leaked like sieves when it rained. The ground got wetter and wetter and so did we. But we knew what steel meant to our country, so we stuck it out. We had a strong sense of discipline. We called it the battle for steel and we went at it as if we were really fighting.'

According to the secretary of the Ten Mile Inn C.Y.L. branch, 'We hardly knew what steel looked like before; but in 1958 eight out of every ten young people in our village smelted it—the same as in

253

other parts of the country. We went all out for the first ten days. We just wouldn't slow down till we'd got the hang of it. One or two comrades like young Li worked five days and nights at a stretch without getting a full night's sleep.' The speaker had done the same himself, it turned out. Girls, too, had stuck to the arduous task for long hours until they mastered it. 'More than twenty of us learnt the whole process,' he went on, 'from making furnaces to turning out the finished product. We've got diplomas from county headquarters.' The young people were obviously proud of these certificates, regarding them as proof of their power to master technique as well as of their capacity for sustained effort and willingness to put up with hardship.

As Commune Party Secretary Jin put it: 'It wasn't just the steel that was tempered, but the people who made the steel.'

The building of the Long Sea Dam, the cutting of the Republic Channel, the struggle against the drought—all these were 'battles'. Competitions were also an important means of stimulating enthusiasm and innovations. They were usually organized for each phase of farm work—sowing, hoeing, harvesting. The tempo and excitement of these competitions and battles appealed to the young people.

The challenge of the new appealed to them too. When one brigade Party committee, because of the shortage of labour, proposed that draught animals should be tended in groups of eight or ten, the older farmers objected. They were not willing to take charge of more than one animal. (This was the tradition, arising from the days when animals were so scarce in the area that only a prosperous minority owned any.) 'You couldn't keep a whole lot of animals fit. They'd get into poor condition and then you'd be criticized for not looking after brigade property,' said one older man. So the brigade leaders called on several young men to accept responsibility for all the animals owned by the brigade. They took on the job, split the animals into four groups and stabled them in the centre of the village where the public could keep an eye on them and see for themselves the effect of collective care.

In Little Yetao more radical innovations were proposed by the Party leadership and carried out by young people, including the use of a *kang* as an incubator for hatching chicks, and of artificial insemination at the breeding station. The technicians were all local primary school graduates scarcely out of their teens.

It was the same with the social services. In Ten Mile Inn, after the first unsuccessful attempt to run the kindergarten with old women in charge, the task was entrusted to young ones.

Such tasks required literacy and at least a foundation of general education. In this respect the young people of the commune had one advantage not possessed by Yangyi youth of any earlier period. They were all literate. And with all the school-age children attending school, in future the commune youth would not only be literate; they would have a general elementary education covering arithmetic, history, geography and natural science. (The present generation of young people, however, still had leeway to make up in general education.)

Though young people were drawn into social services, animal husbandry, poultry raising and capital construction (building dams, channels, terraces), their main field of endeavour was agriculture.

YOUTH TEAMS

The organizing of youth to serve as trail-blazers in farming started with the farming co-operatives. These brought opportunities for forming special teams which would draw on youth's special qualities. From 1956, when the socialist co-operatives were set-up, until 1959, these took the form of 'Youth Production Teams'. During this period work teams were based on households, not individuals, and the Youth Production Teams were composed not of youth alone, but of households in which young people made up a good part of the labour force. In 1958, after the setting-up of the communes, Shexian County had 105 of these teams averaging 30 households each and including practically all the most lively young 'activists'. They were given guidance and help by the Communist Party organizations in their co-operatives, villages or townships, and were often led by labour heroes. This was in order to provide the best possible conditions for proving the worth of the methods and policies advocated by the Party and thus persuading other work teams to adopt them.

In 1959 these Youth Production Teams were to the fore in applying and popularizing the Eight Point Charter. In summing up their work that year, the county leaders found that on all the land they cultivated the average yield exceeded that of ordinary teams by roughly 30 per cent. The most outstanding results in the whole county were achieved by the Ren Wan-he Youth Production Team of Little Yetao. This team was based on 63 households with a total of 183 members and was responsible for the cultivation of 202 *mu*. Its work force included over 50 young people. Labour hero Ren Qing-mei, as secretary of the Little Yetao Communist Party Committee, gave guidance to the team. It achieved such excellent results in every phase of farmwork that the Shexian leaders made a summary of the measures it had adopted and publicized them throughout the county.

In 1960, when the Commune Party Committee took the high yield tracts as 'the main battlefield' (instead of the land worked by ordinary work teams) young people were organized into a different type of team—Youth Shock Teams. These worked on the tracts and were made up of individuals rather than households. Although older farmers were included in them to provide experience, the majority of the members were young men and women. In Shexian County altogether 1,200 such teams were formed.

In Little Yetao brigade there was a 'May 4 Youth Team' (named after the historic anti-imperialist worker and student demonstrations on that day in 1919). In the summer of 1960, when torrential rain and hailstorms following 200 days of drought, wrought havoc with the young maize, the ex-soldiers 'August 1 Team' challenged other teams to compete with them in restoring the ravages of the weather and reaping a good crop in spite of it. The Youth Team took up this challenge at once.

Soon the two teams were racing neck and neck. Then a check showed that the Youth Team was ahead. There were unhealthy yellow leaves on its rivals' tract. The 'August 1 Team's' Party group held a self-criticism meeting, decided that they had been acting with less vigour than the Youth Team and pledged to improve their work. At the height of the hoeing, weeding and fertilizing they slept in the fields so as not to waste time walking back and forth to the village.

Meanwhile the Youth Team had gained another advantage. Their tract ran to the foot of a steep hill. This they made use of as an observation post so that they could see at a glance any yellowish patches in their fields and give them extra water, fertilizer and hoeing. 'August 1' could spot their poor patches only by laboriously combing through the fields. To put themselves on a par with the Youth Team, they built a look-out tower—a thatched hut on ten-foot stilts. This proved a success. They even held on-the-spot conferences in their tower, to work out their tactics.

Next the ex-soldiers found that the corn near the trees on the edge of their fields did not do as well as the rest. This they decided was due to the trees eating up much of the fertilizer and moisture; so they called another meeting and decided to pay special attention to all stalks close to trees. Even after rain, when the rest of the fields needed no watering, they would water these stalks. Soon 'August 1' gained the lead.

The Youth Team was not long in catching up. They re-organized their work, spreading manure in the daytime but carrying it to the fields at night, each person having an agreed quota to fill before going to bed. 'August 1', on the other hand, when it found itself short of labour, went in for technical innovation. Instead of hoeing in the ordinary way, it did so with an old single-bladed plough hitched to a donkey. This greatly stepped-up labour efficiency, for one good man with a hoe could manage only only *mu* a day, while two men and a donkey could do ten *mu*.

In the end, thanks largely to the ex-soldiers' initiative in issuing their challenge and the Youth Team's keenness in taking it up, the

whole brigade surpassed its target; for the other teams also started
setting-up observation towers, using donkey-drawn ploughs for
hoeing and giving extra care to crops near trees. Thus overall production was increased.

These shock teams were a force for promoting the technical
transformation of agriculture. For this their members had to be
educated and members of youth shock teams on high yield tracts
attended courses in general education, advanced technique and
philosophy. Besides all this and doing farmwork their varied
activities included helping build irrigation works, composing poems,
putting on propaganda plays and even building Towers of Heroic
Ambition.

Such varied activities and crowded programmes created a general
air of energy and bustle. One old man, touched by the young
people's efforts, wrote a large poster and hung it on the wall of his
village. It read: 'What revolutionary drive our young people have!
They get up early and go to bed late. They rest little and study much.
Their inventiveness and technique are remarkable.'

There was nothing fortuitous about these achievements. They
were the result of painstaking effort. For the young people had to
understand the significance of a task before they would take it on
with enthusiasm. And this was only the first step. Carrying it
through was harder still. In shock tasks or 'battles' the young
people's tendency was to go all out for speed and quantity while
neglecting quality and cost. They had to learn how to settle down
to study new techniques until they could grasp them, and to keep at
a job without losing heart over setbacks until they finally succeeded.
All this called for skilful and sustained political, ideological and
organizational work. This was undertaken by the Communist Youth
League, under the guidance of the Communist Party.

THE COMMUNIST YOUTH LEAGUE

The Communist Youth League was by definition 'a mass organization of advanced youth led by the Party'.[1] Thus it was organized
differently from the Women's Federation which, though also led by

[1] This definition was based on past successes—and some early defects in
organization. 'During the period of the revolutionary civil wars the Youth League
stressed the need to be an advanced organization, but neglected its mass character.
This led to sectarianism and made the Youth League a second Party. On the other
hand, during the later period of the War of Resistance against Japanese Aggression, the anti-Japanese youth bodies lacked an advanced organization as their
nucleus, and this made them loose and ineffective. That was why the Party, in its
1949 resolution on the establishment of the Youth League, laid down that the
present Youth League must be "a mass organization of advanced youth led by
the Party".' See 'Speech by Hu Yao-pang', in *Documents of the 8th National
Congress of the C.C.P.*, Vol. II, F.L.P., Peking, 1956.

the Party, was a mass organization not restricted to 'advanced' women.

Yangyi had 1,200 League members (almost one-third of the young people in the commune) and there was a League branch in every brigade.[2] Branches were grouped according to districts, Shidong, for example, having eight with a total of 138 members. These were pledged to work for socialism, their three main tasks being: 'to help the Party; to combine labour with national defence;[3] and to be in the forefront in all work.' C.Y.Lers were expected not only to carry out these tasks themselves, but by setting an example to rally all the young people around them to do the same.

One who did this to good effect was twenty-two-year-old Li Wei-guo of Ten Mile Inn, secretary of the Shidong District C.Y.L.

Li Wei-guo came from a family which had twice had the experience of being poor peasants. Li Bao-hui, the father, had been poor in the days before the Communists came to Yangyi and when the 8th Route Army arrived in the area the landlord was on the point of seizing his land for non-payment of a debt. But the Communists roused the villagers to enforce the policy of Reduction of Rent and Interest, whereby usurious interest already paid on a debt was counted towards repayment of the loan. Li Bao-hui was one of the first in the area to stand up for his rights under this law. So his land and house were saved and he remained a poor peasant instead of being thrust down into the ranks of landless labourers.

Soon afterwards the 8th Route Army launched a recruiting drive and several young men whose families had benefited from the communist reforms joined up. Many thought that Li Bao-hui would do the same. But when this was suggested he protested that he did not know one end of a gun from the other and would be no use in the army. Though he found excuses for not volunteering, Li was 'an active element', being organizer of one of the early mutual aid groups and a militant in the land reform campaigns. After land reform, as mutual aid became more efficiently organized, it was possible during the slack season for a few men to do all the field work while others went in for secondary occupations. Li Bao-hui seized this chance to increase his income by buying and selling livestock as a sideline. For a short time he prospered and even became a middle peasant; but before long he was outwitted at the game of buying and selling, fell into debt again and had to sell five *mu* of his newly-won land. Once more he was a poor peasant.

But by now the living standard of poor peasants was better than

---

[2] In the whole of Shexian County there were 51,981 young people, of whom 11,362 were members of the C.Y.L. There were 12 Youth League Committees (one for each commune), 53 General Branches and 509 Ordinary Branches (roughly one for each village).

[3] See Chapter XVI, 'Military Matters and Commune Power'.

it had been (it had reached the level of pre-liberation middle peasants) and Li Bao-hui's second son, Li Wei-guo, unlike his father and elder brother, went to primary school. He was a smart lad and when he left school became work points registrar for one of the first farming co-operatives in the village.

At the age of eighteen he became eligible for the call-up and volunteered. But feeling that his father would disapprove, he did so in secret. Policy, however, called for trying to win the consent of parents, so eventually he broke the news to them. Neighbours and the village Party Branch Secretary all did their best to bring the parents round. Finally they gave their consent and prepared the traditional farewell feast of meat dumplings for the volunteer. After all this, when Li Wei-guo reached the enlistment centre he was turned down as too short and slight. He was disappointed but on returning home went hard at militia training and in time became the crack shot of the village.

That year the socialist farming co-operative was set up and Li Wei-guo, still in his teens, became a team leader. In 1958, the first year of the Great Leap Forward and of the forming of the commune, he was in the thick of things, leading the young people in 'the battle for steel', helping dig the Republic Channel, carrying heavy stones for lining the Ten Mile Inn pond. In 1960 his career nearly came to an end. On the scene when the commune dam burst, he tried to fill the breach with his own body. He was snatched to safety just in time.

(In the midst of all this he found time to get married. 'I'd never have agreed to anything but a free marriage,' he said, 'though my mother was always trying to find what she thought was the right girl for me.' His wife, three years younger than himself, was at school when they met. 'She's a junior middle school graduate,' he said, 'so she's a great help to me in my work.' Before they married, he had made clear he would like his wife to do some work with her hands and not be 'just an intellectual'. She had readily agreed and now worked half-time in the brigade accounts office, half-time in the fields.

Li Wei-guo was proud of his wife. 'As a boy I'd never have dreamed of being able to marry an educated girl,' he said. 'But now such differences don't count. As long as you both want to work for socialism, everything's all right.' The match was considered a good one on both sides. In the old days a girl with nine years' schooling might have married an official, a landlord or a merchant. But with the new standards which made much of labour and devotion to socialism, the wife, for all her education, was thought lucky to have such a husband.)

Li Wei-guo exerted an influence on most of the young people of the Shidong district. Not merely because he was active, alive and

Politics of Yangyi Commune

outgoing and full of jokes and stories. He had an everyday sort of heroism which they felt they could emulate—that of never hesitating to jump into icy water to fix a pump, of giving up his midday rest to do some urgent job in the fields under the broiling summer sun, of staying on to hoe an extra row at the end of a hard day's work. He also inspired them with his vivid picture of what Yangyi Commune would be like in ten years' time, with its tractors, power-lines and reservoirs, its wooded hills and orchards, its research stations and libraries, its college, theatres, hospitals and clinics, its community centres with canteens, club-rooms and bath-houses, its homes with electric lights, radios and even piped water. He also stressed what this future was to be built on—modern, mechanized farming.

Li Wei-guo spoke eloquently on all this, picturing the present generation as revolutionaries transforming agriculture and changing themselves into the socialist-minded, cultured and technically proficient farmers of the future. And what he said carried weight, not merely because of his eloquence, but because his actions matched his words.

Li Wei-guo, of course, was one of the most forward-looking young men of the commune. It was the responsibility of the Communist Youth League to help other young people to emulate him.

Brigade branches of the C.Y.L. held meetings three times a month. Here members checked on the fulfilment of current tasks, organized competitions and emulation, studied and discussed politics and conducted criticism and self-criticism. They also analysed the significance of current policies and related them to their own lives and behaviour. In Ten Mile Inn, in the spring of 1960, for instance, the C.Y.Lers discussed their attitude to eating in the canteens.[4]

When a special team was needed for part of the Long March Tract (which meant working at high tempo and living on the job in temporary huts) every member of the Ten Mile Inn League Branch volunteered and wrote out a pledge to that effect. At first many of the young folk outside of the League had held back, but fired by the members' enthusiasm they came forward and the team was soon made up. After work started on the tract, League members continued to set an example. When tract leaders met to plan the weeding, a time limit of five days was proposed; but Wang Sheng-you, who was secretary of the Ten Mile Inn League Branch, pledged that his team would do it in three. Then he went back, called a meeting of his team, stressed the importance of the job, organized it well and went at it hard himself. The three-day pledge was fulfilled and work on the whole tract went ahead faster.

Of the three branch meetings held every month one was given over to criticism and self-criticism (mainly in connection with how

[4] See Chapter VI.

260

each member had been realizing the League's aims of helping the Party, combining labour and national defence and being in the forefront in all work).

'We C.Y.Lers couldn't stay in the van if we didn't have criticism and self-criticism,' the Ten Mile Inn League Secretary explained. 'In fact we might slide back. At the criticism and self-criticism meetings you report on your work quite concretely. Suppose one of us agrees to hoe three rows and then only hoes two: he has to look into a thing like that and clear it up. If it's something beyond his control, then it's all right. But suppose it was just laziness. Or his mind was on some personal matter. He tries to show why and criticizes himself. If he can't see the thing clearly, then the others help him.

'Take what happened with Wang Yau-he, the head cook of Work Team Two's canteen,' he went on. 'When people complained about his work, we discussed it. And we got to the root of the trouble. He thought he'd been taken out of the front line and sent to the rear. He wanted to work on a shock team, not in a kitchen. We explained to him that the canteens were playing a key role in the building of socialism. And in the end we convinced him. So even though in his heart of hearts perhaps he'd still rather do farmwork, he does his job as a cook much better than before and now there are no complaints to speak of.

'Then there's Li Wei-deng,' he continued. 'He used to be very off-hand about his job as a work-points registrar. Thought he was too good for it. He'd finished senior primary school here in the village and wanted to go to the city to work. He felt that the countryside was a backwater. But he was an old friend of the C.Y.L. District Secretary, Li Wei-guo.' (In fact, as the names indicate, they were cousins.) 'So at a League Branch meeting we compared the two. "Why does Li Wei-guo have such drive? Why is he always in such high spirits?" we asked. "The answer is, he has an aim in life. He wants to work for the people and do something for society."

'That was one point. Another thing we thrashed out with him was the importance of agriculture. How can the countryside be a backwater when agriculture is the base of the whole national economy?

'Of course there was the question of living standards, too. The towns are better off. But, we pointed out, the harder we work, the faster we'll get on with the building of socialism. Then living standards will go up for all of us.

'After a while he said, "All right, if Wei-guo can go all out, so can I." And that's what he's been doing. When the brigade leaders saw how he'd changed, they asked him to take over the accounting for our brigade side-occupations, on top of his ordinary work. He agreed—and still finds time to do some work in the fields. He's doing a really good job all-round now.

'The main thing is, of course, to see the future. That's how criticism and study help us keep in the van.'

<h3>THE CONTRADICTIONS OF YOUTH</h3>

'Youth is the period of the greatest number of contradictions, when problems that have not arisen in childhood may appear, and problems that have been solved by adults may still be unsolved.'[5] Helping the young people to understand the nature of the contradictions in their minds, to find a yard-stick for their behaviour and to pour their energies into the most constructive channels was the function of the Youth League's political and ideological work.

Li Wei-deng's problem—the contradiction between the call of the city and the needs of the countryside—was a common one, especially among young primary school graduates. The traditional view that had prevailed only twenty-five years earlier, before the 8th Route Army came to Yangyi, had not yet disappeared. This was, that any young person with an education was too good for manual work, that there was therefore little scope for him in the countryside and that he should try to find work in a town.

This was only one aspect of the problem. After liberation, as soon as the cities were freed, there was an urgent demand in factories, government offices and trade departments for personnel who were politically reliable. The natural recruiting grounds were the villages of the old Liberated Areas where for over two decades the revolution had been based. So village after village in these areas had families with members working in towns and cities—even in the national capital, Peking. To many young people, going off to these centres to work was not merely satisfying a personal ambition, it was politically correct. With the working class leading the country, they reasoned, it was surely better to work in industry than on the land.

To complicate the contradiction, living standards were higher in the towns. (The difference was not so great, however, as some farmers thought, for money income alone was not a reliable standard of comparison. Unlike the city workers the farmer paid no house rent, nor did he pay for most of his food, which was the product of his own or his group's labour. Clothing was the main expense.)

Thus the pull between town and country resolved itself into a series of issues: the relationship between mental and manual work, between private and public interests, between workers and farmers, industry and agriculture, present and future. The C.Y.L. was concerned with helping its members, and through them the young people in general, to understand and deal with such contradictions.

The relationship between mental and manual work involved the

[5] Hu Yao-pang, Member of the Secretariat of the Central Committee of the Youth League; speech at 8th National Congress of the C.P.C., *Documents*, Vol.II.

262

whole system of values of the old society and the new. Much propaganda had to be done to change the attitude of the educated towards working with their hands, as the struggle for the Party's educational policy revealed.

Settling the question of living standards called for clarifying the actual extent of the differences, the reasons for their existence and how they were being done away with. At the same time it was presented as a problem of communist ethics. This implied that preoccupation with such matters had its roots in selfishness, in desiring to get the best for oneself and leave the worst for others.

Solving the problem of relations between the two classes of workers and farmers and the two branches of the economy, industry and agriculture, depended on theoretical understanding. Study of the 12-year plan for modernizing agriculture showed just how the gap was being bridged. Then in the summer of 1960 the Central Committee's formulation 'agriculture is the base of the economy, industry the leading factor' and 'the front-line of the revolution today is in the countryside', helped convince young people that they were in no backwater. Their own role in social change was stressed and their emergence as a new type of farmer, politically reliable and technically competent—both 'red and expert'. So growing numbers of young people like Li Wei-guo, with his life of action and excitement, or Zhu Xu-mei of the Silver Sea Tract, striving to apply Marxism to agriculture, found plenty to absorb their interest and energy, both mental and physical.

The old pull of the towns had not altogether gone; but it was now being matched by the counter-pull of the villages; and young people from the cities, on leaving school were going in increasing numbers to the countryside. Meanwhile, mental struggle continued. There were still both Li Wei-guo's and Li Wei-deng's and the Youth League kept up its political work among them.

Another problem was the existence of a small group of young people who were satisfied with life, took it as it came and saw no need to exert themselves. One such was attractive Wang Jin-lin of Ten Mile Inn. As a Youth League member she had pledged 'to serve as the Party's right hand'. But she had married young and in 1960, with a fond husband and a plump baby she felt that life was already good enough. While other Youth League members, including her former classmates, were running experimental plots, battling the drought, striving to increase farm yields, attending spare-time school, Jin-lin was content to stay out of the bustle and excitement. There were others like her who, feeling that life in the countryside was now better than it had ever been before, were inspired by no 'heroic ambition'.

The experience of the new generation differed from that of the old. Few of those in their twenties could recall the famine and

263

fighting of their childhood. Within a few years there would be no young people left who had gone through this early tempering. There would certainly be none who had risked their lives by sheltering underground workers, fighting in the militia or smuggling salt and medicine through the Japanese lines.

Thus a new and pressing problem faced the Yangyi Communists: that of raising another generation of revolutionaries to take over from the one which had defeated the Japanese, overthrown the landlords and rich peasants and collectivized agriculture; of educating, organizing and inspiring them to take up the task of modernizing farming and tempering themselves in the revolutionary struggles of their own era.

The Commune Party Committee were satisfied that the mass of Yangyi's youth were taking up this task. 'The young people of our commune,' said Party Secretary Jin, 'following the lead of the Youth League, are always in the van in carrying out Party policy, no matter what the task is. And once they've gone ahead, most of the older people move forward.'

Chapter XXI

ON THE IDEOLOGICAL FRONT

THE SECTOR OF ART AND LITERATURE

ART and literature, radio, cinema and theatre played an important part in commune life, not merely as entertainment but as 'forces on the ideological front'. They brought a new look to the villages round Yangyi following the Great Leap Forward and the forming of the commune in 1958. Within weeks or even days the walls of many houses were whitewashed and decorated with murals by village artists. Where no artist was at hand the task fell to the village teachers, who were looked to as experts in all cultural matters. The main theme was the labouring people's conquest of nature under the lead of the Communist Party. Popular symbols of the rapid advance in production and of general confidence in victory were winged horses flying over the villages and railway engines streaking across the countryside. The confidence aroused by the unprecedented achievements in soil and water conservation was pictured in the brawny figure of a farmer advancing over the landscape with giant strides and cleaving with his hoe the mountains in his path. Beneath this were often inscribed the words of a verse then popular throughout China:

> There's no Jade Emperor in heaven,
> There's no Dragon King on earth.
> I am the Jade Emperor,
> I am the Dragon King.
> Make way you mountain peaks.
> Here I come.

It was around this time, too, that villages set up their permanent exhibitions with portraits of their local heroes and heroines and pictorial village histories highlighting the class struggle, the battle between the two roads and the building of socialism.

In this, music also played its part. Every village, as of old, had its band of drums, cymbals, trumpets and two-stringed fiddles. Now, to their traditional repertoire of folk airs and tunes from local operas, they were adding popular revolutionary songs such as 'Socialism's Fine' or 'Without the Communist Party there'd be no New China'. The band played a prominent part, too, in celebrating such occasions as the awarding of banners to work teams or labour

265

heroes, the building of a dam or improvement of a farm tool—in fact in the general glorification of labour.

Such events were celebrated with especially composed songs and poems recited to an accompaniment of wooden clappers. Poems might also be written in bold characters on large sheets of red paper and presented by a procession, with the band at its head, then pasted on the gate-posts of those being honoured. Or they might be inscribed on whitewashed walls along the village streets.

In fact with the spread of education more and more ordinary folk were expressing in verse their feelings about community and national events—and putting them in writing. Poems would be composed on all and sundry occasions from the seeing-off of volunteers for the army to the setting-up of a high yield tract or the completion of an irrigation project. Slogans about fertilizer and even reports on the carrying out of Party policy, as with Little Yetao's account of its five-sided farming, were often in rhymed form. And County Head Wang De-hen could be counted on to celebrate any notable achievement in Shexian with new couplets.

Village literature also included writing for wall-newspapers and printed newspapers and magazines. Subject matter ranged from reports on irrigation works or experiments in raising sweet potatoes to local history recalling life under the landlords, fighting the Japanese, the struggles for land reform and co-operation. Newly acquired literacy now made possible a mass movement in literature on the basis of which, according to Party policy, artistic standards could be raised. For this the commune drafted ambitious plans, its goal for 1960 being 100,000 items in the form of verses, memoirs, stories and plays.

With the commune, radio had become part of village daily life. There were no individually-owned sets but amplifiers hitched up to a set in the brigade office were fixed at one or more points in a village, depending on its size. When not serving as a public address system relaying brigade announcements or commune news, these were tuned in on county, provincial or national networks. Programmes included folk music and local opera, stories of the revolution and of patriotic heroes and heroines of the last 2,000 years or so, reports on the deeds of labour heroes and heroines and talks on popular science and current affairs, comic satirical dialogues on daily life, and news domestic and foreign.

Once a month the commune's mobile film-unit would visit the villages on the highway and set up its projector on a large threshing floor. A white-washed wall would serve as screen and there was never a shortage of volunteers to run the hand-cranked dynamo. In the summer of 1960, a film on tour in the commune was *Lads and Lasses of our Village*, which showed how the young folk of a mountain village, in the face of their elders' scepticism and despite dangers and

266

hardships, channelled water to their village from distant springs. The most popular form of art and entertainment in the commune, as well as a powerful means of propaganda, was the theatre. In 1960 Shexian County had three travelling repertory companies serving its three hundred thousand odd people, and commune members would walk miles of mountain paths to see their perform- ances. The drama's appeal lay not only in its infinite variety (one piece might be opera, ballet and acrobatics, history, tragedy and comedy combined); but also in its themes, which were both tradi- tional and close to commune life.

There were no regular theatres or halls in the villages. The best facilities in the commune were in Yangyi townlet which had a hall holding several hundred. This had a reed-mat roof and an earthen floor. It did have electric lights over the stage. However, these being none too bright, they were bolstered up during performances by the troupe's own paraffin pressure lamps. In other villages in the com- mune plays were performed in the open, the actors alone having a roof over their heads and the audience sitting on stones or logs unless they brought their own stools with them. In some places the stage might be an old temple platform; in others it was simply a threshing- floor. At reservoir construction sites, high yield tracts or old folks' homes there might be no stage at all.

Each company had a repertoire of over a hundred pieces, about two-thirds of them historical. Among the most popular of these was the *Yang Family Cycle*, a series of plays dealing with a patriotic noble family of the Sung Dynasty (from the tenth to the thirteenth century), famous for the strong character and military prowess of its women. Interest in these pieces was heightened by the legend that the matriarch, Si Tai-jun, was a local woman. But the greatest enthusiasm was for the skill and courage of a maid-servant, a poor member of the noble household, who defeats an arrogant and treacherous enemy general in single combat.

Traditional plays of this type were not taken over without change. The policy towards China's dramatic heritage being: 'Let flowers of all kinds blossom side by side. Weed through the old to let the new emerge,[1] So each company composed new plays in the traditional style or edited and developed old ones, weeding out superstition (chiefly in the form of ghosts), contempt for women and working people, and the placing of filial piety above patriotism. Thus the historical plays, while remaining traditional in form, adopted the new standards of morality. Their period setting, however, pre-

---

[1] This principle was put forward in a directive issued by the Administrative Council of the People's Government in 1951. In 1956 the formula became: 'Let a hundred flowers bloom; Let a hundred schools of thought contend.' The first element of the new double formula, originally applied to the theatre, was now extended to artists and writers in general; the second was applied to scientists.

vented them from coming directly to grips with contemporary problems. This task was undertaken by modern drama.

The first play of this sort to be performed in the Yangyi area had been put on by the staff of the Border Region Bank in 1948, during the last stages of the land reform. This was the celebrated *White Haired Girl*—a musical drama composed in Yenan, based on the life of a poor peasant girl who had been seized by a landlord and forced to become a servant in his household when her father could not pay a debt. Beaten and abused by the landlord's mother and raped by his son, the girl runs away and lives in a mountain cave. She emerges only at night to take the food offered to the gods in a nearby temple and her hair turns white from grief and lack of nourishment and sunlight. In the end she is rescued by an 8th Route Army Land Reform work team and denounces her oppressors at a meeting to 'pour out bitterness' against the landlords.

This first performance of *The White Haired Girl* opened a new era in the local theatre, for it allowed the peasants unprecedented opportunities for identifying themselves with events and characters on the stage. In Ten Mile Inn even an old upper middle peasant woman, whose life had been far more comfortable than most, wept throughout the play and tearfully spoke of herself afterwards as another white-haired girl, recalling her ill-treatment as a young daughter-in-law. On poor peasants the impact was still more powerful.

The next ten years saw the development of modern style drama in Shexian. In 1959 the most popular new play in Yangyi was a musical drama called *Building the North Zhang Channel* (see Chapter VIII). This, like other pieces in the county troupes' repertoire, was written by the actors in collaboration with their audience. It was not only based on actual events, but was tried out before those who took part in them, then modified in the light of their suggestions. The result was a documentary drama of the hewing of the 60-mile channel through the Taihang Mountains.

The curtain rises on the interior of a farmhouse, with the young daughter and daughter-in-law telling of the decision to build the channel. The old folk are sceptical and stress the dangers, difficulties and expense, as well as the disadvantages of diverting labour from agriculture. Soon the sons come in—one a Young Pioneer, the other a Communist. The discussion proceeds in song, verse and prose till the old folk are convinced. In fact the father offers to sell his most treasured possession, his coffin, to help finance the project; and the four youngsters go off to work on the channel with their parents' blessing.

Act two shows the scaling of an almost perpendicular rock face, the lowering of men on ropes over the side of precipices to lay charges of explosives—as well as the fears of those who say that clinging to a cliff, with the high mountains above and the deep river below, is simply suicide. The trail is blazed by the young Communists who climb up 'Monkeys Slip Slope' to hammer in iron pegs for rope-ladders, with the help of which others follow them to start work on a tunnel.

Act three is set in a work site up in the mountains. The girls and women have formed special teams of their own. One is named after the heroine Liu Hu-lan (who at the age of fifteen was beheaded by the Japanese for her revolutionary activities) another after Mu Kuei-ying (a patriotic woman general of the Sung Dynasty). The men name their teams after heroes of the Chinese People's Volunteers in Korea and episodes in the war there. The Young Pioneers, too, have their own hero to inspire them—Luo Cheng of the sixth century Sui Dynasty (who at the age of seventeen won fame as a general). The sixteen old men form a Huang Tzung group (named after an eighty-year-old third century general) and dig a tunnel in 37 days. But not all the workers are heroic. One pessimist thinks it will take a hundred years to finish the job, and it needs a full-scale debate for him to change his mind and volunteer to join a shock brigade. In this act, too, the heroine shyly learns from her sweetheart how to swing a sledge-hammer!

The fourth act opens with the hammer-swinging heroine, in flowered peasant clothes and with bright red ribbons in her long black plaits, washing clothes beside the river. She is wondering how she can suggest to her fiancé that they postpone their wedding till the water flows through the channel. (October 1st, National Day, 1959, has been set as the date.) The boy comes along with the same idea. But the girl speaks first and the boy, inwardly delighted to find his sweetheart so politically conscious, pretends to be offended. The more she lectures him for being 'backward', the happier he is. But he keeps up the pretence, saying that even if he himself agreed, his parents never would. At last it all comes out and they pledge, in a duet, to work, study and improve themselves together; and to get married when the channel is finished. (There were actually two such cases of marriages postponed by mutual consent, among the workers on the channel.)

The fifth and last act, like the others, duplicates real events. Enthusiasm rises. Old and young, men and women compete. Those who at first had doubts criticize themselves. The job is finished ahead of time, in September; the water flows through the channel on National Day—and the young couple arrive with their marriage certificate.

Building the North Zhang Channel was popular not only with commune members. The county leaders praised it for both its art and its effective portrayal of the organized commune members' victory over nature and over backward ideas in their own ranks.

Other successful modern pieces—*The Great Debate* and *The Five Red Flags*—were also created out of life in the county, the former dealing with the struggle between the 'socialist and capitalist roads', the latter with the plan to 'change the face of the county within five years'.

Besides these full-length plays, classical and modern, the companies performed short pieces in various forms, ranging from recitations and satirical dialogues to topical sketches. One of these, called *Pick Up Your Pail*, dealt with the battle against the drought; another, *King Sweet Potato*, with pest control—all the characters from potato to pest using the mask-like make-up, costumes and symbolism of classical drama and engaging in its exciting acrobatics until the pests were finally routed.

Plays on topical themes, however, were still in a minority of roughly one to two in 1960. Later this ratio was to be reversed; for the traditional plays, even though rid of their unacceptable elements, were not the most pointed weapon in ideological struggle. Besides this, in the field of modern drama itself, despite the success of *Building the North Zhang Channel*, it was planned to emphasize the struggle between the two roads even more than the battle against nature. This was to guarantee that politics should stay securely in command.

One of the three companies, which often performed in Yangyi Commune, was the 84-strong Shexian Xiao Laotze troupe (its name indicating its type of acting and singing). This company (which eventually wrote and acted 'The Building of the North Zhang Channel') was formed in 1952 by a handful of village amateurs. 'We had no costumes or properties then,' said the manager, 'just a heap of old clothes. And our acting matched our costumes. The only people satisfied with our performances in those days were the old folk and the children who came to while away the time.' In 1955, with the emergence of the socialist co-operatives in the offing, more resources became available and the company was able to turn professional. 'Even then,' the manager continued, 'you could load all our costumes and props onto a couple of donkeys. And our plays at that time were mostly about petty personal affairs like trying to find a wife, or family quarrels. But we couldn't manage any real fighting.' This meant that there was none of the breathtaking acrobatics practised later. 'And we had no make-up. That was quite a drawback, for to begin with we had only men, all over thirty, even for the young heroines' parts.'

By 1959 the company had 35 women and girls and 50 men and boys, nearly all from poor peasant families, recruited from all parts of the county, including Yangyi Commune. (The fifteen-year-old son of Li Bao-you, chairman of Ten Mile Inn's Poor Peasant League during land reform days, was among those being trained as an

270

acrobat-warrior). And its repertoire and acting were so improved that it won second prize at the regional drama festival in Handan. The company toured far afield. Sometimes the actors would go to mountain villages, climbing the steep paths with costumes and bedding on their backs. In the winter of 1959–60 they went to Xidu, a hamlet of 25 scattered households. No theatre company had ever been there before and the old women, confined to their hill-tops by tiny bound feet, had never seen a play. The company's visit was a gala occasion and the audience turned out in holiday clothes. At the end of the performance a wizened old woman made her way to the front and with the help of the actors clambered on to the make-shift stage. Clasping the hands of each of the performers in turn she said that all her life she had wished to see a play, but with feet like hers she had never ventured down the mountain. In appreciation of the plays 'sent by the Party', the village pledged to increase its output of marketable grain by 3,000 *jin*.

Such incidents were common. So was the exchange between actors and audience of gold-fringed, scarlet congratulatory banners, the company hanging those it received at the side of the stage. Such a banner might read:

To the Shexian Xiao Laotze Opera Company,
Who without thought of self and enduring hardship,
Have inspired us with their plays and helped us with our harvest.
From members of the such-and-such Brigade.

Wherever they went the actors and actresses made a point of working with their hands by day alongside those for whom they acted at night. Their usual practice was to stay in a place four days, performing every evening and rehearsing on two of the days, working in the fields on the other two. During the summer of 1960 they bought themselves sickles out of their own pay, to help with the wheat harvest. When they were on the way from Yangyi to Zhao Village the farmers noted that they picked up manure from the paths and flung it on the fields.

At Mujin, where they were performing for the builders of a reservoir (and helping them on the job), a frost warning came through late at night and all local brigades were called on to cover their seed-beds. The company's Party branch called an emergency meeting (there were thirteen Communists in the troupe), and under its lead the actors and actresses went out to the fields with their bedding and spread it over the seedlings.

Such actions were the outcome of political work, County Head Wang De-hen (himself a theatre fan) giving direct guidance to the company and joining its members in periodical summing-up of their work and discussion of Party policy. This involved study of Mao Tse-tung's writings on art and literature and of Party policy in general. 'It was because we understood that agriculture is the basis of the economy,' said the manager, 'that we bought ourselves sickles and spread our quilts over the seedbeds.'

The company's guiding principle was to 'combine acting, writing, coaching of village amateurs and farming', so that the theatre should 'play its part in changing the face of the countryside'.

A MASS MOVEMENT TO STUDY DIALECTICS

Another 'force on the ideological front' was philosophy.

In the spring of 1960, the Commune Party Committee launched a mass movement for the study of dialectical materialism—the Marxist world outlook.[2] Its aim was to show that theory was essential to everyone and was directly related to day-to-day work, whether one worked in a canteen, a farm tools workshop or on a high yield tract, whether one was a primary school teacher or a farmer. This movement was led by the Commune First Party Secretary, Yang Cai-xun. Three of Mao Tse-tung's philosophical essays were assigned for study: *On Practice, On Contradiction,* and *On the Correct Handling of Contradictions Among the People.*[3]

For the movement to succeed it was necessary first of all to 'scatter the mist'—to dispel any doubts that learning was within the grasp of ordinary farming folk, especially those no longer young, and to end the belief that theory was an impenetrable mystery. Eleven propaganda teams made up of cadres and Party members toured the commune, explaining the importance of studying dialectics and calling on commune members to enroll for regular study. 'Cultivate the Communist spirit of daring to think, speak and act,' they urged, 'and storm the fortress of learning.' Two thousand responded to this call, Party and Youth Leage members taking the lead.

These two thousand started off with a debate on the subject, 'Can

[2] This movement was nation wide in scope and embraced 'hundreds of millions of people'. See Lin Feng, 'The Tasks of China's Cultural Revolution', *Peking Review,* No. 25, 21 June, 1960.

[3] The first two of these, *On Practice* and *On Contradiction,* were originally presented in the form of lectures to the Anti-Japanese Military and Political College in Yenan in the summer of 1937. Their aim was to expose, from a Marxist stand-point, empiricists who relied on their own limited experience, without understanding the importance of theory for revolutionary practice; and dogmatists who relied on phrases taken out of context from Marxist works. The main stress was on combating the latter, on demonstrating that 'Marxism is not a dogma but a guide to action'.

The third essay, *On the Correct Handling of Contradictions Among the People,* was also originally presented as a speech, twenty years later. It was delivered to the Supreme State Conference, a few months after the events in Hungary in 1956. It particularly stressed the distinction between the people and their enemies and contradictions within the ranks of the people.

we make a success of our studies? What do we really think about studying theory?' These questions were discussed in small groups throughout the commune. The students wrote placards stating their own views on the questions and pasted them on the village walls. Meanwhile they urged fellow team members to join in. Drawing in the younger people was not hard, but with the older folk there were difficulties. Some felt that their education was too elementary or their intelligence too limited to cope with philosophy. On the other hand, some said: 'We've done farming all these years and we can still go on doing it whether we study or not. What do we want philosophy for?'

In other words the propaganda teams had persuaded some, but had left others unconvinced that they could or should study. So the debates in the dining-rooms and the placards on the walls touched on a cleavage of opinion. One poster read: 'We farmers and workers are labouring people; we have the richest practical experience. Philosophy and theory are only the product of practice, so we can master them. Of course we'll meet difficulties in our study, so we'll need determination and patience. But the old saying goes: "There's no difficulty under heaven which won't yield to a person who takes pains." ' Supporters of the study movement also pointed to Ren Qing-mei of Little Yetao, who had 'studied for 22 years without a break'. This was to convince older people that they could study, too. Ren's example was also quoted to show the close connection between study of theory and success in practical work. For Little Yetao, despite its poor natural conditions, had become the most prosperous brigade in the commune; and it was generally accepted that this was due to studying and following Party and government policy.

As the debate and placard writing went on, more and more people enrolled. The figure soon rose to 5,000. This included seventy-two-year-old An Yi, who said on signing up: 'I'm old in years but young in heart. After all, how can we do what Chairman Mao says if we don't know what he's talking about.' This little speech was repeated up and down the commune. It helped win over many to the view that: 'There's no harm in having a go.' The end result was a landslide of enrolment sweeping along practically all the adults in the commune. The number of placards on walls in the various villages after a rough count was said to run into tens of thousands.

Side by side with these placards there began to appear promises: 'to strive to master theory,' 'to combine theory and practice,' 'to use theory to improve work.' Close on 20,000 such pledges were made.

To support the study movement the New China Bookshop in Yangyi, instead of waiting for people to come and buy, sent books to all the study stations in the commune and sold 8,500 in a few days.

The next step was to put across the main tenets of dialectical materialism in such a way that the commune members could get a preliminary grasp of them. Once more the method used was group discussions, started off by the Party members and activists each expounding his or her own understanding of some point and illustrating it with examples from life and work in the village, from folk tales or popular classics. Everyone in the group then had his say on the subject—often just thinking aloud. When group members, with the aid of such informal discussion, had worked out their ideas, they were encouraged to put them into writing in the form of brief articles. These were posted up to stimulate further discussion. In this way, exceptionally lively contributions made in one group might be spread to others.

The aim of the discussions was for each person to explain various dialectical concepts in the light of his own experience, to make them part of his own thinking; then to see how these newly-grasped concepts might be applied in his own work. There was no set standard for judging contributions. Learning to think more effectively and so to become more efficient at one's work was bound to take time. Even a confused notion might mark the beginning of the process. Systematically and persistently developed it could bring results.

One study group which achieved some success was made up of the staff of a small brigade-run restaurant, near Yangyi bus-stop, which catered to travellers and transport workers on the highway between Wu-an and Shexian county town (Yangyi being about halfway between them). Mao Tse-tung's philosophical concept of 'the generality and the particularity of contradiction' seemed clearer to this group when one of the cooks declared: 'This is the way I see it. Everybody gets hungry and everybody eats. That's the generality of the contradiction between hunger and eating. But some people like noodles and some prefer bread: some don't feel satisfied unless they get heavy, solid food; others can only digest a light, soft diet. That's the particularity of the contradiction.' As to applying this principle to everyday work, he went on: 'It's no good for us cooks to think we've done our job as long as we've provided the customers with any sort of food. A Marxist cook has to investigate and find out what sort of food suits the people he's serving. That is he has to analyse the particularity of the contradiction and provide different dishes for people with different tastes.' The outcome of this particular philosophical discussion was that the restaurant staff began to investigate the tastes of the truck and bus drivers and their passengers and to vary their menu accordingly.

On the Silver Sea Tract the 'Five Mei's' (the 'Five Flowering Plums' of cotton-growing and basket-ball fame) had been attending classes at the tract's 'Red and Expert' school. They had learned a good deal from practical experience as well as from books about the sowing, pruning and general management of cotton plants. And when in their study of philosophy they reached Lesson Five, dealing with the relationship of 'perceptual' and 'rational' knowledge, they concluded that they needed an experimental plot to try out some of the 'rational' knowledge they had gained from study.

At the Ten Mile Inn Primary School the principal summed up the staff's gains from studying the three philosophical works in this way:

'In the first place we've all come to grips with the fact that there are two world outlooks and two points of view. The two world outlooks are those of the working-class and the bourgeoisie. The two points of view are the advanced and the backward. Both of these points of view are to be found among people with a working-class outlook; but some people whose general outlook is correct, sort out problems properly and are forward-looking; others aren't. Once you're clear about the existence of the two world outlooks and the two viewpoints, you need to get rid of a bourgeois outlook and to cultivate a working-class one; to develop a proper way of looking at things and of thinking about them. And when you come across right and wrong ways of doing things, you have to consider your own thoughts and actions and see how they measure up. This means that you have to become more politically conscious and change all your old ideas.

'Through studying Chairman Mao's works on contradiction we've come to realize that there are contradictions in everything—and of course that includes our work as teachers. The main contradictions that we've sorted out in our teaching are:

1. Between the mass movement to improve teaching and studying—and our poor material conditions.
2. Between the idea of making slow but sure progress—and that of making great leaps forward.
3. Between working hard and enthusiastically—and just doing enough to get by.
4. Between doing things in an organised and disciplined way—and doing them haphazardly or carelessly.

'We're tackling all these problems and we've already learnt how to look at things and analyse them, so that we can solve whatever problems may crop up in our work.'

Some groups were more lively and successful than others. One of the decisive factors were the amateur 'tutors'—Party and Youth League members or 'activists' who launched the discussions. These tutors read the essays to be studied ahead of time and prepared illustrations of the key points by relating them to familiar stories and sayings and applying newly-grasped concepts to work.

A few of these new-fledged tutors had a flair for putting things in a vivid, homely way. A woman assistant in one of the Yangyi shops gained such a name for being able to make knotty philosophical points clear that people were constantly dropping in to ask her questions. Eventually a corner of the shop counter was set aside especially for these consultations.

On the Silver Sea Tract the discussions were considered to have been particularly lively and successful. This was partly attributed to the lecture notes prepared by the tract's team of tutors, which included twenty-two-year-old Zhu Xu-mei (of the 'Five Mei's'), ex-8th Route Armyman Fei, Commune Party Secretary Jin Han-cheng and ten others. They had gone over the three philosophical essays, worked out the main ideas to be covered and provided homely illustrations of them.

At an early stage of the movement, study groups in the brigades around the tract also began to use these notes to aid their own discussions. The commune leaders took note of this and passed on a copy of the notes to the County Head. The latter considered them to be just what was needed to help amateur tutors launch newly-literate commune members on the study of dialectical materialism. So he asked the Silver Sea tutors to prepare their notes for publication. While doing this they revised and improved the material by incorporating striking sayings and experiences which had been brought up in discussion by tract or brigade members.

Thus one of the results of Yangyi Commune's movement to study Mao Tse-tung's three essays was the publication in August 1960 of a 72-page booklet entitled *Lecture Notes for Farmers Studying Philosophy*, by the Silver Sea Research Group for Theoretical Study. On its green paper cover was a picture of the tract's 'Tower of Heroic Ambition' and on the flyleaf Lenin's words: 'Without revolutionary theory there can be no revolutionary movement.' As frontispiece there was quatrains composed by County Head Wang De-hen, and Commune Party Secretaries Yang Cai-xun and Jin Han-cheng. County Head Wang's verse read:

> The will to build our Silver Sea
> Ascends like the sun in the east.
> Fresh flowers of theory burst in bloom,
> Ten thousand mauves, a thousand shades of red.

The booklet consisted of thirty lessons and was divided into three parts of ten lessons each, one part on each of Mao Tse-tung's three philosophical essays.

It expounded such concepts as dogmatism, empiricism, subjectivism, metaphysics, the generality and the particularity of contradictions, the principal contradiction and its major aspects. In doing so it made Marxist philosophy meaningful and applicable for ordinary commune members by relating it to their own experiences.

Lesson Three, for example, asks the question: What is dogmatism? and answers:

On the Ideological Front

There's an old story about a man who went to market to buy himself some shoes. Before leaving home he measured his feet with a piece of string. But when he got to the market he couldn't find the string and ran all over the place looking for it. Someone said to him: 'Can't you try the shoes on?' 'No,' he answered. 'I trust that string, not my feet.' We must oppose such dogmatism; but at the same time we must oppose empiricism. What is this empiricism? It's like this. Once there was a man who went up into the mountains to cut wood and accidentally dropped his axe over a cliff. As it was already getting dark he couldn't go down after it; so he made a mark at the edge of the cliff where he'd dropped it and the next day he went back and found it. Some time after that he was crossing a river in a boat and accidentally dropped his knife overboard. He at once made a nick on the edge of the boat to mark where it had fallen; and when the boat reached the opposite bank he got into the water underneath the nick and started looking for his knife. These two stories describe: a man who was not flexible, who mechanically used a set formula and was therefore a dogmatist; and a 'nick-the-boat-and-find-the-knife' empiricist, who blindly worshipped his past experience, not realizing that when time, place and conditions change, you must use new methods. Both these men failed and became laughing-stocks.

The nature of contradiction was dealt with in this way:

Some people say, 'I've seen all sorts of things but I've never seen a contradiction'. But contradictions are not hard to see. In the past landlords used to oppress their hired hands and the hired hands wanted to rise up and fight back. That was a contradiction. It was solved by the struggle against the landlords and the distribution of the land. On the question of planned purchase and supply there is a contradiction between us and the upper-middle peasants. We say: 'Fine. We're better off.' They say: 'There's no freedom.' That is a struggle between the capitalist and the socialist roads, and it is a contradiction. We want close planting, but some say: 'Wide furrows bring flourishing corn.' That is a contradiction between progressive and conservative ways of thinking. If it doesn't rain we fight the drought and if it rains too much we fight flood. Those are contradictions between man and nature. . . .

There are contradictions in everything under the sun. That's nothing to be afraid of. When there is a contradiction we solve it, for we can only make progress by developing and changing things. When we have finished our course, we shall know how to discover and solve contradictions and we shall be able to grasp their laws and push forward our work smoothly and successfully.

Metaphysics is dealt with under the heading of 'Two World Outlooks', as follows:

The metaphysical outlook, or the outlook of vulgar evolutionists, consists in looking at the world from an isolated, static and one-sided viewpoint. It regards all things as changeless: or it regards whatever changes there are as merely an increase or decrease in quantity, and their cause as external forces. This is a reactionary outlook of the bourgeoisie. They say that the old, capitalist society will never change and pass away. This is only for the purpose of maintaining their own dark rule. We say that the capitalist system will collapse and fall to pieces and the whole of humanity will enter communist society. . . .

Here on the tract, for example, we have 80 women working. They have broken old traditions and moved to the tract to live . . . But people with a bourgeois outlook think that women should be oppressed and ruled over and that all they can do is cooking and housework. We think that women can take part in socialist construction, that they can do anything—haven't the Five Mei's an experimental plot on which they are aiming at a yield of 2,000 *jin* of cotton per *mu*?

The Commune Party Committee had put much effort into making the movement to study dialectical materialism a success and into making study in general regular and systematic. By the late summer of 1960 when the achievements of the movement were summed up, over 25,000 articles had been written by commune members on various aspects of their studies. Farmers who had taken part in preparing material for the launching of group discussion, and could now be considered 'tutors', numbered 356. In addition there were 20 commune cadres and 10 workers who brought the total number of philosophy tutors in the commune to 386.

The study of dialectical materialism, as well as general and technical education was a contribution to the technical revolution in the countryside. It did not, of course, bring an immediate spate of inventions and innovations, and even those that did follow quite soon needed a period and modification. But there were some immediate results, such as two separately devised pulleys, one on the Silver Sea Tract for shifting earth, one at Little Yetao for lifting manure from pig-pens in the valley bottom to terraces on the hillsides. These were seen as a sign of things to come.

After the summary, plans were drawn up for the next two years of study of political theory. In 1961, following upon the study of dialectical materialism in 1960, political economy was to be tackled as well as works on the general nature of socialism. In 1962 communism was to be the main topic, based on reading of relevant passages from Marx, Engels, Lenin, Stalin and Mao Tse-tung. The number of political study tutors was to be more than doubled by 1961, the plan calling for 859; by 1962 the number was to reach

On the Ideological Front

1,696. By the end of that year, too, the commune as a whole planned to have altogether 55 Party-and-Youth-League and 'Red and Expert' schools. The commune centre in Yangyi townlet was to set up a reading-room for Mao Tse-tung's works by 1961 and another for Marxist-Leninist classics by 1962. By the end of that year it was to establish a research institute.

These plans were inspired by Mao Tse-tung's words: 'The wealth of society is created by the workers, peasants and working intellectuals. If they take their destiny into their own hands, use Marxism-Leninism as their guide, and energetically tackle problems instead of evading them, there is no difficulty in the world which they cannot overcome.[4]

[4] Introduction to 'The Party Secretary Takes the Lead and All the Party Members Help Run the Co-operatives', in *Socialist Upsurge in China's Countryside*, F.L.P., Peking, 1957.

EPILOGUE

WHAT we saw in Yangyi People's Commune flew in the face of much that was being written about communes in the West.

The commune did not come into being in obedience to an edict from Peking. It arose as a popular response to the need for co-ordinating local management and administration, for concentrating manpower and capital to control nature and to modernize and diversify farming. It did not aggravate the harm of natural disasters. It staved them off. The commune was bringing, not a withering, but a flowering of human personality and self-expression—for women, for the rising generation, for all those willing to live by their own labour and work for the advance of society. The family and marriage, with more mutual respect based on social and economic equality, rising standards of education and richer cultural life, was becoming more stable and harmonious, not less.

Briefly, our investigation showed that the commune was a success, not a failure.

Our visits to a dozen communes in half a dozen provinces spanning a thousand miles, talks with travellers to still other parts, and the study of reports, all suggested that this was true of communes throughout China.

After 1962, when facts forced acknowledgement of striking advances, some said that they were made despite the communes, not because of them. Others maintained that the communes were not what they used to be, that a retreat had been beaten back to co-operatives.

As evidence of this, certain changes were cited:

The first concerned size. Communes did drop in size from an average of around 5,000 to roughly 1,800 households, or conversely tripled in number from 26,000 to 74,000 by the end of 1962. (Yangyi split up into four communes with an average of 2,500 households in each.) This change was made partly to cope with transport and communications difficulties in mountainous areas, partly to simplify the tasks of planning and administration.

Second was the transfer of the basic unit of management and accounting from brigade to work team level. This was done in many communes where the chief source of power was human muscle, where farm work was still done mainly with hoe and sickle. This lowering in the level of the basic unit was partly to simplify planning and administration, but mainly to rationalize distribution. By

Epilogue

linking income more directly to effort it spurred on production. Third was the narrowing down of commune industry. The three years of natural disasters made clearer than ever that agriculture must be the main task of the communes. In the first flush of enthusiasm for it, commune industry over-extended itself, absorbing some labour that agriculture could not spare and producing some goods that it did not need. The more significant change was not that industry was reduced, but that it was geared to agriculture's uneven seasonal demands and placed directly at its service.

Fourth was the closing down of year-round canteens. The drive to release women from housework, like the development of industry, was overtaken by the natural disasters. These placed a premium on every grain of cereal, every ounce of manpower, every pound of fuel. Efficient running of canteens demanded skilled labour, while leaving the light household labour of the old and young unused; it consumed coal without satisfying the need for domestic space-heating. Such factors, coupled with the customary preference for home-cooking, led to a great reduction of the number and scope of canteens. Generally speaking these now function only during rush seaons; or they cater only to special needs (of kindergartens, old folks' homes, commune headquarters etc.). But the goal which inspired canteens: the revolutionizing of the most backward and scattered sector of the economy—that of the household; and the release of women for productive employment—all this remains.

These adjustments so far from meaning 'liquidation of the communes' and a 'return to co-operatives' enhance the advantages of the commune over the co-operative. Of these, size is the most obvious, the 74,000 communes of today being roughly ten times as big as the 740,000 socialist co-operatives of early 1958. The commune with its concentration of manpower and material resources is a far stronger force than the co-operative was to free farming from the tyranny of flood, drought and wind, and to advance to modern mechanized agriculture.

The commune, embracing as it does farming, industry, trade, education and military matters, has at all times had a far broader scope than the co-operative. The gradual working out of the relations of these five aspects to each other, and placing them at the service of agriculture has not only produced a leap forward in the commune itself. It has improved national economic planning and speeded China's general economic advance.

The commune's three-level structure makes it adaptable to advances in the forces of production. The summing-up of experience since 1958 has shown that the fixing of one or another of these as the basic level of management and accounting depends on the level of productive forces. Where much if not most of a commune's output is achieved with such implements as the hoe and the sickle, the basic

281

level is the work team; where it is achieved with machines such as tractors and combine harvesters, the basic level will be the commune. During the transition from one stage to the other, with widespread use of both animal-drawn implements and small machines such as electric irrigation pumps, the basic level will be the brigade.

Finally, the commune is the smallest unit of state power. This means that it includes not only collective ownership at three levels, but the potentiality for 'ownership by the whole people.'

The commune is thus a vehicle for carrying China's five hundred million farming people to communism. Its unique integration of social and economic with political functions may well prove to be the commune's historic contribution—a significant step towards bridging the gap between worker and farmer, town and country, mental and manual labour, towards the era when the 'government of men' gives way to the 'management of things'.

INDEX

accounting, 101, 130-3
accumulation, 45, 46, 95, 100, 102
administration, 195 ff.; costs, 46
afforestation, 26, 27, 93, 96, 109, 112, 113
'Agricultural Co-operation, The Question of', Mao Tse-tung, 12
'agriculture the base of the economy', 75, 97, 117, 261, 263, 272
airing of views, 72; *dazibao*, 81, 82, 174, 223
animal husbandry, 98, 104, 109, 112-14
anti-rightist campaign, 1957-8, 22, 174
appraisal of work, 129-30; among teachers, 176
artificial insemination, 115
awards, 84

banking, 144
bonuses, 48
bourgeois rightists, 186
bridging the gap between town and country, 173
brigade, 35, 44-6, 78, 105, 123-4; regrouping, 58; cadres, 59; enterprises, 66; disposal of income, 100; financial plan, 132; welfare committee, 152, 155
'bureaucracy, sectarianism and subjectivism', 62, 63, 74
bureaucrat capitalists, 199 fn.
business management, 132-3

cadres, def., xiii fn.; policy, 13, 197-8; election, 218, 219

calendar of farming, 109
call-up, 40, 191, 259
canteens; *see* community dining rooms
capitalist trade, 145; socialist transformation, 148
check-up on co-operatives, 22-3
class: definition of rural classes, 4 (table 1) ;analysis, 71; struggle, 15; differentiation reappearing, 6; line, 20, 204 ff.; ideology, 205 ff.
climate, 55, 87, 93 fn.
close planting, 50-2
Commune Communist Party Conference, April 1959, 43
Commune Congress, 39, 40, 45, 100, 133
Commune Council, 35, 40, 45, 90, 101, 105
'Communique of the 8th Plenary Session of the 8th Central Committee of the Chinese Communist Party', 1959, 26
'Communique of the 6th Plenary Session of the 8th Central Committee of the Chinese Communist Party', 1958, 121
'Communique of the 10th Plenary Session of the 8th Central Committee of the Chinese Communist Party', 1962, 203
Communist Party, 195 ff.; organization, 200 ff.; membership qualifications, 198; tasks, 201 ff.; history in Yangyi, 198 ff.
Sixth Plenary session, 1958, 121; Eighth Plenary session, 1959, 26, 60; Tenth Plenary session, 1962, 203
Communist Youth League, 40, 51, 69, 80, 82, 91, 97, 102, 132, 155, 176, 178, 257-62

Index

General Line for Socialist Construction, 30–3, 60, 72
grading of the land, 123
grading of the working force, 39
'Grain the key lever', 117
grain output; see output
'Grasping each end to pull forward the middle', 233 ff.
Great Debate, The, 21–5, 61
Great Leap Forward, The, 26, 60–1, 63, 72, 76, 95, 178, 265
'Guarantee of work and output', 39

irrigation, 26, 27, 28, 75, 79, 81, 93–4, 104; North Zhang Channel, 55–7

joint state-private enterprises, 148

kindergartens, 151, 159–61

hail, 90–1
handicraft co-operatives, 29
high level co-operatives; see farming co-operatives, socialist
high yield tracts, 75, 76–86, 97
homes for the aged, 151, 161–4
housework, 68, 240, 244–5
housing, 115
'How a Youth League Branch Established a Course in Work Point Recording', Socialist Upsurge in China's Countryside, 178
'hundred flowers bloom, a hundred schools contend, let a', 267 fn.
Hu Yao-pang, Speech at the 8th National Congress of the CCP, 1956, 257, 262

ideological front, the, 265–79
ideological revolution, the, 61–75
improvement of farm tools; see inventions and innovations
incentives, material, 124, 224
income; disposal of brigade income, 100, 101; cash, 102, 117
'increase production and serve the people', 143–4
industry, 40, 98, 104, 136–42
inspection terms, 65, 101
inventions and innovations, 136–7, 139, 141–2, 254, 278
iron mine, 137
iron and steel works, 137–8

labour, 45, 76, 95–9, 102, 124–6, 142
labour heroes and heroines: Ren Qing-mei, 14–15; Ma Zhan-yan, 53; Guo Qing-chun, 65; Li Shun-ta, 112; Guo Heng-de, 16–19, 88, 236–7
land, reclamation, 111; utilization, 121–2; assessment, 123
land reform, 65, 95, 111
landlords, 4 (table 1), 65; industry, 140; see ex-landlords
leadership, 220–38
'leading on the job', 225 ff.
'levelling and transferring', 42
Liao Lu-yen, Minister of Agriculture, 75 fn.
'The Whole Party and the Whole People Go in for Agriculture in a Big Way', 1960, 93
literacy drives, 176–80
Liu-Shao-chi, 31; The Class Character of Man, 204; 'The Mass Line of the Party', How to be a Good Communist, 221; 'Report on the Work of the Central Committee of the CCP to the 2nd Session of the 8th National Party Congress', 1958, 26
livestock; see animal husbandry
living standards, 73–4, 82, 117–18, 144–5, 262–3
loans, state, 57, 113
low level co-operatives; see farming co-operatives, semi-socialist
Lu Ting-yi, 'Education Must be Combined with Productive Labour', 158, 173

For Product Safety Concerns and Information please contact our EU
representative GPSR@taylorandfrancis.com
Taylor & Francis Verlag GmbH, Kaufingerstraße 24, 80331 München, Germany

* 9 7 8 1 1 3 8 8 7 3 7 6 6 *